MONETARY ECONOMICS IN THE 1990s

Monetary Economics in the 1990s

The Henry Thornton Lectures, Numbers 9–17

Edited by

Forrest Capie
Professor of Economic History
City University
London

and

Geoffrey E. Wood
Professor of Economics
City University
London

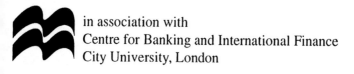

in association with
Centre for Banking and International Finance
City University, London

First published in Great Britain 1996 by
MACMILLAN PRESS LTD
Houndmills, Basingstoke, Hampshire RG21 6XS
and London
Companies and representatives
throughout the world

A catalogue record for this book is available
from the British Library.

ISBN 0–333–57561–X

First published in the United States of America 1996 by
ST. MARTIN'S PRESS, INC.,
Scholarly and Reference Division,
175 Fifth Avenue,
New York, N.Y. 10010

ISBN 0–312–16219–7

Library of Congress Cataloging-in-Publication Data
Monetary economics in the 1990s : the Henry Thornton lectures,
numbers 9–17 / edited by Forrest Capie and Geoffrey E. Wood.
    p.   cm.
"In association with Centre for Banking and International Finance,
City University, London."
Includes bibliographical references and index.
ISBN 0–312–16219–7
1. Monetary policy.   I. Capie, Forrest.   II. Wood, Geoffrey
Edward.   III. City University (London, England).   Centre for Banking
and International Finance.
HG230.3.M6352   1996
332.4'6—dc20   96–17556
                                                                     CIP

10   9   8   7   6   5   4   3   2   1
05   04   03   02   01   00   99   98   97   96

Printed and bound in Great Britain by
Antony Rowe Ltd, Chippenham, Wiltshire

Contents

Notes on the Contributors

The editors

Forrest Capie is Professor of Economic History at City University, London.

Geoffrey E. Wood is Professor of Economics at City University, London.

Robert J. Barro is Robert C. Waggoner Professor of Economics at Harvard University and a Senior Fellow of the Hoover Institution. He is also a contributing editor of *the Wall Street Journal*. Since 1989, he and Paul Romer have directed a programme on economic growth through Harvard University and the National Bureau of Economic Research. His books include *Economic Growth* (co-authored with Xavier Sala-i-Martin); *Macroeconomics*; *Modern Business Cycle Theory*; and *Money, Expectations, and Business Cycles*. He has written extensively in professional journals and recently published the popular book, *Getting It Right: Markets and Choices in a Free Society*. He holds a PhD in economics from Harvard University and a BS in physics from the California Institute of Technology. He is a fellow of the American Academy of Arts & Sciences and the Econometric Society and has served as an officer of the American Economic Association. In February 1996, he was the Lionel Robbins Lecturer at the London School of Economics.

Otmar Issing is a Member of the Board of the Deutsche Bundesbank and a Member of the Policy-Making Central Bank Council. He is in charge of the Bundesbank's Economic Research and Statistical Departments. He was previously Professor of Economics at the Universities of Würzburg and Nuremberg. From 1988 to 1990 he was a Member of the German Council of Economic Experts. In 1991 he became an elected Member of the Academy of Sciences and Literature, Mainz. Apart from numerous contributions to learned journals and collective volumes, he published (among his books) two leading textbooks in monetary economics, *Einführung in die Geldtheorie* (Introduction to Monetary Theory, 10th edn, 1995) and *Einführung in die Geldpolitik* (Introduction to Monetary Policy, 5th edn, 1993).

Charles P. Kindleberger is Ford International Professor of Economics, Emeritus. He took his BA at the University of Pennsylvania in 1932 and his PhD at Columbia University in 1937. After ten years in government, central banking and military service, he taught international economics and economic history at the Massachusetts Institute of Technology from 1948 to 1981, where he is now. Among his numerous books are *The World in Depression, 1929–1939* (2nd. edn, 1986), *Manias, Panics and Crashes* (3rd edn, 1996), *The Financial History of Western Europe* (2nd edn, 1989), and *World Economic Primacy, 1500–1990* (1996).

David Laidler is Professor of Economics at the University of Western Ontario, London. He was educated at the London School of Economics (BSc Econ. 1959), University of Syracuse (MA 1960) and the University of Chicago (PhD 1964). He has held teaching appointments at the University of California, Berkeley (1963–6), the University of Essex (1966–9), and the University of Manchester (1969–75). Professor Laidler has written numerous books and articles on monetary economics and the history of economic thought in the course of his career. However, he remains particularly proud of the fact that his first paid employment as an economist was as Anna Schwartz's research assistant on *The Monetary History of the United States*.

Michael Mussa is the Economic Counsellor and the Director of the Department of Research at the International Monetary Fund, a position he has held since September of 1991. In this capacity, he is responsible for advising the management of the Fund and the Fund's Executive Board on broad issues of economic policy and in providing analysis of ongoing developments in the world economy. In addition, he supervises the activities of the Research Department, including preparation of the *World Economic Outlook*, the reports on international capital markets, and a variety of other materials related to the Fund's economic surveillance activities, as well as a wide ranging programme of research on issues of relevance to the Fund. Before joining the staff of the Fund, Michael Mussa was a long time member of the faculty of the Graduate School of Business of the University of Chicago, starting as an Associate Professor in 1976 and being promoted to the William H. Abbott Professorship of International Business in 1980. From 1971 to 1976, he was on the faculty of the Department of Economics at the University of Rochester. During this period he also served as a visiting faculty member at the Graduate Center of the City University of New York, the London School of Economics, and the Graduate Institute of International Studies in Geneva,

Switzerland. Dr Mussa's main areas of research are international economics, macroeconomics, monetary economics and municipal finance. He has published widely in these fields in professional journals and research volumes. He is a Research Fellow of the National Bureau of Economic Research. In 1981, the University of Geneva awarded Dr Mussa the Prix Mondial Nessim Habif for his research in international economics. In 1987 Dr Mussa was elected a Fellow of the Econometric Society. By appointment of President Ronald Reagan, Dr Mussa served as a Member of the US Council of Economic Advisors from August 1986 to September 1988.

Helmut Schlesinger is a Member of the Board of Directors of the Bank for International Settlements. He is an honorary professor at the University of Administrative Sciences in Speyer, was a visiting professor at Princeton University and is a guest professor at the Humboldt University in Berlin. He studied economics at the University of Munich. From 1949 to 1952, he worked at the IFO Institute for Economic Research, before joining what was later to become the Deutsche Bundesbank in 1952. After serving as Head of the Research and Statistics Department from 1964 to 1972, he became a Member of the Board of the Deutsche Bundesbank in July 1972. In 1980, Dr Schlesinger was appointed Deputy President of the Deutsche Bundesbank and Deputy Chairman of the Central Bank Council. From 1991 to 1993, he held the office of President of the Deutsche Bundesbank and Chairman of the Central Bank Council. In 1981 he was awarded the Ludwig Erhard Prize for economic journalism and received honorary doctorates from Johann Wolfgang Goethe University in Frankfurt, Georg-August University in Göttingen and St Gallen University.

Robert Shiller is the Stanley B. Resor Professor of Economics, Cowles Foundation for Research in Economics, Yale University. He received his PhD in economics from the Massachusetts Institute of Technology in 1972. He is Research Associate of the National Bureau of Economic Research, a fellow of the American Academy of Arts and Sciences, a fellow of the Econometric Society, a member of the Academic Advisory Panel for the Federal Reserve Bank of New York, and a recent recipient of a Guggenheim fellowship. He has written widely on financial markets, macroeconomics, real estate, statistical methods, behavioural economics, and on public attitudes, opinions, and moral judgments regarding markets. His 1989 book *Market Volatility* was a mathematical and behavioural analysis of price fluctuations in speculative markets. His 1993 book *Macro Markets: Creating Institutions for Managing Society's Largest Economic*

Risks proposed a variety of new risk-management contracts, such as futures contracts in national incomes or in real estate, that would revolutionize the management of risks to standards of living. He is co-founder of Case Shiller Weiss, Inc., a real estate research firm.

Niels Thygesen is Professor of Economics at the University of Copenhagen. He has served as Head of the Monetary Division, OECD, as Economic Adviser to the Minister of Finance of Malaysia and as Adviser to Danmarks Nationalbank. He has served on several expert groups on monetary integration and macroeconomic cooperation in the European Communities, including the Committee for Monetary Union in Europe (the Schmidt–Giscard Committee). He has been a Senior Research Fellow of the Centre for European Policy Studies in Brussels since 1982. He was President of SUERF (Société Universitaire Européenne de Recherches Financières), 1988–91. Niels Thygesen was nominated at the European Council Meeting in June 1988 as one of the three independent expert members of the Delors Committee on the study of economic and monetary union in the European Communities (the Delors Committee). He was nominated in December 1992 by the Swedish government as member of the Commission on the crisis in the Swedish economy. He has published widely on international economics and on European integration, most recently in Daniel Gros and Niels Thygesen, *European Monetary Integration: From the European Monetary System to Economic and Monetary Union*, 1992.

Roland Vaubel is Professor of Economics at the University of Mannheim, Germany. He received a BA in philosophy, politics and economics from the University of Oxford, an MA from Columbia University, New York, and a doctorate from the University of Kiel, Germany. He has been a staff member of the Institute for World Economics in Kiel, Professor of Economics at Erasmus University Rotterdam and Visiting Professor of International Economics at the University of Chicago (Graduate School of Business). He is a member of the Advisory Council to the German Federal Ministry of Economics and of the Institute of Economic Affairs, London.

Introduction

In 1979 the Centre for Banking and International Finance at City University established an annual Henry Thornton Lecture, in honour of that great monetary economist of the late eighteenth and early nineteenth centuries. The lectures were also published, for limited circulation, by City University. Subsequently, the first eight lectures in the series were presented in *Monetary Economics in the 1980s* (1989). The present volume contains the subsequent nine lectures in the series.

In the introduction to that first volume a brief account was given of Henry Thornton's life and of his extensive political and philanthropic work as well as his remarkable contribution to economics. The present essay is therefore confined to economics. A brief outline of some of Thornton's contributions was provided by Anna Schwartz, in the second Henry Thornton Lecture (1981):

> He understood:
> the fallacy of the real-bills doctrine;
> the distinction between the first-round and ultimate effects of monetary change;
> the lag in effect of monetary change;
> the problem market participants faced in distinguishing relative from general price changes;
> the distinction between internal and external gold drains;
> the factors influencing the foreign exchanges including the role of purchasing power parity;
> how to bring inflation under control;
> the relation of the Bank of England to other English banks;
> types of effects of monetary disturbances on interest rates;
> the distinction between the market rate and the natural rate of interest and between nominal and real rates of interest.
>
> (Schwartz, 1981)

That does not exhaust the total of his contributions. He recognised that one type of money could readily substitute for another, with the result that if one type of money is controlled, a close substitute will emerge. His understanding of velocity, and the importance for it both of interest rates and of expectations, was sophisticated. He maintained a clear distinction

1

between real and nominal magnitudes, noting, as Ricardo did not, the important difference between the impact of a real and of a nominal disturbance on a country's balance of payments (Perlman, 1986). He anticipated Wicksell's development of the concepts of the market and the natural rate of interest (Humphrey, 1986) and set out how money wage stickiness produced temporary non-neutrality of money. It is remarkable how much of modern monetary economics comprises developments of what appeared in Thornton's *Paper Credit*, first published in 1802.

A fuller account of Thornton's contributions is contained in the introduction to *Monetary Economics in the 1980s* (1989), and in the references cited therein, notably Hayek's introduction (1939) to the republication of *Paper Credit*. We now turn in this introduction to a discussion of the essays in the present volume, and to relating them to themes in Thornton's work.

The nine essays divide into four groups. There are the three (Thygesen, 1990; Vaubel, 1988; and Issing, 1995) on institutional design. Two (Schlesinger, 1993; and Kindleberger, 1992) discuss the conduct of monetary policy. Two (Laidler, 1991; and Mussa, 1994) deal with the economic background against which policy is conducted. And the remaining two (Barro, 1987; and Schiller, 1989) deal with fundamental issues in markets and public finance.

We discuss the lectures in these four groups.

INSTITUTIONAL DESIGN

Thornton's *Paper Credit* combined developing monetary theory with analysing the workings of the financial system of his day. Two of the lectures in this volume develop that latter aspect of his work. One of these is that by Professor Neils Thygesen (delivered in 1990), in which he considered what structure would be appropriate for the European Central Bank.

Taking as given that we are to have a single European money, Professor Thygesen considers what structure of the central bank which manages it would best ensure appropriate monetary performance. By appropriate he means one which ensures low inflation. As he puts it (p. 77), 'All net benefits from monetary union ... could be more than offset if a deterioration were to occur in the average inflationary performance of the union relative to what would have been observable under a more decentralised system of policy-making.'

How can this be ensured? As he notes (p. 78), 'It would be a mistake to attach exclusive importance to legal texts.' The attitude of policy makers generally, and of the public, is important. These attitudes have changed in recent years in many countries. There is much wider recognition that low inflation is not only compatible with satisfactory economic growth, but may well be a condition necessary for sustainable growth.[1]

Nevertheless, although voters' attitudes are crucial, the central bank's mandate should manifestly be consistent with this revealed preference for low inflation. Professor Thygesen suggests that this will involve several aspects of the bank's constitution. The bank should be forbidden from direct financing of government deficits; such financing has been at the root of almost all great inflations (Capie, 1986). What of indirect financing, of carrying out open market operations in government debt? Professor Thygesen considers that to forbid that is unnecessary, for such temporary financing has not caused serious inflationary problems in the past. However, he argues, there should be procedures to ensure it is plain that the bank is not, 'smooth(ing) out emerging differences in borrowing costs for national governments due to different perceptions of risk in the markets ... since market discipline would otherwise be weakened' (p. 81).

He is aware that exchange rate intervention can offset domestic monetary actions. To remove, or at least weaken, pressure for such intervention, Professor Thygesen argues that fiscal co-ordination within EMU is important. He suggests this will be necessary to prevent uncoordinated fiscal expansion (for example) against a background of anti-inflationary policy leading to an appreciation of the currency, such as resulted from such a situation in the USA from 1981 to 1984.

There are also formal, legal points to help preserve autonomy and freedom from pressures to inflate. Members of the governing body should have long terms of office and security of tenure. The central bank should have financial dependence, in the sense of being free to determine both its salary structure and its audit system. This conclusion he argues by observing the consequences of the opposite for the US Federal Reserve (p. 84). There should, of course, be provision to ensure that the bank does not operate in a political vacuum. Otherwise the electoral consent that must, however ingenious the bank's constitution, ultimately underpin its commitment to price stability, would be eroded. This can, he suggests, be achieved by having an annual report presented to the European Parliament by the President of the Bank, and having the President also appear before a specialised committee of that bank on a regular, more frequently than annual, basis, to account for the bank's conduct. This could be supplemented by having a fairly clearly defined price objective to facilitate monitoring of performance.

This is a cautious and carefully thought out framework, and it shows concern, too, for transitional difficulties; Professor Thygesen notes the likely difficulties of relying on monetary aggregates in the immediate aftermath of EMU. (On this point, see also Wood, 1990.)

The lecture concludes with a brief discussion of whether a gradualist strategy of moving towards EMU by gradual abandoning of national monetary sovereignty is feasible. In some respects, Professor Thygesen suggests, there will remain a role for what were national central banks. They are, for example, well suited to maintaining relations with their national financial institutions. But rapid centralisation of monetary policy-making power is, once a common currency is in plane, essential. Otherwise, he writes, 'A situation might develop akin to the first two decades after the start of the Federal Reserve in which the Board was unable on some occasions to assert authority upon the more firmly established regional banks. This proved to be a recipe for indecisiveness' (p. 86).

Professor Thygesen's lecture is a careful examination of both transitional and long-term aspects of the creation of a European Central Bank. It recognises the importance of appropriate institutional design for appropriate institutional performance, and is a most welcome addition to a body of literature where expressions of hope are too common, and careful attention to important detail too rare. It brings to the discussion the kind of realism which was always present in Thornton's work.

In his lecture, Neils Thygesen considered how a proposed institution, the European Central Bank, should be designed so as to deliver its assigned objective of price stability. The lecture by Roland Vaubel complements that perfectly, for its considers how an existing monetary institution, the IMF, actually functions. Such an analysis is usually approached from the starting assumption that policy makers in such an institution wish to maximise, subject to any unavoidable constraints, the welfare of whichever group with whose care they are charged. Neils Thygesen's prescriptions for the ECB are derived from such a framework, for his proposals are largely designed to protect the staff of that body from outside pressures which could impede the achieving of their objective. Professor Vaubel rejects that usual starting assumption, and starts from the public choice perspective. This approach, he writes, 'assumes that policy makers can, and often do, act against the public interest. It tries to explain economic policy by their personal preferences and restrictions' (p. 33).

Roland Vaubel chooses to apply his analysis to the IMF not from any suspicion that it is worse (or better) than any other institution, but because it is a particularly promising body to investigate from the public choice perspective. It is:

far removed from the attention and control of the voters... Language barriers and sheer distance raise the cost of gathering information... The issues to be decided are relatively technical. Since representatives of several countries participate in the decisions, the rate of return on information about those issues is even lower than in domestic policies.'

(p. 33)

He applies his analysis to IMF lending and IMF conditionality. The conclusion is that subsidised IMF lending is an inefficient form of aid and that the present form of conditionality is an inefficient way of giving advice. Both persist, despite the fact that 'many dedicated civil servants are at work in the International Monetary Fund' (p. 52), because the Fund faces a perverse incentive pattern.

These conclusions are important, and not just for any future reforms of the IMF. They manifestly have implications for the design of prospective institutions such as the ECB. It must be protected not just from perverse *external* pressures; it must also be protected from any incentive structure which produces *internal* ones. Professor Vaubel's paper is of major practical significance; a very fitting paper indeed in a lecture series in honour of Henry Thornton.

In his paper, Professor Issing broadened very substantially the range of issues usually considered in current discussions. Economists usually focus on technical matters – of analysis, of interpretation of data, of advising on policy and of devising appropriate incentive structures. That is understandable. There are major questions to resolve. It is not surprising that all previous Henry Thornton lectures have confined themselves to such technical issues. But sometimes it is necessary to go beyond these. It is necessary, for example, if we can attain one objective only at the expense of another; if, in other words, there is a long term trade off between the objectives. Fortunately, there is no such trade off for monetary policy. But other difficulties remain. Ever since the world abandoned a monetary system based on precious metals there has been debate over how monetary policy can best be guided. Reliance on purely discretionary decision making has, as Professor Issing explains, been unsatisfactory. But it has been difficult, in view of the uncertainty associated with the outcome of policy decisions, to advance monetary rules or constitutions which can be followed mechanically, and litigable contracts enforcing 'good' behaviour are also thus, Professor Issing argues, hard to design. Judgement has so far remained necessary. The problem Professor Issing has brought to our attention is how we are to choose who can be relied upon to exercise the best available judgement, perhaps against their own narrow interests. A simple way of putting the matter is to ask how we can be sure that good judgement will always be exercised. There is no straightfoward answer but it is both necessary and welcome that the question be brought to our attention.

THE CONDUCT OF POLICY

In this lecture Dr Schlesinger set out how monetary policy was inevitably affected by economic openness, but that nevertheless, 'any successful monetary policy invariably begins at home' (p. 138). And the objective of that policy should be price stability, not least because, 'A currency which has a stable value at home makes it easier to meet international obligations and to take the international context into adequate account' (p. 138).

In Germany, the Bundesbank has pursued price stability by targeting money growth; this has been done because 'monetary relations – that between the money stock and prices, demand for money, the trend in the velocity of circulation – are comparatively stable' (p. 138). There is thus no fundamental contrast between German monetary policy and that of countries such as Britain, which had from September 1992 a direct target for inflation. There is simply a difference of approach, a difference reflecting different monetary conditions. (One of the key differences is the short-term behaviour of the velocity of circulation of money, a subject which, as Dr Schlesinger notes, was discussed extensively by Henry Thornton in *Paper Credit*.)

When an economy is open the exchange rate regime is of manifest significance for the monetary authorities. This significance has several aspects. If the rate is floating, its behaviour may give information on the future trend in prices. 'It would be an illusion to believe it to be possible to safeguard the value of money at home and at the same time to ignore the exchange rate trend of one's own currency' (p. 139). Floating of course allows domestic monetary autonomy. But that may be at the cost of considerable exchange rate volatility, in consequence perhaps of monetary or fiscal policies elsewhere. Although transitory, such turbulence can cause problems through the relative stickiness of domestic prices. This had led, *inter alia*, to the desire to create a 'zone of monetary stability' in Europe. So far this has resulted in the EMS, the system to which the DM provides the anchor. The system depends of course on willingness to adapt national policies to maintain the link with that anchor. This willingness has varied from time to time, but must eventually be displayed otherwise the stable anchor of the system will be overwhelmed by inflows from abroad. The system requires a stable anchor – otherwise it is not worth joining – and stability of the anchor requires action from both the country whose currency it is, and from the others in the system. Responsibility runs both ways.

As this becomes more widely recognised, the possibilities of enlarged ERM membership increase. There are still, however, as Dr Schlesinger points out, substantial differences in the operating techniques of monetary policy. A move to full EMU is, he suggests, increasingly possible as the overwhelming importance of price stability is recognised. Such a move will require harmonisation of the methods of operation of monetary policy as well as of its objective.

Dr Schlesinger's lecture concludes with a brief discussion of EMU. He reiterates the importance of price stability, and therefore urges strict compliance with the Maastricht Treaty convergence criteria and the use of monetary targets as a way of operating monetary policy in the new system. There should also be, he writes, the introduction of 'minimum reserve requirements for all money creating institutions' (p. 144). Without price stability, any benefits that might emerge from a monetary union would soon be eroded. This lecture by Dr Schlesinger is a forceful and lucid elaboration of that point.

Professor Kindleberger directs our attention to the essence of central banking. The role of the central bank and the nature of its functions have been back at the centre of the stage in the last decade. A great deal of this discussion settled on the issue of independence. This in turn was a consequence of unsatisfactory behaviour of the price level in the preceding thirty years or so and a growing acceptance of the view that monetary stability could produce price stability. An institution free of political interference could, it has come to be believed, provide monetary stability, and hence price stability. But while that solved the long-run problem it left open what might happen in a financial crisis, or indeed its immediate predecessor, a rise in demand for liquidity. In other words what was the role of the lender of last resort. Unfortunately, this issue is still the subject of some debate and even confusion. At the heart of this is whether the lender of last resort means coming to the rescue of a financial institution that finds itself in difficulty, or whether it should limit itself to providing the market as a whole with sufficient liquidity for institutions to work with.

In his wide-ranging paper Charles Kindleberger demonstrates his considerable knowledge of history and theory and inclines to the former role: that the central bank has an obligation to aid institutions in some cases at least. He cites Ashton's view that the Bank of England was the lender of last resort in the eighteenth century, that is before it acquired monopoly of note issue and was still a large private institution pursuing commercial

business and profit. Kindleberger argues that the central bank in its role of
lender of last resort should sometimes bail out individual institutions, but
that it should not always do it; and by adopting such behaviour it can
reduce moral hazard somewhat. This is a view which understandably has
wide appeal and support but the issue of the extent of remaining moral
hazard, and its costs, will certainly continue to be debated.

BACKGROUND TO POLICY

Professor Laidler's paper is on the most difficult of all areas in macroeconomics, that of explaining business cycles. For most of the twentieth
century this has been what macroeconomics has been about. And at the
centre of the debate has been the role of wages and prices and their respective stickiness. In recent times explanations have been characterised as
either Neo-Classical or New Keynesian. In the former real variables
change because prices change, in the latter quantities change because
prices do not. But Laidler argues that classical and neo-classical economists believed that money wages and prices could be sticky. He then
takes us through an exemplary exploration of these concepts in the history
of economic thought from Hume and Cantillon through Mill and on to the
Phillips curve and beyond.

Laidler shows that the idea that money wages and prices are sticky
has a very long history, but that economists have nevertheless improved
their (and others') understanding of the significance of this for the analysis of economic fluctuations. Along the way he corrects many views on
the supposed role of money wage/real wage and price stickiness in the
respective schools of thought, but the main point he wishes to make is
that up until the 1970s the debate on these issues was always between
greater or lesser stickiness. He points out that prior to the 1970s the
phrases 'wage flexibility' and 'price flexibility' were not in use, since no
school of thought believed that markets always cleared by price alone.
Laidler argues that the return in the 1970s and 1980s to examining stickiness 'represents a return to a line of investigation which began in the
mid-eighteenth century and has more than proved its value in the
intervening years'.

While Henry Thornton was concerned with the nature of paper credit,
for him a relatively recent phenomenon, Michael Mussa glories in the
triumph of paper credit, the fact that in the last fifty years it has established itself as the basis of all monetary systems. Metallic monetary
standards are a thing of the past.

Mussa argues that metallic money held prices stable over the long-run, whereas currently and for the foreseeable future long-run stability has gone. Under modern paper standards monetary policy is not constrained by the objective of price-level stability. Under metallic standards deflation occurred, whereas under paper standards deflation is not politically feasible. The consequence is that long-run stability of prices can no longer be sustained. Nevertheless, there can still be disinflation and that brings some pain. Under metallic standards there were frequently bouts of deflation that brought the price level back to the original level following any inflationary period. That was painful. In the analogy that Mussa uses it was like old-fashioned dentistry without painkillers. That is no longer acceptable. Modern monetary systems no longer have deflation, but they involve occasional disinflation – like dentistry with painkillers, not pleasant but accepted as necessary. It is worth emphasising that Mussa ascribes the positive trend of price levels over the past fifty or so years to this dislike of deflation. He rejects the argument that it is the result of the time in consistency of a policy which promises price stability.

Mussa draws some lessons from the diversity of experience across several countries in the last fifty years. The first is that there is no long-run trade-off between inflation and economic activity. He argues that while economists knew this, from the work of Friedman and Phelps, by the beginning of the 1970s, it was the experience of the 1970s and 1980s that persuaded the public and policy makers. Further, that while disinflation has painful short-run costs, there is a willingness on the part of the public to bear these costs in order to reduce inflation. And finally, there is a growing understanding of the need for policies that guard against inflationary pressures developing. (This is doubtless what was behind the recent, growing interest in central bank independence.)

There are implications for the international monetary system. Given that we now live in a world where prices will drift upwards, albeit at as a slow pace, Mussa argues we will be bound to have floating exchange rates. However, he believes the exchange rate has lost much of its potency as a symbol of national strength, and no longer gives rise to the concern that it once did

MARKETS AND PUBLIC FINANCE

Robert Barro's 1987 lecture set out and reconsidered a view of the significance of government budget deficits that was discussed by David Ricardo and which Barro had revived in 1974. For many years the conventional view of budget deficits had been that they reduced net national saving. What Barro calls the 'standard model' (p. 13) starts from 'the assumption that the substitution of a budget deficit for current taxation leads to an expansion of aggregate consumer demand. In other words, desired private saving increases by less than the tax cut, so that desired national saving declines.' This assumption leads to the conclusions that a budget deficit stimulates demand, and that by raising the interest rate, it also reduces the stock of productive capital (or, in a small open economy, produces a current account deficit). But as Barro points out, given government spending, a deficit-financed tax cut implies higher future taxes of the same present value as the tax cut. This follows from the fact that, like everybody else, the government faces a budget constraint: 'government spending must be paid for now or later' (p. 15). The moment this is accepted, along with the belief that householders are aware of this, the conventional view of the impact of budget deficits must be rejected. 'The substitution of a budget deficit for current taxes (or any other rearrangement of the timing of taxes) has no impact on the aggregate demand for goods' (p. 15).

There are, as Barro notes, objections to this conclusion, but none of them reinstates the conventional view. He considers four major objections – finite horizons, imperfect loan markets, uncertainty about future taxes, and departures from lump sum taxes. All these objections have implications for 'Ricardian Equivalence' – for example, the last lets deficits be used for tax smoothing – but, he argues the 'Ricardian' approach provides a 'benchmark model for assessing fiscal policy' (p. 28). He reinforces this conclusion by examining the effects of budgets on interest rates, on saving, and on current account deficits. His review suggests that the evidence either supports the Ricardian view on balance or, if it does not, lends clear support to neither the Ricardian nor the conventional position.

This lecture is a forceful and clear statement of a theoretical conclusion with major practical implications.

Robert Shiller was at the fore-front of research on the efficient markets hypothesis that became a focus for work in the 1980s and 1990s when markets were again gaining in favour. Shiller asks why it is that asset markets from time to time produce quite dramatic bubbles – speculative booms often followed by crashes. Such booms and crashes appear to have been around since markets were first formed, and in the late 1980s we were reminded sharply again of violent movements. The view that was developing in the 1980s, and indeed becoming dominant, was that markets, particularly financial markets, were efficient, the efficiency deriving from rational investor behaviour. And yet if they were so efficient what could explain these apparently wild and irrational bubbles? Or could a bubble be rational? Shiller reports on some of his own work examining booms in the property market, and crashes in the stock market. His approach was an alternative to most of the other work going on in economics, laying stress as he did on the need to discover, as far as possible, what motivated the behaviour of those participating in the markets. Shiller and co-workers did this by means of questionnaires to participants, asking questions particularly on expected price changes under different types of markets conditions. And they followed this up with telephone interviews on what participants were thinking at the time of the crash. (In the case of the late 1980s they did this immediately after the crash.) Shiller concludes that such techniques reveal important insights into the causes of these booms and crashes.

CONCLUSIONS

The lectures in this volume range widely in both subject and in approach. They thereby demonstrate the continuing vigour of monetary economics and the wide variety of subjects that lies within its domain. Very remarkably, despite their variety and their relevance to current issues in economic policy, they are all developments of topics considered in Thornton's work. We hope that these lectures, tributes to Thornton, will encourage interest in his writings; there is still much to be learned and much intellectual stimulus to be gained from them.

Note

1. Robert Barro (1995) provides evidence in support of this last point for a large number of countries. Of particular importance he finds that even inflation in low single figures harms growth.

References

Barro, R. (1995) 'Inflation and Economic Growth', *Bank of England Quarterly Bulletin*, May, Vol. 35, No. 2, pp. 166–76.

Capie, F.H. (1986) 'Conditions in which Hyperinflation has Appeared', in Brunner and Meltzer (eds.), *Carnegie Rochester Public Policy Series*, March. Reprinted in Capie (ed.), *Major Inflations in History*.

Capie, F.H., and Wood, G.E. (1989) *Monetary Economics in the 1980s* (London: Macmillan).

Hayek, F.A. (1932) 'Introduction' to Thornton's *Paper Credit* (New York: Rinehart).

Humphrey, T. (1986) 'Cumulative Process Models from Thornton to Wicksell', *Federal Reserve Bank of Richmond Review*, Vol. 72, May/June.

Perlman, M. (1986) 'The Bullionist Controversy Revisited', *Journal of Political Economy*, Vol. 94, No. 4, August.
Wood, G.E. (1990) 'One Money for Europe', *Journal of Monetary Economics*, No. 25.

1 Ricardo and Budget Deficits[*]

Robert Barro

In recent years there has been a lot of discussion about US budget deficits. Many economists and other observers have viewed these deficits as harmful to the US and world economies. The supposed harmful effects, predicted by theories of the life-cycle type, include high real interest rates, low saving, low rates of economic growth, large current-account deficits in the United States and other countries with large budget deficits, and either a high or low dollar (depending apparently on the time period). On the other hand, this crisis scenario has been hard to maintain along with the robust performance of the US economy since late 1982. This performance features high average growth rates of real GNP, declining unemployment, much lower inflation than before, a sharp decrease in nominal interest rates and some decline in expected real interest rates, high values of real investment expenditures, and a dramatic boom in the stock market.

Persistent budget deficits have increased economists' interest in theories and evidence about fiscal policy. At the same time, the conflict between standard predictions and actual outcomes in the US economy has, I think, increased economists' willingness to consider approaches that depart from the standard paradigm. In this paper I will focus on the alternative theory that is associated with the name of David Ricardo.

THE STANDARD MODEL OF BUDGET DEFICITS

Before developing the Ricardian approach, I will sketch the standard model. The starting point is the assumption that the substitution of a budget deficit for current taxation leads to an expansion of aggregate consumer demand. In other words, desired private saving rises by less than the tax cut, so that desired national saving declines. It follows for a closed

---

* This lecture was delivered in November 1987 and first published in booklet form by City University Business School, Dept of Banking and Finance.

economy that the expected real interest rate would have to rise to restore
equality between desired national saving and investment demand. The
higher real interest rate crowds out investment, which shows up in the
long run as a small stock of productive capital. Thereby, in the language of
Franco Modigliani (1961), the public debt is an intergenerational burden
in that it leads to a smaller stock of capital for future generations. Similar
reasoning applies to pay-as-you-go social security programmes, as has
been stressed by Martin Feldstein (1974). An increase in the scope of
these programmes raises the aggregate demand for goods, and thereby
leads to a higher real interest rate and a smaller stock of productive capital.

In an open economy, a small country's budget deficits or social security
programmes would have negligible effects on the real interest rate on
international capital markets. Therefore, in the standard analysis, the home
country's decision to substitute a budget deficit for current taxes leads
mainly to increased borrowing from abroad, rather than to a higher real
interest rate. That is, budget deficits lead to current-account deficits.
Expected real interest rates rise for the home country only if it is large
enough to influence world markets, or if the increased national debt
induces foreign lenders to demand higher expected returns on this
country's obligations. In any event, there is a weaker tendency for a
country's budget deficits to crowd out its domestic investment in the short
run and its stock of capital in the long run. However, in the long run, the
current-account deficits show up as a reduced stock of national wealth,
which corresponds to the greater claims of foreigners.

If the whole world runs budget deficits or expands the scale of its social
insurance programmes, then real interest rates rise on international capital
markets, and crowding-out of investment occurs in each country.
Correspondingly, the world's stock of capital is lower in the long run.
These effects for the world parallel those for a single closed economy, as
discussed before.

THE RICARDIAN ALTERNATIVE

The Ricardian modification to the standard analysis begins with the
observation that, for a given path of government spending, a deficit-
financed cut in current taxes leads to higher future taxes that have the
same present value as the initial cut. This result follows from the government's budget constraint, which equates total expenditures for each period
(including interest payments) to revenues from taxation or other sources
and the net issue of interest-bearing public debt. Abstracting from chain-

letter cases where the public debt can grow forever at the rate of interest or higher, the present value of taxes (and other revenues) cannot change unless the government changes the present value of its expenditures. This point amounts to economists' standard notion of the absence of a free lunch – government spending must be paid for now or later, with the total present value of receipts fixed by the total present value of spending. Hence, holding fixed the path of government expenditures and non-tax revenues, a cut in today's taxes must be matched by a corresponding increase in the present value of future taxes.[1]

Suppose now that households' demands for goods depend on the expected present value of taxes – that is, each household subtracts its share of this present value from the expected present value of its income to determine its net wealth position. Then fiscal policy would affect aggregate consumer demand only if it altered the expected present value of taxes. But the preceding argument was that the present value of taxes would not change as long as the present value of spending did not change. Therefore, the substitution of a budget deficit for current taxes (or any other rearrangement of the timing of taxes) has no impact on the aggregate demand for goods. In this sense, budget deficits and taxation have equivalent effects on the economy – hence, the term, 'Ricardian equivalence theorem'.[2] To put the equivalence result another way, a decrease in the government's saving (that is, a current budget deficit) leads to an offsetting increase in desired private saving, and hence to no change in desired national saving.

Since desired national saving does not change, the real interest rate does not have to rise in a closed economy to maintain balance between desired national saving and investment demand. Hence, there is no effect on investment, and no burden of the public debt or social security in the sense of Modigliani (1961) and Feldstein (1974). In a setting of an open economy there would also be no effect on the current-account balance because desired private saving rises by enough to avoid having to borrow from abroad. Therefore, budget deficits would not cause current-account deficits.

THEORETICAL OBJECTIONS TO RICARDIAN EQUIVALENCE

I shall discuss four major theoretical objections that have been raised against the Ricardian conclusions. The first is that people do not live forever, and hence do not care about taxes that are levied after their death. The second is that private capital markets are 'imperfect', with the typical person's real discount rate exceeding that of the government. The third is that future taxes and incomes are uncertain. The fourth is that taxes are not lump sum, since they depend typically on income, spending, wealth, and so on. I assume throughout that the path of government spending is given. The Ricardian analysis applies to shifts in budget deficits and taxes for a given pattern of government expenditures; in particular, the approach is consistent with real effects from changes in the level or timing of government purchases and public services.

It turns out that each of the four issues implies that budget deficits matter, and are in that sense non-Ricardian. However, it is important in each case to consider not only whether the Ricardian view remains intact, but also what alternative conclusions emerge. Many economists raise points that invalidate strict Ricardian equivalence, and then simply assume that the points support a specific alternative; usually the standard view that a budget deficit lowers desired national saving and thereby drives up real interest rates or leads to a current-account deficit. Many criticisms of the Ricardian position are also inconsistent with this standard view.

Finite Horizons and Related Issues

The idea of finite horizons, motivated by the finiteness of life, is central to life-cycle models – see, for example, Franco Modigliani and Richard Brumberg (1954) and Albert Ando and Franco Modigliani (1963). In these models individuals capitalize only the taxes that they expect to face before dying. Consider a deficit-financed tax cut, and assume that the higher future taxes occur partly during the typical person's expected lifetime and partly thereafter. Then the present value of the first portion must fall short of the initial tax cut, since a full balance results only if the second portion is included. Hence the net wealth of persons currently alive rises, which motivates an increase in consumption demand. The rise in consumer demand means that desired private saving does not rise by enough to offset fully the decline in government saving; hence desired national saving falls. It follows in a closed economy that the current real interest rate increases, which reduces investment demand in the short run and the stock of capital in the long run. For an open economy, the short-run response is a current-account deficit, which leads in the long run to a small stock of national wealth.

A finite horizon seems to generate the standard result that a budget deficit reduces desired national saving. However, the argument works only if the typical person feels better off when the government shifts a tax burden to his or her descendants. The argument fails if the typical person is already giving to his or her children out of altruism. In this case people react to the government's imposed intergenerational transfers, which are implied by budget deficits or social security, with a compensating increase in voluntary transfers (see Robert Barro, 1974). For example, parents adjust their bequests or the amounts given to children while the parents are still living (or, equivalently, children raise their transfers to aged parents).

The main point is that a network of intergenerational transfers makes the typical person a part of an extended family that goes on indefinitely. In this setting, households capitalize the entire array of expected future taxes, and thereby plan effectively with an infinite horizon. In other words, the Ricardian results, which seemed to depend on infinite horizons, can remain valid in a model with finite lifetimes.

Two important points should be stressed. First, intergenerational transfers do not have to be 'large'; what is necessary is that transfers based on altruism be operative at the margin for the typical person.[3] Specifically, most people must be away from the corner solution of zero transfers, where they would, if permitted, opt for negative payments to their children. (However, the results also go through if children typically support their aged parents.) Second, the transfers do not have to show up as bequests at death. Other forms of intergenerational transfers work in a similar manner.

One objection to Ricardian equivalence is that some persons, such as those without children, are not connected to future generations (see James Tobin and Willem Buiter, 1980, pp. 86ff.). Persons in this situation tend to be made wealthier when the government substitutes a budget deficit for taxes. At least this conclusion obtains to the extent that the interest and principal payments on the extra public debt are not financed by higher taxes during the remaining lifetimes of people currently alive. However, the quantitative effects on consumption tend to be small. For example, for someone with 30 years of remaining life who consumes at a constant rate, a one-time budget deficit of $1 would increase real consumption demand by 1.4 cents per year if the annual real interest rate is 5 per cent, and by 2.1 cents per year if the real interest rate is 3 per cent.[4]

The aggregate effect from the existence of childless persons is even smaller because people with more than the average number of descendants experience a decrease in wealth when taxes are replaced by budget deficits. (In effect, although some people have no children, all children must have parents.) The presumption for a net effect on aggregate consumer demand depends on different propensities to consume out of wealth for people with and without children. Since the propensity for those without children tends to be larger (because of the shorter horizon), a positive net effect on aggregate consumer demand would be predicted. However, the quantitative effect is likely to be trivial. Making the same assumptions as in the previous example, a budget deficit of $1 would raise aggregate real consumption demand by 0.3 cents per year if the real interest rate is 5 per cent and by 0.9 cents if the real interest rate is 3 per cent.

Michael Darby (1979, Ch. 3) and Laurence Kotlikoff and Lawrence Summers (1981) calculate that the accumulation of households' assets in the United States for the purpose of intergenerational transfers is far more important than that associated with the life cycle. This observation suggests that intergenerational transfers would be operative for most people, which supports the Ricardian position as noted above.

Douglas Bernheim, Andrei Shleifer and Lawrence Summers (1985) note that the motivation behind intergenerational transfers matters for the results. These authors consider the possibility that bequests, instead of being driven by altruism, are a strategic device whereby parents induce their children to behave properly. Some imaginative evidence is presented (involving how often children visit and communicate with their parents) to document the importance of strategic bequests.

This enforcement theory of giving has different implications for the effects of budget deficits and social security. If the government redistributes income from young to old (by running a deficit or raising social security benefits), then the old have no reason in this model to raise transfers to offset fully the government's actions. Instead, the old end up better off at the expense of the young, and aggregate consumer demand rises. Then, as in the standard approach, real interest rates increase or domestic residents borrow more from abroad.

One shortcoming of this approach is that it treats the interaction between parents and children as equivalent to the purchases of services on markets. In this setting parents would tend to pay wages to children, rather than using bequests or other forms of intergenerational transfers. These features – as well as the observation that most parents seem to care about their children's welfare – can be better explained by introducing altruism along with a desire to influence children's behaviour. In this case Ricardian equivalence may or may not obtain. Consider the utility that a parent would allocate to his or her child if there were no difficulty in motivating the child to perform properly. Suppose that the parent can design a credible threat involving bequests that entails the loss of some part of this utility for the child. (Note that if no threats are credible, the whole basis for strategic bequests disappears.) If the threat is large enough to induce the child's behaviour that the parent desires, Ricardian equivalence still holds. For example, if the government runs a budget deficit, the parent increases transfers to the child, and thereby preserves the child's level of utility, as well as the behaviour sought by the parent. On the other hand, the parent may have to allow excess utility to the child in order to secure a better threat against bad performance. Then a budget deficit enables the parent to reduce the child's utility (as desired), while maintaining or even enhancing the threat that influences the child's behaviour. In this case Ricardian equivalence does not hold.

Imperfect Loan Markets

Many economists argue that the imperfection of private credit markets is central to an analysis of the public debt; see, for example, Robert Mundell (1971). To incorporate this element, assume that a closed economy consists of two types of infinite-lived economic agents; those of group A who have the same discount rate, r, as the government (and are therefore willing to hold the government's debt), and those of group B who have the higher discount rate r̃ > r. The constituents of group A would include many large businesses and some individuals. The members of group B, such as small businesses and many households, possess poor collateral; therefore, loans to these people imply large costs of evaluation and enforcement. It follows that the members of group B face higher borrowing rates (even after an allowance for default risk) than the government.

Suppose that the government cuts current taxes and runs a budget deficit. Further, assume that the division of the tax cut between groups A and B – say fifty-fifty – is the same as the division of the higher future taxes needed to service the extra debt. Then, as in the Ricardian setting, those from group A experience no net change in wealth. But, since r̃ > r, the present value of group B's extra future taxes falls short of that group's share of the tax cut. Therefore, those from group B react to their increased wealth by raising consumption demand. Moreover, as current consumption increases, the discount rate r̃ tends to fall, which motivates an increase in investment demand. For example, if a small business uses its tax cut to raise current investment, the fall in r̃ reflects the diminishing marginal return to investment.

In the aggregate a budget deficit now raises aggregate demand, or equivalently, the aggregate of desired private saving increases by less than one-to-one with the government's deficit. It follows that the real interest rate r, which applies to group A and the government, rises to induce people to hold the extra public debt. Hence there is crowding out of consumption and investment by members of group A. However, since the discount rate r̃ for group B declines on net, the expenditures of this group are encouraged. The main result is a diversion of expenditures from group A to group B, and a corresponding narrowing of the spread between the two discount rates, r and r̃. In the aggregate investment may either rise or fall, and the long-term effect on the capital stock is uncertain. However, the major change is a better channelling of resources to their ultimate uses. Namely the persons from group B – who have relatively high values for rates of time preference and for marginal returns to investment – command a greater share of current output. In any event the outcomes are non-neutral, and in that sense non-Ricardian.

The important finding from the inclusion of imperfect loan markets is that the government's issue of public debt can amount to a useful form of financial intermediation. The government induces people with good access to credit markets (group A) to hold more than their share of the extra public debt. Those with poor access (group B) hold less than their share, and thereby effectively receive loans from the first group. This process works because the government implicitly guarantees the repayment of loans through its tax collections and debt payments. Thus loans between A and B take place even though such loans were not viable (because of 'transaction costs') on the imperfect private and credit market.

This much of the argument may be valid, although it credits the government with too much skill in the collection of taxes from people with poor collateral (which is the underlying source of the problem for private lenders). But even if the government is more efficient, the conclusions do not resemble those from the standard analysis. As discussed before, budget deficits can amount to more financial intermediation, and are in that sense equivalent to a technological advance that improves the functioning of loan markets. From this perspective it is reasonable to find a reduced spread between various discount rates and an improvement in the allocation of resources. If the government really is better at the process of intermediating, then more of this activity – that is, more public debt – raises perceived wealth because it actually improves the workings of the economy.

Instead of introducing costs of enforcing the collection of loans, Toshiki Yotsuzuka (1986) extends the analysis of Mervyn King (1984) and Fumio Hayashi (1985) by allowing for adverse selection among borrowers with different risk characteristics. Individuals know their probabilities of default, but the lenders' only possibility for learning these probabilities comes from observing the chosen levels of borrowing at going interest rates. In this setting the government's borrowing amounts to a loan to a group that pools the various risk classes. Such borrowing matters if the private equilibrium does not involve similar pooling. However, by considering the incentives of lenders to exchange or not exchange information about their customers, Yotsuzuka argues that the private equilibrium typically involves a pooled loan of limited quantity at a relatively low interest rate. Then the high-risk types may borrow additional amounts at a high interest rate. In this case the government's borrowing replaces the private pooled lending, and leads to no real effects. That is, Ricardian equivalence holds despite the imperfect private loan market where high-risk people face high marginal borrowing rates. The general lesson again is that Ricardian equivalence fails because of imperfect credit markets only if the government does things in the loan market that are different from, and perhaps better than, those carried out privately.

Uncertainty about Future Taxes and Incomes

Some economists argue that the uncertainty about individuals' future taxes – or the complexity in estimating them – implies a high rate of discount in capitalizing these future liabilities (see Martin Bailey, 1971, pp. 157–8; James Buchanan and Ricard Wagner, 1977, pp. 17, 101, 130; and Martin Feldstein, 1976, p. 335). In this case, a substitution of a budget deficit for current taxes raises net wealth because the present value of the higher expected future taxes falls short of the current tax cut. It then follows that budget deficits raise aggregate consumer demand and lower desired national saving.

A proper treatment of uncertainty leads to different conclusions. Louis Chan (1983) first considers the case of lump-sum taxes that have a known distribution across households. However, the aggregate of future taxes and the real value of future payments on public debt are subject to uncertainty. In this case a deficit-financed tax cut has no real effects. Individuals hold their share of the extra debt because the debt is a perfect hedge against the uncertainty of the future taxes. (This analysis assumes that private credit markets have no 'imperfections' of the sort discussed earlier.)

Suppose now that future taxes are still lump sum but have an uncertain incidence across individuals. Furthermore, assume that there are no insurance markets for relative tax risks. Then a budget deficit tends to increase the uncertainty about each individual's future disposable income. Chan (1983, p. 363) shows for the 'usual case' (of non-increasing absolute risk aversion) that people react by reducing current consumption and hence, by raising current private saving by more than the tax cut. Consequently, the effects on real interest rates, investment, the current account, and so on are the opposites of the standard ones.

The results are different for an income tax (Chan, 1983, pp. 364–6 and Robert Barsky, Gregory Mankiw and Stephen Zeldes, 1986). Suppose that each person pays the tax ry_i, where y_i is the person's uncertain future income. Suppose that there are no insurance markets for individual income risks, and that r is known. (The analysis thus abstracts from uncertainties in relative tax rates across individuals.) In this case a budget deficit raises the future value of r and thereby reduces the uncertainty about each individual's future disposable income. In effect, the government shares the risks about individual disposable income to a greater extent. It follows that the results are opposite to those found before; namely, a budget deficit tends to raise current consumption and hence, to raise private saving by less than the tax cut.

Overall, the conclusions depend on the net effect of higher mean future tax collections on the uncertainty associated with individuals' future disposable incomes. Desired national saving tends to rise with a budget deficit if this uncertainty increases, and vice versa.

The Timing of Taxes

Departures from Ricardian equivalence arise also if taxes are not lump sum; for example, with an income tax. In this situation budget deficits change the timing of income taxes, which affects people's incentives to work and produce in different periods. It follows that variations in deficits are non-neutral, although the results tend also to be inconsistent with the standard view.

Suppose, for example, that the current income-tax rate, r_1, declines, the expected rate for the next period, r_2, rises. To simplify matters, assume that today's budget deficit is matched by enough of a surplus next period so that the public debt does not change in later periods. Because the tax rate applies to income, people are motivated to work and produce more than usual in period 1 and less than usual in period 2. Since the tax rate does not apply to expenditures (and since wealth effects are negligible here), it follows that desired national saving rises in period 1 and falls in period 2. Therefore, in a closed economy, after-tax real interest rates tend to be relatively low in period 1 – along with the budget deficit – and relatively high in period 2 – along with the surplus. In an open economy, a current-account surplus accompanies the budget deficit, and vice versa.[5] Hence the results are non-Ricardian, but also counter to the standard view. (Temporary variations in consumption taxes tend to generate the standard pattern where real interest rates, current-account deficits, and budget deficits are positively correlated.)

Unlike in the Ricardian case where debt and deficits do not matter, it is possible in a world of distorting taxes to determine the optimal path of the budget deficit, which corresponds to the optimal time pattern of taxes. In effect, the theory of debt management becomes a branch of public finance; specifically, an application of the theory of optimal taxation.

One important observation is that budget deficits can be used to smooth tax rates over time, despite fluctuations in government expenditures and the tax base. For example, if time periods are identical except for the quantity of government purchases – which are assumed not to interact directly with labour supply decisions – then optimality dictates uniform taxation of labour income over time. This constancy of tax rates requires budget deficits when government spending is unusually high, such as in wartime, and surpluses when spending is unusually low.

Constant tax rates over time will not be optimal in general;[6] for example, it may be that optimal tax rates on labour income would vary over the business cycle. To the extent that some smoothing is called for, budget deficits would occur in recessions, and surpluses in booms. If optimal tax rates are lower than normal in recessions and higher than normal in booms, then the countercyclical pattern of budget deficits is even more vigorous. The well-known concept of the full-employment deficit, as discussed in Cary Brown (1956) and Council of Economic Advisors (1962, pp. 78–82), adjusts for this cyclical behaviour of budget deficits.

The tax-smoothing view has implications for the interaction between inflation and budget deficits if the public debt is denominated in nominal terms. Basically, the fiscal authority's objective involves the path of tax rates and other real variables. Therefore, other things equal, a higher rate of expected inflation (presumably reflecting a higher rate of monetary growth) motivates a correspondingly higher growth rate of the nominal, interest-bearing debt. This response keeps the planned path of the real public debt invariant with expected inflation. This behaviour means that differences in expected rates of inflation can account for substantial variations in budget deficits if deficits are measured in the conventional way to correspond to the change in the government's nominal liabilities. However, this element is less important for an inflation-adjusted budget deficit, which corresponds to the change in the government's real obligations (see Jeremy Siegel, 1979).

With perfect foresight, the strict tax-smoothing model implies constant tax rates. More realistically, new information about the path of government spending, national income, and so on, would lead to revisions of tax rates. However, the sign of these revisions would not be predictable. Thus, in the presence of uncertainty, tax smoothing implies that tax rates would behave roughly like random walks.

It is possible to use the tax-smoothing approach as a positive theory of how the government operates, rather than as a normative model of how it should act.[7] Barro (1979, 1986) shows that this framework explains much of the behaviour of US federal deficits from 1916 to 1983, although the deficits since 1984 turn out to be substantially higher than predicted. Over the full sample, the major departures from the theory are an excessive reaction of budget deficits to the business cycle (so that tax rates fall below 'normal' during recessions) and an insufficient reaction to temporary military spending (so that tax rates rise above normal during wars). These departures are found also by Chaipat Sahasakul (1986), who looks directly at the behaviour of average marginal tax rates. Robert Barro (1987, Section 3) finds for the British data from the early 1700s through 1918 that temporary military spending is the major determinant of budget deficits. Also, unlike the US case, the results indicate a one-to-one response of budget deficits to temporary spending.

Gregory Mankiw (1987) used the tax-smoothing model for a joint analysis of the inflation tax and other taxes. This perspective can explain why short-term nominal interest rates, which are the tax rate associated with money, have been close to a random walk since the founding of the Federal Reserve System in 1914 (see Gregory Mankiw and Jeffrey Miron, 1986). Moreover, Mankiw (1987) finds, for the United States from 1952 to 1985, that changes in nominal interest rates are positively associated with changes in the ratio of federal tax receipts to GNP or with changes in average marginal tax rates. These results accord with a model where nominal interest rates and other tax rates are jointly determined from an optimal-tax perspective.

EMPIRICAL EVIDENCE ON THE ECONOMIC EFFECTS OF BUDGET DEFICITS

It is easy on the theoretical grounds to raise points that invalidate strict Ricardian equivalence. Nevertheless, it may still be that the Ricardian view provides a useful framework for assessing the first-order effects of fiscal policy. Furthermore, it is unclear theoretically that the standard analysis offers a more accurate guide. For these reasons it is especially important to examine empirical evidence.

The Ricardian and standard views have different predictions about the effects of fiscal policy on a number of economic variables. The next two sections summarize the empirical evidence on interest rates and saving.

Although these variables have received considerable attention, the theories also have divergent implications for other variables, such as the current-account balance and exchange rates. However, because less empirical work has been done, even less is known about these variables than about interest rates and saving.

Interest Rates

The Ricardian view predicts no effect of budget deficits on real interest rates, whereas the standard view predicts a positive effect, at least in the context of a closed economy. Many economists have tested these propositions empirically (for a summary, see US Treasury Department, 1984). Typical results show little relationship between budget deficits and interest rates. For example, Charles Plosser (1982, p. 339) finds for quarterly US data from 1954 to 1978 that unexpected movements in privately-held federal debt do not raise the nominal yield on government securities of various maturities. In fact, there is a weak tendency for yields to decline with innovations in federal debt. Plosser's (1987, Tables VIII and XI) later study, which includes data through 1985, reaches similar conclusions for nominal and expected real yields. Paul Evans (1987b) obtains similar results for nominal yields with quarterly data from 1974 to 1985 for Canada, France, Germany, Japan, the United Kingdom, and the United States.

Paul Evans (1987a, Tables 4–6) finds from annual US data for 1931 to 1979 that current and past real federal deficits have no significant association with nominal interest rates on commercial paper or corporate bonds, or with realized real interest rates on commercial paper. Over the longer period from 1908 to 1984, using monthly data, there is some indication of a negative relation between deficits and nominal or real interest rates (Evans, 1987a, Tables 1–3). Evans also explores the effects of expected future budget deficits or surpluses. He assumes that people would have expected future deficits in advance of tax cuts, such as in 1981, and future surpluses in advance of tax hikes. But interest rates turn out typically not to rise in advance of tax cuts and not to fall in advance of tax hikes. If anything, interest rates tended to move with the opposite pattern. Mankiw's (1987) analysis, which views the nominal interest rate as a form of tax rate, is consistent with these findings.

Overall, the empirical results on interest rates support the Ricardian view. Given these findings it is remarkable that most macroeconomists remain confident that budget deficits raise interest rates.

Consumption and Saving

Most empirical results on the interplay between budget deficits and saving come from the estimate coefficients of fiscal variables in consumption or saving functions. Examples of this work are Kochin, 1974, Ernest Tanner, 1979, Martin Feldstein, 1982, Roger Kormendi, 1983, John Seater and Robert Mariano, 1985, and Franco Modigliani and Arlie Sterling, 1986. The majority of these (selected) studies finds that fiscal policy has little effect on consumer demand, but Feldstein and Modigliani/Sterling reach opposite conclusions.

The consumption-function approach has also been used to assess the effect of retirement programmes under social security. When funded on a pay-as-you-go basis, such programmes are similar to budget deficits in terms of their theoretical effects on national saving. Feldstein (1974, 1977) initially concluded that more generous social security programmes depressed national saving. However, this finding was contested in subsequent research (see, for example, Robert Barro, 1978, Darby, 1979, Louis Esposit, 1978, Arlie Sterling, 1977, Robert Barro and Glenn MacDonald, 1979, and Dean Leimer and Selig Lesnoy, 1982). Overall, the evidence from the US time series and from a cross-section of countries fails to demonstrate a clear link between social security and national saving.

The empirical studies mentioned above rely on estimates of consumption functions, which involve well-known identification problems. For example, the approach does not deal satisfactorily with the simultaneity among consumption, income, and real interest rates. Another difficulty concerns the definitions of wealth and income; the inclusion of capital gains has dramatic effects on measures of US saving (see James Poterba and Lawrence Summers, 1986, Appendix Table A–2). Other problems concern the fiscal variables that enter as regressors. These variables can play a signalling role for future income or government expenditure, which affects the interpretation of estimated coefficients. For example, if the government adjusts its budget deficits to smooth out tax rates, as suggested before, then the current tax rate proxies for the expected long-run ratio of government expenditure to income, which influences current consumption demand (see Levis Kochin, Daniel Benjamin, and Mark Meador, 1985). Similarly, the correlation of the deficit with recessions, wars, and so on affects the analysis.

Chris Carroll and Lawrence Summers (1987) compare private saving in the United States and Canada. They note that the private saving rates were similar in the two countries until the early 1970s, but have since diverged; for 1983–5 the Canadian rate was higher by about 6 percentage points.

After holding fixed some macroeconomic variables and aspects of the tax systems that influence saving, the authors isolate a roughly one-to-one, positive effect of government budget deficits on private saving. That is, as implied by the Ricardian view, the relative values of net national saving in the United States and Canada appeared to be invariant with the relative values of the budget deficits. These results are particularly interesting because the focus on relative performance in the United States and Canada holds constant the many forces that have common influences on the two countries. It may be that this procedure lessens the problems of identification that hamper most studies of consumption functions.

Current-Account Deficits

Popular opinion attributes the large current-account deficits in the United States since 1983 to the effects of budget deficits. There has not been much careful analysis of this relationship, but the data reveal a positive association between the two deficits only if the experience since 1983 is included.

On data since 1948 to 1982 there is no association between the ratio of the total government budget surplus (national accounts' version) to GNP (solid line) and the ratio of net foreign investment to GNP (dotted line).[8] (correlation = −.02). However, including the data since 1983 raises the correlation to .36. In effect, the US data since World War II reveal just a single incident – the period since 1983 – when budget and current-account deficits have been high at the same time. While this recent co-movement is interesting, it does not provide strong support for the view that budget deficits cause current-account deficits. It would be useful to investigate this relationship further, possibly with data from other countries.

CONCLUDING OBSERVATIONS

The Ricardian approach to budget deficits amounts to the statement that the government's fiscal impact is summarized by the present value of its expenditures. Given this present value, rearrangements of the timing of taxes – as implied by budget deficits – have no first-order effect on the economy. Second-order effects arise for various reasons, which include the distorting effects of taxes, the uncertainties about individual incomes and tax obligations, the imperfections of credit markets, and the finiteness of life. To say that these effects are second order is not to say that they are uninteresting; in fact, the analysis of differential taxation in the theory of public finance is second order in the same sense. However, careful analysis of these effects tends to deliver predictions about budget deficits that differ from those of standard macroeconomic models.

I have argued that empirical findings tend mainly to support the Ricardian viewpoint. However, these findings deal primarily with interest rates and consumption/saving, and the results are sometimes inconclusive. It would be useful to assemble additional evidence, especially in an international context.

Although the majority of economists still lean toward standard macroeconomic models of fiscal policy, it is remarkable how respectable the Ricardian approach has become in the last decade. Most macroeconomists now feel obligated to state the Ricardian position, even if they then go on to argue that it is either theoretically or empirically in error. I predict that this trend will continue and that the Ricardian approach will become the benchmark model for assessing fiscal policy. This is not to say that most analysts will embrace Ricardian equivalence and therefore conclude that fiscal policy is irrelevant. But satisfactory analyses will feature explicit modelling of elements that lead to departures from Ricardian equivalence, and the predicted consequences of fiscal policies will flow directly from these elements.

Notes

1. The calculations use the government's interest rate in each period to calculate present values, and assume perfect foresight with respect to future government expenditures and taxes. For further discussion see Ben McCallum (1984) and Robert Barro (1988, Section 5).

2. The term, Ricardian equivalence theorem, was introduced to macroeconomists by James Buchanan (1976). After Gerald O'Driscoll (1977) documented Ricardo's reservations about this result, some economists have referred to the equivalence finding as being non-Ricardian. But, as far as I have been able to discover, David Ricardo (1951) was the first to articulate this theory. Therefore, the attribution of the equivalence theorem to Ricardo is appropriate even if he had doubts about some of the theorem's assumptions. As to whether the presence of this idea in Ricardo's writings is important for scientific progress, I would refer to Nathan Rosenberg's (1976, p. 79) general views on innovations in the social sciences:

> what often happens in economics is that, as concern mounts over a particular problem ... an increasing number of professionals commit their time and energies to it. We then eventually realize that there were all sorts of treatments of the subject in the earlier literature ... We then proceed to read much of our more sophisticated present-day understanding back into the work of earlier writers whose analysis was inevitably more fragmen-

tary and incomplete than the later achievement. It was this retrospective view which doubtless inspired Whitehead to say somewhere that everything of importance has been said before – but by someone who did not discover it.

3.   Philippe Weil (1987) and Miles Kimball (1987) analyse conditions that ensure an interior solution for intergenerational transfers. Douglas Bernheim and Kyle Bagwell (1986) argue that difficulties arise if altruistic transfers are pervasive. See Robert Barro (1988, Section 5) for a discussion of their analysis.

4.   The assumption is the real debt remains permanently higher by $1. For some related calculations, see Merton Miller and Charles Upton (1974, Chapter 8) and James Poterba and Lawrence Summers (1987, Section I).

5.   These results follow if the effects on investment demand are small. With adjustment costs, investment would tend to respond little to this kind of temporary change in income taxes.

6.   The conditions for optimality, based on results from optimal taxation theory, appear in David Aschauer and Jeremy Greenwood (1985). On the notion of tax smoothing, see A.C. Pigou (1928, Chapter 6), Robert Barro (1979, 1986), and Finn Kydland and Edward Prescott (1980).

7.   A colleague of mine argues that a 'normative' model should be defined as a model that fits the data badly.

8.   The data are quarterly, seasonally-adjusted values from Citibase. The results are similar if the federal surplus is used instead of the total government surplus.

References

Ando, Albert and Franco Modigliani (1963) 'The "Life Cycle" Hypothesis of Saving: Aggregate Implications and Tests', *American Economic Review*, 53, March, pp. 55–84.

Aschauer, David A. and Jeremy Greenwood (1985) 'Macroeconomic Effects of Fiscal Policy', *Carnegie-Rochester Conference Series on Public Policy*, 23, Autumn, pp. 91–138.

Bailey, Martin J. (1971) *National Income and the Price Level*, 2nd edition (New York: McGraw Hill).

Barro, Robert J. (1974) 'Are Government Bonds Net Wealth?' *Journal of Political Economy*, 82, November/December, pp. 1095–117.

Barro, Robert J. (1978) *The Impact of Social Security on Private Saving: Evidence from the U.S. Time Series* (Washington D.C.: American Enterprise Institute).

Barro, Robert J. (1979) 'On the Determination of the Public Debt', *Journal of Political Economy*, 87, October, pp. 940–71.

Barro, Robert J. (1986) 'U.S. Deficits since World War I', *Scandinavian Journal of Economics*, 88, No. 1, pp. 195–222.

Barro, Robert J. (1987) 'Government Spending, Interest Rates, Prices, and Budget Deficits in the United Kingdom, 1701–1918', *Journal of Monetary Economics*, 20, September.

Barro, Robert J. (1988) 'The Neoclassical Approach to Fiscal Policy', in Robert J. Barro (ed.) *Handbook of Modern Business Cycle Theory* (New York: Wiley).

Barro, Robert J. and Glenn M. MacDonald (1979) 'Social Security and Consumer Spending in an International Cross Section', *Journal of Public Economics*, 11, pp. 275–89.

Barsky, Robert B., N. Gregory Mankiw, and Stephen P. Zeldes (1986) 'Ricardian Consumers with Keynesian Propensities', *American Economic Review*, 76, September, pp. 676–91.

Bernheim, B. Douglas, Andrei Shleifer, and Lawrence H. Summers (1985) 'The Strategic Bequest Motive', *Journal of Political Economy*, 93, December, pp. 1045–76.

Bernheim, B. Douglas and Kyle Bagwell (1986) 'Is Everything Neutral?' unpublished, Stanford University, July.

Brown, E. Cary (1956) 'Fiscal Policy in the Thirties: a Reappraisal', *Journal of Political Economy*, 46, December, pp. 857–79.

Buchanan, James M. (1976) 'Barro on the Ricardian Equivalence Theorem', *Journal of Political Economy*, 84, April, pp. 337–42.

Buchanan, James M. and Richard E. Wagner (1977) *Democracy in Deficit* (New York: Academic Press).

Carroll, Chris and Lawrence H. Summers (1987) 'Why Have Private Savings Rates in the United States and Canada Diverged?' *Journal of Monetary Economics*, 20, 1987

Chan, Louis K.C. (1983) 'Uncertainty and the Neutrality of Government Financing Policy', *Journal of Monetary Economics*, 11, May, pp. 351–72.

Council of Economic Advisors (1962) *Annual Report* (Washington D.C.: U.S. Government Printing Office).

Darby, Michael R. (1979) *The Effects of Social Security on Income and the Capital Stock* (Washington D.C.: American Enterprise Institute).

Esposito, Louis (1978) 'Effect of Social Security on Saving: Review of Studies Using U.S. Time-Series Data', *Social Security Bulletin*, 41, May, pp. 9–17.

Evans, Paul (1987a) 'Interest Rates and Expected Future Budget Deficits in the United States', *Journal of Political Economy*, 95, February, pp. 34–58.

Evans, Paul (1987b) 'Do Budget Deficits Raise Nominal Interest Rates? Evidence from Six Industrial Countries', *Journal of Monetary Economics*, 20, September.

Feldstein, Martin S. (1974) 'Social Security, Induced Retirement, and Aggregate Capital Accumulation', *Journal of Political Economy*, 82, September/October, pp. 905–26.

Feldstein, Martin S. (1976) 'Perceived Wealth in Bonds and Social Security: a Comment', *Journal of Political Economy*, 84, April, pp. 331–6.

Feldstein, Martin S. (1977) 'Social Security and Private Savings: International Evidence in an Extended Life Cycle Model', in Martin S. Feldstein and Robert Inman (eds) *The Economics of Public Services* (London: Macmillan).

Feldstein, Martin S. (1982) 'Government Deficits and Aggregate Demand', *Journal of Monetary Economics*, 9, January, pp. 1–20.

Hayashi, Fumio (1985) 'Tests for Liquidity Constraints: a Critical Survey', National Bureau of Economic Research, Working Paper No. 1720, October.

Kimball, M.S. (1987) 'Making Sense of Two-Sided Altruism', *Journal of Monetary Economics*, 20, September,

King, Mervyn A. (1986) 'Tax Policy and Consumption Smoothing', unpublished, London School of Economics, April.

Kochin, Levis A. (1974) 'Are Future Taxes Anticipated by Consumers?' *Journal of Money, Credit and Banking*, 6, August, pp. 385–94.

Kochin, Levis A., Daniel K. Benjamin and Mark Meador (1985) 'The Observational Equivalence of Rational and Irrational Consumers if Taxation is Efficient', in Federal Reserve Bank of San Francisco, *Seventh West Coast Academic Conference*, San Francisco.

Kormendi, Roger C. (1983) 'Government Debt, Government Spending, and Private Sector Behavior', *American Economic Review*, 73, December, pp. 994–1010.

Kotlikoff, Laurence J. and Lawrence H. Summers (1981) 'The Role of Intergenerational Transfers in Aggregate Capital Accumulation', *Journal of Political Economy*, 89, August, pp. 706–32.

Kydland, Finn E. and Edward C. Prescott 'A Competitive Theory of Fluctuations and the Feasibility and Desirability of Stabilization Policy', in Stanley Fischer (ed.) *Rational Expectations and Economic Policy* (Chicago: University of Chicago Press).

Leimer, Dean R. and Selig D. Lesnoy (1982) 'Social Security and Private Saving: New Time-Series Evidence', *Journal of Political Economy*, 90, June, pp. 606–29.

Mankiw, N. Gregory (1987) 'The Optimal Collection of Seigniorage: Theory and Evidence', *Journal of Monetary Economics*, 20, September.

Mankiw, N. Gregory and Jeffrey A. Miron (1986) 'The Changing Behaviour of the Term Structure of Interest Rates', *Quarterly Journal of Economics*, 101, May, pp. 211–28.

McCallum, Ben T. (1984) 'Are Bond-financed Deficits Inflationary? A Ricardian Analysis', *Journal of Political Economy*, 92, February, pp. 123–35.

Miller, Merton H. and Charles W. Upton (1974) *Macroeconomics, a Neoclassical Introduction* (Homewood Ill.: Irwin).

Modigliani, Franco (1961) 'Long-run Implications of Alternative Fiscal Policies and the Burden of the National Debt', *Economic Journal*, 71, December, pp. 730–55.

Modigliani, Franco and Richard Brumberg (1954) 'Utility Analysis and the Consumption Function: an Interpretation of Cross-Section Data', in K.K. Kurihara (ed.) *Post-Keynesian Economics* (New Brunswick, New Jersey: Rutgers University Press).

Modigliani, Franco and Arlie G. Sterling (1986) 'Government Debt, Government Spending and Private Sector Behaviour: a Comment', *American Economic Review*, 76, December, pp. 1168–79.

Mundell, Robert A. (1971) 'Money, Debt, and the Rate of Interest', in R.A Mundell, *Monetary Theory* (Pacific Palisades, California: Goodyear)

O'Driscoll, Gerald P. (1977) 'The Ricardian Nonequivalence Theorem', *Journal of Political Economy*, 85, February pp. 207–10

Pigou, A.C. (1928) *A Study in Public Finance* (London: Macmillan).

Plosser, Charles I. (1982) 'Government Financing Decisions and Asset Returns', *Journal of Monetary Economics*, 9, May, pp. 325–52.

Plosser, Charles I. (1987) 'Further Evidence on the Relation between Fiscal Policy and the Term Structure', *Journal of Monetary Economics*, 20, September.

Poterba, James M. and Lawrence H. Summers (1986) 'Finite Lifetimes and the Savings Effects of Budget Deficits', unpublished, Harvard University, October.

Poterba, James M. and Lawrence H. Summers (1987) 'Finite Lifetimes and the Savings Effects of Budget Deficits', *Journal of Monetary Economics*, 20, September.

Ricardo, David (1951) 'Funding System', in Piero Sraffa (ed.) *The Works and Correspondence of David Ricardo, volume IV, Pamphlets and Papers*. 1815–1823 (Cambridge: Cambridge University Press).

Rosenberg, Nathan (1976) *Perspectives on Technology* (Cambridge: Cambridge University Press).

Sahasakul, Chaipat (1986) 'The U.S. Evidence on Optimal Taxation over Time', *Journal of Monetary Economics*, 18, November, pp. 251–75.

Seater, James J. and Robert S. Mariano (1985) 'New Tests of the Life Cycle and Tax Discounting Hypotheses', *Journal of Monetary Economics*, 15, March, pp. 195–215.

Siegel, Jeremy J. (1979) 'Inflation-Induced Distortions in Government and Private Saving Statistics', *Review of Economics & Statistics*, 61, April, pp. 83–90.

Sterling, Arlie G. (1977) 'An Investigation of the Determinants of the Long-Run Savings Ratio', unpublished, M.I.T., May.

Tanner, J. Ernest (1979) 'An Empirical Investigation of Tax Discounting', *Journal of Money, Credit and Banking*, 11, May, pp. 214–18.

Tobin, James and Willem Buiter (1980) 'Fiscal and Monetary Policies, Capital Formation, and Economic Activity', in George M. von Furstenberg (ed.) *The Government and Capital Formation* (Cambridge Mass.: Ballinger).

US Treasury Department (1984) *The Effects of Deficits on Prices of Financial Assets: Theory and Evidence* (Washington D.C.: US Government Printing Office).

Weil, Philippe (1987) 'Love Thy Children: Reflections on the Barro Debt Neutrality Theorem', *Journal of Monetary Economics*, 19, May, pp. 377–91.

Yotsuzuka, Toshiki (1987) 'Ricardian Equivalence in the Presence of Capital Market Imperfections', *Journal of Monetary Economics*, 20, September.

2 The Political Economy of International Money and Finance*
Roland Vaubel

Political economy tries to explain the conduct of economic policy. There are two approaches. One is to assume that economic policy makers want to maximize a – somehow defined – welfare function of their people. This is the public interest view of government. It treats nations as the basic decision units. The other approach is the public choice perspective. It assumes that economic policy makers can, and often do, act against the public interest. It tries to explain economic policy by their personal preferences and restrictions. Since policy makers always claim to be guided by the public interest, the public choice approach is inherently critical and distrustful. Since policy makers try to justify their actions with normative economic theories, the public choice theorist faces a double task: he must show that these normative arguments are false or inapplicable, and he must present his own alternative explanation.

The public choice approach is most promising in fields which are far removed from the attention and control of the voters. International economic policy is such a field. Language barriers and sheer distance raise the cost of gathering first-hand information about foreign countries. The issues to be decided are relatively technical. Since representatives of several countries participate in the decisions, the rate of return on information about these issues is even lower than in domestic politics. This holds for the voters as well as the politicians they elect. The national politician has less of an incentive to monitor international organizations than to control his own civil servants. By monitoring international agencies, he would generate external benefits abroad which he cannot appropriate.

Almost all public choice analyses of international economic policy have been concerned with international trade policy and development aid. Yet, rational voter ignorance is at least as likely in the international monetary

---

* This lecture was delivered in November 1988 under the title, 'The Political Economy of International Organisations in International Money and Finance', and first published in booklet form by City University Business School, Dept of Banking and Finance.

field. This lecture is a first attempt to apply the theory of public choice to the most important international organization in the field of international money and finance, to the International Monetary Fund.

IMF LENDING

Normative Analysis

The Bretton Woods Era

Under the Bretton Woods System, the aim of maintaining stable exchange rates seemed to justify IMF credits. They served to finance foreign exchange interventions. Even given the aims of the system, this justification raised three questions:

(i) Is foreign exchange intervention always, or indeed ever, the most efficient instrument of adjusting the money supply to the exchange rate target – bearing in mind that the intervention represents a form of public capital export or import and that it interferes with the money supply policy of the foreign central bank?

(ii) If foreign exchange intervention is efficient, why should it be financed with credits from the IMF rather than by borrowing in the market or by drawing down foreign exchange reserves?

(iii) Why should the IMF lend at lower interest rates than the market (as it did)?

According to some adherents of parity systems, a monetary authority that maintains a stable exchange rate between its currency and a foreign currency confers an external benefit on the other country. Can the interest subsidy be viewed as compensation for this benefit? But in this case, compensation ought to have been paid for any exchange-rate-oriented monetary policy – not only for foreign exchange interventions and not only to countries with balance of payments problems.

Moreover, if access to cheap IMF credits is conditional upon a balance of payments crisis, the incentive to avoid such a crisis is weakened. Losses of international reserves in a fixed exchange rate system are a consequence of excessive monetary expansion. This is a point which Henry Thornton emphasized (for example, in Chapter 5 of his 'Enquiry into the Nature and Effects of the Paper Credit in Great Britain', 1802/1965). Edwards (1984, Section 5) has confirmed it for 23 developing countries under fixed exchange rates in 1965–72. Even an unpublished IMF study conducted in 1981 concluded that, in 1964–73, overly expansionary demand policies had been the principal cause of balance of payments problems in the borrowing countries, while exogenous factors had been least important (Killick, 1984, p. 188).

Can public choice theory explain these features of IMF lending?

Real Adjustment to the Oil Price Shocks

After the collapse of the Bretton Woods System, the justification of IMF lending shifted from monetary to real adjustment. IMF lending was to offset the adverse consequences of temporary real disturbances from abroad and to permit a gradual adjustment to permanent ones.

This justification was weaker than the earlier ones in at least three respects:

(i)   While monetary adjustment requires action by the central bank, that is, by a public agency, the choice between real adjustment and financing is something that can be left to the individual. Each person can attain his optimal speed of adjustment by appropriately borrowing in the market. This is not a case of market failure. Politicians and international civil servants, by contrast, do not and cannot know the optimal speed of adjustment, and even if they knew it, they would probably lack the incentive to bring it about.

(ii) A government that borrows from the IMF increases the monetary base of the currency it receives and uses. This effect contributes to exchange rate stabilization, that is, monetary adjustment, but it is neither helpful nor desirable in the context of real adjustment.

(iii) While monetary adjustment to stabilize the exchange rate can confer Pareto-relevant external benefits upon the n-th currency country, borrowing for optimal real adjustment does not have this effect. What was the appropriate interest rate for balance of payments financing, once the exchange rate system of Bretton Woods had been abandoned?

Almost all IMF credits contain open or hidden subsidies. Open subsidies have been available through the Oil Facility Subsidy Account, the Supplementary Financing Subsidy Account, the Trust Fund and, more recently (1988), the Enhanced Structural Adjustment Facility. Substantial hidden subsidies are granted because high-risk borrowers are never charged more than the rate which first-class borrowers pay in the market. In the case of ordinary resources, this is the interest rate on US government securities. In the case of borrowed resources, the charges are equal to the cost of borrowing by the Fund plus a small margin of 0.2–0.325 per cent a year. In the case of SDR drawings, a weighted average of treasury bill rates in the five leading industrial countries applies. Even in the case of arrears, no more than the SDR interest rate is charged. If the debtor government cannot borrow in the market at all, that is, if its market interest rate is infinite, the present value of the IMF subsidy is equal to the amount of the loan.

According to Chandavarkar (1984, p. 58), a member of the IMF's staff, statements about IMF subsidies have to be 'qualified to take account ... that concessionality is also linked to the requirement of adjustment ... by members'. The acceptance and implementation of appropriate policy conditions, it is true, reduces the credit risk to the Fund and justifies a lower interest rate. But it also reduces the credit risk for private lenders. It cannot justify the fact that the IMF lends at lower interest rates than the market.

The perverse incentive effects of subsidized IMF lending have already been noted in the context of the Bretton Woods System. They are also present under flexible exchange rates. In the words of Jürg Niehans (1985, pp. 67f.),

> balance of payments crises result primarily from a country's own policies. They can be produced at will, virtually overnight, simply by overvaluating the exchange rate. The fact that IMF lending, despite the collapse of the Bretton Woods System, still is largely conditional on a balance-of-payments crisis creates an incentive for a country to let itself slip into such a crisis whenever IMF lending is desired.

Magee and Brock (1986, p. 191) believe that this incentive is indeed effective:

> The IMF unwittingly promotes ... adverse political selection in LDC borrowing by its encouragement of macroeconomic crises. If powerful political insiders are going to profit from economic crises, we should not be surprised at their frequency in the LDCs.

There is a considerable body of evidence that the balance of payments problems of IMF borrowers in the seventies were largely of their own making. A study by Reichmann (1978) shows that overexpansionary demand policies were the major factor in 15 out of 21 developing countries that had standby arrangements with the Fund during 1973–5. An analysis by Khan and Knight (1983) concludes that, over the whole period of 1973–80, the budget deficit (relative to GDP) was the second most important factor explaining the current account balances of developing countries (after the terms of trade). And an unpublished IMF study by

Donovan (1984), which is 'not for public use', demonstrates that over-expansionary monetary and fiscal policies also contributed to the debt servicing problems: in the five years prior to debt crisis, the rescheduling countries had

- considerably higher rates of net credit expansion to government (13.4 per cent annually) than the non-rescheduling countries (5.9 per cent annually);
- considerably higher rates of monetary expansion (M2: 31.9 per cent annually) than the non-rescheduling countries (22.8 per cent annually); and, not surprisingly,
- considerably higher consumer price inflation (23.8 per cent annually) than the non-rescheduling countries (14.3 per cent annually).

Donovan also finds that the rescheduling countries were less prudent in their debt management: in 1981, for example, the proportion of external medium and long-term debt contracted at variable interest rates was much larger for the rescheduling countries (51 per cent) than for the non-rescheduling countries (35 per cent). By contrast, the terms of trade of the rescheduling countries did not deteriorate during the five years prior to the debt crisis; they improved by more than 13 per cent.

Since, according to the Articles of Agreement (V.8.d and XX.2), the IMF has to charge uniform interest rates to all borrowers and since its interest rate is also independent of the size of the loan, the IMF pays the largest subsidies to the least creditworthy. Since, contrary to the Articles of Agreement (V.8.b), the rates of charge are also normally independent of the duration of the loan,[1] the IMF tends to give the largest subsidies to long-term debtors.

The uniformity of interest charges does not only aggravate the moral hazard problem. It also results in adverse selection. In the words of Fratianni and de Grauwe (1984, p. 160), the IMF has 'saddled itself with a "lemon" problem'. Max Corden (1983, p. 228), who confines himself to SDR lending, adds:

> The uniform interest rate ... seems to me an important consideration that weighs against the SDRs. It is clearly efficient for interest rates to include margins for risk; in this important respect, then, the SDR is inefficient.

The interest rate subsidy also generates an incentive to delay adjustment once a credit has been obtained; for, according to Article V, Section 7b of the Agreement, each member is normally expected to repay its credits (even before maturity!) 'as its balance of payments and reserve position improves'. The incentive to delay adjustment runs directly counter to the objective laid down in Article 1 (vi) that the Fund should 'shorten the duration ... of disequilibrium in the international balances of payments of members'.

The interest rate subsidy might be regarded as an insurance benefit.[2] But the insurance is not actuarially fair because premia do not differ according to risk. From 1960 to 1982, 42 member countries accounted for 78 per cent of all standby and extended credits from the IMF (Vaubel, 1983). This is not an outcome to be expected if members had been hit by random accidents. Moreover, cross-section regressions by Officer (1982, Table 4) and Cornelius (1988, pp. 197–204) show that, between 1974 and 1980, the flow of IMF credits to individual member governments tended to bear a significantly positive correlation with the outstanding stock of previous IMF credits. What all this evidence amounts to is that the Fund is a continuous provider of aid, in the form of subsidized insurance cover, to a particular group of its member governments. This raises four questions:

(i)   Why do the donor governments grant their aid in the form of subsidies to insurance cover?
(ii)   Why do they grant the largest subsidies to the most negligent member governments?
(iii) Why is the insurance offered to governments rather than to individuals?
(iv)   Why is the subsidy confined to insurance with an international public insurance monopoly, the International Monetary Fund?[3]

The International Debt Crisis

When the international debt crisis broke out in 1982, three additional justifications of IMF lending were added.

According to the first, the IMF was to maintain the stability of the international banking system. But should banks which have overestimated the creditworthiness of their debtors, receive assistance from governmental institutions spending taxpayers' money? This became known as the 'bailout' problem. To maintain the money supply is not necessary to maintain insolvent banks. Alternatively, if the banks were merely regarded as illiquid and their difficulties as temporary, they ought to have received loans from the central bank at a penalty. Official subsidized lending to their debtors was not efficient for the purpose, the more so as the debtors had also borrowed from many banks which were not in trouble. As under the European agricultural policy, output subsidization for the entire industry took the place of direct transfers to the needy.

The second justification emphasized IMF conditionality. For several reasons, to which I turn later, the IMF is said to enjoy a comparative advantage in identifying, negotiating and enforcing the economic policy changes that would re-establish the creditworthiness of the debtor governments. The Fund's 'seal of approval' is a signal to the banks and serves as a 'catalyst' for their lending. All this may be true but it cannot justify IMF lending. It merely justifies the provision of information, negotiation and enforcement services. It has been suggested (by John Williamson, 1980, p. 274) that the IMF should be 'in a position to put up a fair bit of money directly' because, by doing so, it renders its advice more credible. Should governments bet on all their announcements? Can they increase their credibility by committing taxpayers money? Would it not be more efficient if IMF officials committed a portion of their salaries?

Finally, the IMF was viewed as the optimal coordinator of the banks' lending. Central coordination was considered necessary because, in a debt crisis, additional lending by one bank can generate external benefits for the other creditor banks. The IMF was to prevent free riding[4]. There are three problems with this justification:

(i)   Why could the creditor banks not solve the coordination problem among themselves, given that they managed to form 'steering committees' and to found the Institute of International Finance?

(ii)   Why was the cost of coordination not borne by the banks but, contrary to Art. V.2.b, by the IMF, that is, ultimately by the taxpayer?[5]

(iii)   Even if the IMF was the optimal coordinator, why did it also lend?

The theory of public choice ought to explain why the international debt crisis resulted in a large increase of subsidized IMF lending and in the provision of various free services to creditor banks.

Positive Analysis

The Actors

The lending policies of the International Monetary Fund are determined by five distinct groups of actors.

First of all, there are the politicians of the national member governments. They are interested in power and prestige. They try to maximise the value of their objective function subject to the restriction of having to be re-elected. In the case of the IMF, national politicians, usually the Ministers of Finance, are members of the Board of Governors and its Interim Committee. The Board of Governors is the highest authority of the Fund. Since the voting weights are related to the countries' quotas, the governments of the main industrial countries (the Group of Ten) have a majority of votes on the Board. However, for some decisions of fundamental importance, qualified majorities of 70 or 85 per cent are required. A quota increase, for example, requires 85 per cent of the votes (Art. III. 2.c).

The national civil servants form a second group of actors. They also enjoy power and prestige and, in addition, a comfortable life. They are not subject to the re-election constraint.

The third group of actors consists of the national delegates. They constitute the Board of Executive Directors, which also decides by weighted voting. Since the delegates tend to return to their national civil service after some time, they want to avoid conflict between the Fund and their government. But their preference for power, prestige and also income leads them to favour more powers and resources for 'their' international organization. Moreover, as Frey and Gygi (1989) emphasize, there is a self-selection process at work: 'bureaucrats with a favourable view of an international organization are more inclined to apply to, and accept, such an assignment' (p. 10).

The fourth group are the international civil servants or 'bureaucrats': the IMF staff, which is headed by a Managing Director. The staff is interested in power, prestige, income, all sorts of non-pecuniary benefits and, as a prerequisite, in the survival of the institution. All these objectives are positively related to the Fund's resources, that is, its operating budget and its lending potential. Moreover, if the number of monitors – that is, of Executive Directors – is constant, more resources yield more autonomy.

Finally, IMF lending can be influenced by interest groups, for example, by the banking and the export industries. Their aim is to protect their profits. Most probably, they will try to influence IMF policies by lobbying the national minister of finance and the members of parliament.

If these are the actors and their preference functions, how can we derive explanations of the puzzles we have noted?

The Bretton Woods Era

The first puzzle was the fact that the member governments are interested in the opportunity to borrow from an international organization rather than the market. Their support for the IMF has been independent of their creditworthiness and of the degree of capital market liberalization.

From a public choice perspective, the treasury origins of the IMF are indicative. As Makin (1984, p. 183) has noted, the IMF serves the interests of the treasuries of the member governments by flexibly accommodating their borrowing and debt servicing 'needs' at minimum cost[6]. By charging low and uniform interest rates, the IMF protects its member governments against the judgement of the market. It insures them against the electoral damage which a visibly poor credit standing might otherwise cause. The IMF staff are also likely to prefer uniform interest rates. They help to avoid conflict with potential borrowers, especially if the latter do not also borrow in the international market at an observable market rate. For similar reasons, national social insurance systems and public insurance schemes for export credits and foreign investments do not usually charge premia according to risk. Moreover, by paying larger subsidies to the least creditworthy, the Fund, like the national social insurance schemes, can try to justify its activities with humanitarian goals. As is well known from social insurance economics, however, the poor need not be bad risks. The debt crisis was a case in point: the governments of rich developing countries proved to be least creditworthy. Redistribution through public insurance systems is not well targeted. It is an inefficient instrument of alleviating poverty.

Our second puzzle was the IMF's practice of subsidizing foreign exchange interventions rather than any monetary policy conducive to stable exchange rates. From a public choice perspective, it is important to note that foreign-exchange interventions give a government some leeway for domestic demand management in spite of exchange rate fixity. The money supply increase that is compatible with a given exchange rate is larger when domestic credit expansion is accompanied by a sale of foreign exchange. How much difference it makes depends on whether it is sterilized by the foreign central bank. A non-sterilized intervention which increases the foreign money supply gives more leeway than a sterilized one which merely augments the supply of bonds denominated in the foreign currency. But it still makes a difference as long as bonds in different currencies are imperfect substitutes in a portfolio of risky assets. If monetary policy or domestic credit expansion in the key currency country is geared towards maintaining domestic price stability or gold convertibility, foreign exchange interventions enable the governments of the other countries to affect their domestic business cycles. (Lord Keynes must have been aware of this when he negotiated the Bretton Woods agreement.) The politicians in government try to influence the domestic business cycle in their favour, by generating a boom at election time, and reversing the impulse thereafter. IMF lending facilitates the expansion. IMF conditionality facilitates the contraction. In this way, the Fund contributes to the generation of political business cycles.

Real Adjustment to the Oil Price Shocks

I turn to our third puzzle, the rapid growth of IMF lending after the first oil price increase: from 1970 to 1975 the volume of IMF lending more than doubled in real terms. Under the headline 'Do We Need an IMF?', the *Economist* asked in 1976: 'The IMF did its best to resist the change to floating. Now that it has had to be accepted, why is the IMF still bent on credit creation?'

Most public choice explanations focus on the interests of the IMF staff. Gottfried Haberler (1974, p. 156) wrote:

> The Bretton Woods system finally broke down in March 1973 when extensive floating of all major currencies started. Needless to add that the International Monetary Fund as a bureaucratic institution continues to function – international institutions may change their names or lose their function but they never die.

As another example Haberler mentions the Bank for International Settlements 'which had been solemnly declared dead and ordered to be interred (in an annex by the Bretton Woods charter for the IMF), but is still very much alive' (note 17a). Further examples come to mind: the World Bank was founded to assist in the reconstruction of the European economies after World War II but was later reoriented towards the less developed countries; the OEEC was established to administer the Marshall Plan but was later – under a new name (OECD) – permitted to engage in other activities, and so on.

With the par value system abandoned, many observers expected the demise of the IMF or at least of its lending operations. Not only the building, but also the institution, of the Fund appeared to be an 'empty shell' (Niehans). However, what seemed to be a serious threat turned out to be a major opportunity. What started as a struggle for self-preservation ended with a significant increase of power, prestige and resources for the IMF staff. Its strategy can be analysed with the help of the economic theory of bureaucracy. Indeed, the IMF staff is a particularly suitable object for such an analysis because it enjoys a considerable degree of autonomy from elected governments.

The IMF has always been keen to increase its resources. It usually asked for more than it got. It has preferred permanent increases in its own capital (quota increases) to more borrowing ('enlarged access' and so on) and to additional SDR allocations. But it has also welcomed the establishment of various new lending facilities and SDR expansion. It wanted the substitution account but did not get it. Against opposition from the EEC countries, it insisted that the developing countries should be permitted to participate in the SDR scheme (though it has not been in favour of the 'link').[7] It repeatedly demanded additional SDR allocations but did not succeed.

It also made sure that, by the time of the next quota review, its lending capacity was fully, or at least highly, utilized. My analysis of the six quota increases reveals the following pattern. In the last year before the approval of the quota increase by the Board of Governors, the use of Fund credit relative to quotas rose on average by 27 per cent.[8] In the preceding year, which sets the stage for the deliberations of the Board of Executive Directors and of the Interim Committee, the increase was on average 58 per cent. If we move further back by one or two years, we observe a stable and low degree of capacity utilisation. Quite obviously, the IMF staff engages in hurry-up lending. The choice which it faces is not 'to use it or lose it', it tries to obtain more resources.

This goal can also explain our fourth puzzle, the persistence of interest subsidies under floating exchange rates. General subsidization of IMF credit was not foreseen in the Articles of Agreement. But it helps the IMF staff to increase the demand for its own services. When demand increases, the Fund can lend more and improve its bargaining position *vis-à-vis* potential borrowers. If IMF credits were not subsidized, no member government might demand them. If the interest subsidy is viewed as an insurance benefit which developing countries can obtain at a subsidized price, the IMF also has a vital interest in being the only insurance that can offer this subsidy. The phenomenon is similar to the monopoly of subsidized social insurance agencies at the national level. Since the IMF cannot hope to insure individuals, it insists that governments rather than individuals ought to choose between adjustment and financing. The member governments are inclined to support this view: the timing of real adjustment may have to depend on the electoral cycle.

Since the Fund wants to increase demand for its credits, it tends to prefer financing to adjustment. Under the Bretton Woods system, it had lacked the incentive to welcome appropriate adjustments of nominal exchange rates.[9] After 1973, its interests were biased against speedy adjustment to permanent real shocks. By slowing down the adjustment, the IMF could increase the size and duration of its lending and extend the period of policy supervision.

The IMF's interest in lending and supervising may also explain our fifth puzzle: the surprising fact that, even under flexible exchange rates, eligibility for IMF credits continues to depend on the state of the balance of payments. In the words of Article V, Section 3.b. (ii), of the Agreement,

a member shall be entitled to purchase the currencies of other members from the Fund ... subject to the ... condition ... [that] it has a need to make the purchase because of its balance of payments or its reserve position or development of its reserves.

If it is true that the IMF staff wants to maximize its lending and supervision, it cannot be interested in legal restrictions of eligibility that might effectively bar potential borrowers, nor, of course, can the borrowers. The balance of payments criterion, as we have noted, is not an effective barrier. Any member government can easily engineer a decline in the current account balance by increasing the budget deficit or expanding the money supply, and it is even easier to run down the country's foreign exchange reserves by altering the composition of monetary expansion.

In view of this, Dell and Lawrence (1980, p. 129) have suggested that

> in determining the appropriate volume of balance of payments support and the conditions required for the provision of that support ... it is important to distinguish between those elements of the balance of payments deficit for which a developing country is itself responsible and those elements that are due to factors beyond its control.

Such restrictions of eligibility are not the IMF's interest.

The International Debt Crisis

There can be no doubt that the IMF staff seized the opportunity of the international debt crisis with determination. The years since 1977 had been difficult. The use of Fund credit had been declining: in 1979/80 it was 36 per cent lower than in 1976/7. The creation of another oil facility in 1979 was rejected on the ground that the first oil facility had made it too easy to postpone adjustment (Williamson, 1983, p. 647). The incoming Reagan Administration favoured a restrictive course for IMF lending.

The debt crisis was an ideal opportunity for the IMF because it was primarily a threat to US banks and a problem for the US government, the IMF's main adversary. The benefits of increased IMF lending would be concentrated with the largest industrial country and probably with some major debtor countries; the costs, being widely dispersed over the other industrial countries, would hardly be noticed by their citizens, the more so as no national tax laws had to be changed. Finally, by raising the risk premia which many of these debtor governments would have to pay in the market, the crisis increased the interest subsidy to be obtained from the IMF and, hence, the demand for IMF credits.

The abrupt and complete turnaround of the US government between August and December 1982 has been documented in some detail,[10] usually with considerable 'Schadenfreude'. There is widespread agreement that this conversion was not motivated by charity for the developing countries but by fears for the US banking system. As Sachs (1987, p. 34) has emphasized, this explains why lending concentrated on just a few large debtor countries which seemed to pose a serious risk for the major US banks. The Reagan Administration came to regard the IMF as 'a convenient conduit for US influence' (as Assistant Treasury Secretary Marc Leland put it[11]). It did so for at least three reasons:

(i)   The IMF enabled the US government to shift the cost of saving the banks largely on to the other industrialized countries. The US government even refused to participate in the 1983 loan to the IMF.

(ii)   In some cases, the IMF may have served to induce non-US-creditor banks to contribute fresh money.

(iii)   Policy conditions from the IMF may have been more acceptable to the debtor governments than pressure from US banks or the US government. When, by 1985, US influence on the IMF had become increasingly evident, Secretary Baker shifted the emphasis from the Fund to the World Bank (Cohen, 1986, p. 231).

This strategy was complemented by an acceleration of US monetary expansion which reduced the debtors' real interest-rate burden and generated an economic upswing in 1984, an election year. US policy was clearly inconsistent with Ronald Reagan's conviction that private losses, arising from voluntary contracts, should not be passed on to the general taxpayer or money holder. But the Secretary of the Treasury, himself a former investment banker, apparently agreed with John Williamson (1983, p. 654) that this was not 'the right point in history to establish this principle'. Donald Regan was the driving force behind the campaign to obtain congressional approval for the quota increase. 'I lobbied 400 out of 435 Congressmen before that vote', he is reported to have said (*Financial Times*, 26 September 1983). He was strongly supported by his undersecretary Beryl Sprinkel, another former banker, and by the chairman of the Federal Reserve Board, which – in the absence of IMF action – would have had to take some unpleasant decisions.

The banks testified strongly in favour of the quota increase (Lomax, 1986, p. 237). As Fratianni and de Grauwe (1984, p. 168) emphasize, 'the high concentration of troubled loans among a small number of US banks [made] it likely that these banks [engaged] in collective action aimed at shifting their losses onto the rest of society'. Their cost of organizing collective action was low, they could internalize a large part of the benefit from lobbying, and they had the largest threat potential. They could benefit from IMF action in several ways:

(i)   Subsidized IMF lending would improve the debtors' solvency and the market value of the loans.
(ii)   IMF lending might facilitate the servicing of the debt.
(iii)   IMF conditionality would improve the creditworthiness of the debtors.
(iv)   The IMF would provide free information, negotiation and enforcement services to the banks.

The banks also founded the Washington-based Institute of International Finance which has continued their lobbying effort. Its managing director, Horst Schulmann, recently recommended a doubling of Special Drawing Rights.[12] Since SDRs are unconditional credit lines, they could be freely used to repay the banks; conditional IMF lending, by contrast, can be, and has been, made conditional upon the provision of 'fresh money' from the creditor banks. In this way, the IMF extracts from the banks part of the gain which its lending confers to them. By asking the banks to co-finance its loans, the IMF improves the quality of its assets. This is one explanation of why the Managing Director of the Fund has asked for a doubling of quotas rather than of SDRs (IMF Survey, 10/17/88, p. 308).

In a recent article (Vaubel, 1986), I have argued that the tasks which national governments delegate to international organizations tend to be unpleasant activities ('dirty work') which the national politicians consider necessary to gain or maintain the support of some interest groups, but for which they do not want to take direct responsibility:

> International organization raises information costs more for the general public which has to pay than for the well-organized pressure groups which benefit. If some countries receive more than they pay, international organization may also serve to disperse the costs of such programmes more widely than would be possible on a national basis.
>
> (p. 48)

My prime example was the European agricultural policy. It now turns out that the same is true for the IMF's role in the debt crisis. The IMF serves as a smokescreen for subsidies to major US banks and, possibly, to favourite debtor governments. A former member of the IMF staff (Finch, 1988, p. 19) has suggested the same interpretation: 'Support via the IMF and World Bank permits the cost of political alliances to be hidden from normal budgetary controls'.

To say that the IMF serves the interests of the creditor banks is not to imply that it acts against the interests of the debtor governments. However, in the opinion of some economists, the Fund is helping to exploit the debtor countries. Rüdiger Dornbusch (1986) writes:

The IMF set itself up to save the system, organizing banks into a lenders' cartel and holding the debtor countries up for a classical mugging. The IMF ... provided the essential mechanism to ... extract resources from Latin America.

(pp. 140, 148)

It is difficult to tell whether the IMF's subsidies to the debtor countries were large enough to compensate their potential losses from subsidized banking collusion. But, surely, there is something of a difference between joint protection of property rights and 'mugging'.

Our public-choice analysis of subsidized lending and coordination by the IMF shows that the puzzles which we noted in the context of the normative theory can be solved with the help of interest group theory and international information asymmetries among the IMF member countries. The major banks and the government of the principal member country became allies of the IMF staff. How did the IMF staff respond to this opportunity?

At the end of 1987, total IMF credit commitments, measured in real US dollars, were 32 per cent larger than in 1980 and four times larger than in 1970.[13] In 1985, the ratio of IMF credits to world exports was 74 per cent larger than in 1980. From 1980 to 1986, the IMF staff grew by 18 per cent. Its long-term rate of growth, say, since 1958, has been 5.3 per cent per annum, compared with 3.4 per cent for the staff of the Federal Reserve Board. From 1978 to 1988 IMF staff per member country was on average 70 per cent larger than two decades ago (1958–67); the ratio of IMF staff to the number of new standby and extended arrangements was 129 per cent larger.

Since the outbreak of the debt crisis, several new credit facilities have been set up. Two of them, the Structural Adjustment Facility (March 1986) and the Enhanced Structural Adjustment Facility (August 1988) are confined to the low-income developing countries. They focus especially on the sub-Saharan African countries 'whose difficulties in repaying the Fund ... appeared to threaten the system' (Kahler, 1986, p. 270). The British Chancellor of the Exchequer was frank enough to recommend 'backdated drawing on the Enhanced Structural Adjustment Facility to help clear arrears' (IMF Survey, 10/17/88, p. 323). In this way, the IMF joined the international Ponzi scheme of lending the interest that is due. Since the creation of the new facilities was not accompanied by equivalent cuts elsewhere, the Fund was also enabled to lend more to the other developing countries to the extent that the low-income LDCs can be taken out of the regular facilities.

The two structural facilities have served to reduce the number of member countries which are, or may become, ineligible due to their arrears. At the same time, eligibility has been extended under the Compensatory Financing Facility which is now called Compensatory and Contingency Financing Facility (August 1988). As a result of this change, the Fund may not only lend to compensate for export shortfalls and unusual cereal import costs but also for deviations from projected interest rates, workers' remittances and tourist receipts. The Fund's power is also increased because contingency financing will be subject to policy conditions.

Nevertheless, the IMF staff faces some serious problems for the future. When the immediate crisis was over, the Fund had to move increasingly into longer-term lending. This led to several difficulties:[14]

(i)   the willingness to accept IMF programmes declined,
(ii)   the probability of rapid abrogation grew, and
(iii)   the IMF moved into a field where it had to compete, probably at a comparative disadvantage, with another international organization, the World Bank.

It is well known from public choice theory that bureaucracies are afraid of overlapping competences. Competition among organizations endangers the information monopoly on which the bureaucracy's power rests. Moreover, exclusive responsibility raises its prestige. There are now signs (the World Bank loan to Argentina in September 1988) that collusion between the Fund and the Bank is weakening. This may indicate that one member of the cartel (in this case the World Bank) expects to win.

Finally, what will happen once the major US creditor banks have built up their reserves to such an extent that they can survive default by the Latin American debtor governments? Will the US government continue to support IMF expansion, and will the other major members concur?

IMF CONDITIONALITY

Normative Analysis

The case for IMF conditionality has been based on the following arguments:[15]

(i)   The IMF knows better than the banks what the debtor governments ought to do; its information cost is lower.

(ii)   The IMF is providing new and generally useful knowledge, an international public good.

(iii)   The IMF is a useful scapegoat for unpopular policy reforms in the debtor countries;[16] it improves the bargaining position of the elected politicians against local interest groups or of the national civil service against the elected politicians; it is a more useful scapegoat than foreign governments or foreign banks could ever be.

(iv)   IMF conditionality reduces the moral hazard of IMF lending or insurance.

(v)   The IMF is in a better position to enforce adherence to agreed policy conditions (which is said to be another public good).

The first argument is debatable; the last is irrelevant,[17] but the argument from moral hazard (iv) certainly isn't. IMF conditionality, it is true, cannot justify IMF lending. But IMF lending can justify IMF conditionality.

The moral hazard argument is usually meant to imply that IMF conditionality prevents the debtor governments from wasting the funds they have borrowed. This is not moral hazard in the strict sense in which this concept is used in insurance economics. An insurance does not care about the uses to which its payments are put by the recipients. The use of the money is important for a lending institution but not for an insurance. The problem of the insurance, its moral hazard problem, is how to make sure that the insurance cover does not induce the client to become careless with respect to damage prevention. IMF conditionality does not set in before the damage is there. It can, if effective, prevent the borrowing governments from staying in trouble to get more money. But it does not prevent them from getting into trouble in the first place. Why does IMF conditionality only operate *ex post* and not *ex ante*? This is a puzzle which public choice theory has to explain.

Second, even in the case of *ex post* conditionality, the Fund could reduce moral hazard by preannouncing rules for its policy conditions. If all potential borrowers knew in advance that the Fund's conditions are uniform and non-negotiable, they could not hope to get away with a special deal. Strict rules for conditionality would also prevent the creditor governments from interfering. As one former member of the IMF staff complains,

> the debt strategy [is] losing its substance ... when the IMF and the World Bank are forced by the major governments to lend without regard to repayability. The pressures on the staff and management of IMF and

World Bank to accept inadequate assurances of reform ... can be over-whelming.

(Finch, 1988, pp. 18f.)

Why does the Fund stick to *ad hoc* conditionality, its 'case-by-case approach'?

Third, policy conditions are more likely to be implemented if they are made public. New knowledge about the necessary policy reforms is an international public good; it ought to be disclosed. Why does the Fund not publish its agreements?

Fourth, monitoring by the Fund, the banks and the general public would be easier and more effective if the policy conditions were simple and small in number. Why does the Fund negotiate a multiplicity of apparently complicated policy conditions?

Fifth, policy conditions, to be effective, must relate to easily control-lable variables, either to instruments or to close intermediate targets.[18] Otherwise, it is not clear whether the violation of the agreement is due to policy failures or to unforeseeable disturbances. Without controllability, there can be no responsibility. Targets for hardly controllable variables are not only likely to be missed, as IMF experience shows;[19] they are also unlikely to exert much influence on the conduct of economic policy. However, IMF policy conditions tend to focus on remote endogenous variables such as the current account balance, for which the Fund itself has a particularly poor forecasting record (Artis, 1988).[20] The theory of public choice ought to explain this puzzle.

Finally, several authors (Williamson, 1983; Cooper, 1983; Cornelius, 1988) have noted that IMF conditionality varies procyclically: it is stricter when the world is in a recession than when there is a boom. The period from 1979 to 1982 has been a favourite example. There is also econometric evidence (Cornelius, 1988, pp. 197–207) that a tightening of conditionality reduces the volume of IMF credits. One need not be a Keynesian to be against procyclical government lending and spending. Why does the IMF reinforce the cycle?

Positive Analysis

Public choice theory suggests that the IMF staff enjoys both lending and conditionality. The power to stipulate policy conditions increases its influence and prestige. For the staff, this is another reason to prefer quota increases to additional SDR allocations.

Why does the Fund not favour *ex ante* conditionality? Why does it not, for example, exclude all applicants who have exceeded some limit for monetary expansion in excess of trend real economic growth, or for the budget deficit relative to GDP, or who have imposed unacceptable exchange restrictions, trade barriers, minimum wages, price controls or interest ceilings, or who have expropriated investors without adequate compensation? Clearly, the IMF staff is not interested in such *ex ante* conditions because they restrict eligibility, the scope for IMF lending and bargaining.

Nor is the Fund interested in strict *ex post* conditionality rules. They would diminish its room for discretion which is the basis of its power *vis-à-vis* individual applicants.[21] In the case of rules, the Fund's role would be reduced to monitoring; the banks or their Institute might even do it themselves. Fixed rules would also prevent the Fund from varying the tightness of its policy conditions so as to maintain a high level of lending when the demand for its credits is weak and to enjoy a high degree of conditionality when the demand for its credits is strong. The major creditor governments share the Fund's distaste for rules because rules would also diminish their influence.[22]

The confidentiality of IMF policy conditions, by contrast, seems to be in the common interest of the debtor governments and the IMF staff. The debtor governments prefer secret commitments for two reasons. If they intend to comply, secrecy enables them to use the Fund as a scapegoat for any policy change, even one which the Fund has not demanded. If they intend to renege on the agreement, secrecy will help them to save face; only the Fund will know.[23] The IMF staff, it is true, could put more pressure on the debtors to implement the conditions, if the conditions were publicly known. But the Fund itself could also be monitored more easily. If the agreements prescribe policies which the debtor governments would have adopted anyway, the Fund would be seen to be ineffective. If the agreements prescribe policies which are not implemented, the Fund would also appear to be ineffective.[24]

Mosley (1987, p. 2) implies that the transition to supply-side-related policy conditions has weakened the Fund's bargaining position because they are more likely to meet deep-rooted resistance from domestic interest groups and because they are more difficult to monitor. Nevertheless, the IMF staff has been quite willing to include supply-side conditions. A possible public-choice explanation is that a large number of policy conditions reduces the scope for outside control and criticism of the Fund's effectiveness.[25] A multiplicity of conditions is confusing to the external observer, and a low degree of implementation can easily be attributed to conflicts among them. The Fund's desire to protect itself against outside monitoring may also explain why it prefers highly variable *ad hoc* conditions to simple conditionality rules.

The choice of remote endogenous target variables can serve a similar purpose. When the target is missed, this can almost always be attributed to unforeseeable disturbances. In this way, the debtor governments can conceal their non-compliance, and the IMF staff can conceal the ineffectiveness of its policy conditions.

Finally, the Fund's procyclical variation of conditionality is easily explained by its objective function. The IMF staff derives utility from lending as well as from far-reaching policy conditions. If demand for IMF lending increases, the staff raises its utility by lending more (if possible) as well as by tightening its policy conditions.[26] Since a world recession, as in 1981/2, raises the demand for IMF credits, it leads to tighter conditionality.[27] Since a boom, as in 1978/9, reduces the demand for IMF credits, it leads to easier, conditionality.[28] Since the interest rate for IMF credits is largely predetermined and irrelevant for the staff's remuneration, the Fund uses variations of conditionality as a substitute for interest rate adjustment. If this explanation is correct, it follows that Richard Cooper's (1983) proposal for a countercyclical use of IMF conditionality is not feasible because it is not in the IMF's bureaucratic interest to implement it.

CONCLUSION

This analysis has been confined to IMF lending and IMF conditionality. It would be interesting to look also at IMF surveillance and coordination but too little is known about it (which may indicate that it is ineffective). Analysis of IMF forecasts has revealed an optimistic bias with respect to output growth (Artis 1988); this bias is in the interest of incumbent member governments. The Fund's practice of inviting the Ministers of Finance to give public speeches at the Annual Meeting and of giving them much publicity also serves to please the Fund's principals and to ensure its survival. Invitations to external academic researchers increase the Fund's prestige and reduce the likelihood of scholarly criticism. The periodic country visits, reports and recommendations and other activities which are not provided for in the Articles of Agreement, reveal the Fund's drive for expansion and influence.

It has not been the purpose of this study to deny that many dedicated civil servants are at work in the International Monetary Fund. But they are exposed to a perverse incentive pattern. Since there is little else on which four Fund economists from five countries can agree, this is where their interests meet. It is the same in any department of economics.

Milton Friedman is reported to have said in 1983: 'I strongly oppose any increase of the IMF's quota and prefer to move in the opposite direction to see how we can dismantle the IMF and get rid of it.'[29] My analysis has more modest implications. It implies that subsidized IMF lending, conditional upon balance-of-payments or debt-servicing problems, is an inefficient form of aid and ought not to be continued. It also implies that the present form of *ex post, ad hoc* and procyclical conditionality is an inefficient way of giving policy advice, and that the Fund would be a more impartial advisor and monitor if it did not have the power to lend.[30]

If these conclusions are correct, we should welcome the decision of the British government not to participate in any IMF quota increase in 1989. However, for the public choice theorist, it is a decision that is difficult to explain.

Notes

1. According to Article V, Section 8b, of the Articles of Agreement, 'the rates of charge normally shall rise at intervals during the period in which balances are held'. The charges under the Enlarged Access are a rare case conforming to this rule.
2. See also Corden (1983, pp. 225 ff.) and Vaubel (1983, pp. 72 ff.). Corden regards the quotes themselves 'as part of a sovereign insurance system' (p. 226).
3. The Multilateral Investment Guaranty Agency, which has recently been established, is an analogous case. It receives subsidies which are denied to private insurance companies (see Vaubel, 1985).
4. Banks which refuse to increase their lending are not necessarily free riders, however. They may simply not want to 'throw good money after bad'.
5. Article V, Section 2b, of the Articles of Agreement reads as follows: 'If requested, the Fund may decide to perform financial and technical services ... that are consistent with the purpose of the Fund. Operations involved in the performance of such financial services shall not be on the account of the Fund.'
6. The treasury origins of the Fund distinguish it from the BIS, which is a central bankers' club.
7. See, for example, Ferguson (1988, pp. 122, 125, 137).
8. In 1982/3, under the Enlarged Access, it even granted credits before securing their financing. This *fait accompli* was to underline the urgency of the quota increase.
9. Especially the last few years of the Bretton Woods system 'had the IMF on a sweeping run around the liquidity side ... when the right call was to run to the opposite, adjustment side. The goal for the IMF was realization of its potential as a world central bank' (Makin, 1984, p. 180).

10. See, for example, Cohen (1986, pp. 226 ff.), Lomax (1986, p. 102) and Makin (1984, pp. 226 ff.).

11. Cohen (1986, p. 229).

12. See IMF Survey (4/4/88, pp. 103–6). Schulmann suggests that 'the plan as such has no financial costs for G-7 governments, since SDRs are created by the IMF with no outlays from its members, and it has no impact on global inflation' (p. 104). The truth is that the central banks and the governments of the industrial countries would lose seigniorage, and that SDR drawings entail additional money creation in the creditor countries.

13. The increase of quotas was, of course, much smaller because it did not reflect the expansion of IMF borrowing and the allocation of SDRs. This may explain why the IMF staff tend to refer exclusively to the evolution of IMF quotas.

14. See also Kahler (1986, p. 250).

15. For details see Vaubel (1983). More recently, Lomax (1986, p. 240) and Mosley (1987, p. 6) have elaborated on argument (iii), Corden (1983, pp. 225 f.) on argument (iv) and Sachs (1987, pp. 25, 31) on argument (v).

16. The same hypothesis has been advanced with respect to national central banks: '... as an institution. The Fed's ultimate political purpose is to serve as an economic policy scapegoat for incumbent politicians ... Fed officials are expected to let Congressmen and Senators blame them for whatever financial and economic developments their constitutents back home dislike. In exchange for playing economic policy scapegoat, Fed officials are offered unusually long terms of office and substantial budgetary autonomy' (Kane, 1986, pp. 189, 196).

17. If the first argument were correct, we would expect that the Fund also produces superior forecasts. This is not the case (Artis, 1988). The banks may prefer IMF conditionality simply because it is supplied free of charge. The last argument is irrelevant: to enforce contracts, it is not necessary that the enforcer is a party to the contracts.

18. This has also been suggested by Williamson (1983, p. 635), Cooper (1983) and Mosley (1987, p. 34). Spraos (1986) takes the opposite view.

19. The low compliance rate has been documented by a large number of studies. For an essentially complete list see Cornelius (1988, p. 186). He concludes that the studies published by the Fund tend to arrive at a more favourable evaluation of IMF programmes than do the external studies.

20. In the case of the current account balance, there is the additional problem that no politician or economist can know its optimal size. Only the play of market forces can reveal the optimal allocation of the world capital stock.

21. If the Fund wishes to prevent moral hazard (which it does not), it could, of course, use its discretion to punish the applicants for past 'misbehaviour'.

22. Kane (1986, p. 193) suggests that, for the same reason, elected politicians do not like monetary policy rules for their central bank.

23. As Kahler (1988, p. 13) points out, the confidentiality of ordinary IMF consultants can be explained in the same way.

24. Chant and Acheson (1986, p. 109) apply the same reasoning to explain why central bankers like the instrument of moral suasion: 'Maintenance of autonomy and self-preservation of the bureau are forces which would seem to lead

officials of the bureau to prefer covert to overt methods. By use of covert methods combined with a skilfully created mythology, the management of any bureau can increase its immunity to critical investigation. In the absence of information on the bureau's operation, the potential critic is disarmed and becomes a reduced threat to the bureau's autonomy and existence. Moreover, covert methods provide the management with the possibility of magnifying its successes and minimizing apparent failures'. The authors also mention covert loans among central banks as an example (pp. 120 f.).

25. Chant and Acheson (1986, p. 110) use the same reasoning to explain why central banks do not confine themselves to open-market operations.

26. Both time-series and cross-sectional variations of conditionality may be explained by variations of the demand for credit. Mosley (1983) observes with respect to World Bank lending: 'The relative bargaining strength of donor and recipient, rather more than considerations of strict economic appropriateness, may have exerted an influence on the World Bank's conditional aid packages' (p. 22). 'Tight conditions were generally negotiated with the poorest countries, those with the worst balance-of-payments problems, and those most dependent of SAL finance for official capital flows from abroad' (p. 20).

27. At the same time, the Reagan Administration was pressing for stricter conditionality. The IMF was able to use it as a scapegoat for what its own bureaucratic interest implied.

28. An additional explanation is that 'in mid-1979 the Fund was embarrassed at its success in raising money for the supplementary financing facility, virtually none of which had been lent' (Williamson, 1983, p. 647).

29. *Journal of Commerce*, 13 October 1983, reprinted in: Deutsche Bundesbank, *Auszüge aus Presseartikeln*, 20 October 1983, p. 4.

30. The conclusion that, in the case of the Fund, 'the credit-assessment role directly conflicts with the lending role' has also been reached by Fred Smith (1984, p. 220) – though for somewhat different reasons.

References

Artis, M.J. (1988) 'How Accurate Is the World Economic Outlook?', Staff Studies for the World Economic Outlook, International Monetary Fund, July.

Chandavarkar, Anand G. (1984) *The International Monetary Fund: Its Financial Organization and Activities*, IMF Pamphlet Series, No. 42.

Chant, John F., Keith Acheson (1986) 'The Choice of Monetary Instruments and the Theory of Bureaucracy', in Eugenia F. and Mark Toma (eds) *Central Bankers, Bureaucratic Incentives, and Monetary Policy* (Dordrecht) pp. 107–28.

Cohen, Benjamin J. (1986) *In Whose Interest? International Banking and American Foreign Policy* (New Haven, London).

Cooper, Richard N. (1983) 'Panel Discussion', in John Williamson (ed.) *IMF Conditionality* (Cambridge, Mass.: M.I.T. Press), pp. 596–77.

Corden, W. Max (1983) 'Is There an Important Role for an International Reserve Asset Such as the SDR?' in George M. von Furstenberg (ed.) *International Money and Credit: The Policy Roles* (Washington, D.C: American Enterprise Institute), pp. 213–47.

Cornelius, Peter (1988) *Das Prinzip der Konditionalität bei Krediten des Internationalen Währungsfonds* (München).

Dell, Sidney, Roger Lawrence (1980) *The Balance of Payments Adjustment Process in Developing Countries* (New York).

Donovan, Donal J. (1984) *The Sources of Current External Debt Servicing Difficulties: Some Empirical Evidence*, International Monetary Fund (DM/84/15), Washington, March; summarized in: *Finance and Development*, 1984, No. 4, pp. 22–5.

Dornbusch, Rüdiger (1986) *Dollars, Debts, and Deficits* (Cambridge, Mass.: M.I.T. Press).

Edwards, Sebastian (1984) 'The Role of International Reserves and Foreign Debt in the External Adjustment Process', in Joaquin Muns (ed.) *Adjustment, Conditionality, and International Financing* (Washington, D.C.), pp. 143–73.

Ferguson, Tyrone (1988) *The Third World and Decision Making in the International Monetary Fund* (London, New York).

Finch, C. David (1988) *Annual Meetings in the Past and the Future: Issues for the IMF and the World Bank* (Institute for International Economics, Washington, D.C.) mimeo, 25 p.

Fratianni, Michele and Paul de Grauwe (1984) 'The Political Economy of International Lending', *Cato Journal*, Spring/Summer, pp. 147–70.

Frey, Bruno S., Beat Gygi (1989) 'The International Organizations from the Constitutional Point of View', in Roland Vaubel, Thomas D. Willett (eds) *The Political Economy of International Organizations* (Boulder,)

Haberler, Gottfried (1974) *Economic Growth and Stability* (Los Angeles).

Kahler, Miles (1986) 'Conclusion: Politics and Proposals for Reform', in M. Kahler (ed.) *The Politics of International Debt* (Ithaca: Cornell University Press), pp. 245–72.

Kahler, Miles (1988) 'Organization and Cooperation: International Institutions and Policy Coordination', paper prepared for the Conference on Blending Economic and Political Analysis of International Financial Relations, Claremont College and University of Southern California, May, 28 p.

Kane, Edward J. (1986) 'Politics and Fed Policymaking: The More Things Change the More They Remain the Same', in Eugenia F. and Mark Toma (eds) *Central Bankers, Bureaucratic Incentives, and Monetary Policy* (Dordrecht: Kluwer), pp. 185–98.

Khan, Mohsin S. and Malcolm D. Knight (1983) 'Determinants of Current Account Balances of Non-Oil Developing Countries in the 1970s', IMF Staff Papers, 30, pp. 819–42.

Killick, Tony (1984) 'IMF Stabilisation Programmes', in T. Killick (ed.) *The Quest for Economic Stabilisation: The IMF and the Third World* (Aldershot: Gower), pp. 183–226.

Lomax, David F. (1986) *The Developing Country Debt Crisis* (London: Macmillan)

Magee, Stephen P. and William A. Brock (1986) 'Third World Debt and International Capital Market Failure as a Consequence of Redistributive Political Risk Sharing', in Michael P. Clandon (ed.) *World Debt Crisis: International Lending on Trial* (Cambridge, Mass.: M.I.T. Press), pp. 173–98.

Makin, John H. (1984) *The Global Debt Crisis. America's Growing Involvement* (New York).

Mosley, Paul (1987) 'Conditionality as a Bargaining Process: Structural Adjustment Lending, 1980–86', *Essays in International Finance*, No. 168, Princeton University.

Niehans, Jürg (1985) 'International Debt with Unenforceable Claims', *Economic Review*, Federal Reserve Bank of San Francisco, Winter pp. 65–79.

Officer, Lawrence H. (1982) 'The Differential Use of the IMF Resources by Industrial, Other Developed, and Less Developed Countries: A Historical Approach', *Journal of Developing Areas*, 16, pp. 401–20.

Reichmann, Thomas M. (1978) 'The Fund's Conditional Assistance and the Problems of Adjustment, 1973–75', *Finance and Development*, 15, Dec., pp. 38–41.

Sachs, Jeffrey D. (1987) 'International Policy Coordination: The Case of the Developing Country Debt Crisis', National Bureau of Economic Research, Working Paper No. 2287, 59 p.

Smith, Fred (1984), 'The Politics of IMF Lending', *Cato Journal*, Spring/Summer, 211–241.

Spraos, John (1986) 'IMF Conditionality: Ineffectual, Inefficient, Mistargeted', *Essays in International Finance*, No. 166, Princeton University.

Vaubel, Roland (1983) 'The Moral Hazard of IMF Lending', in Allan H. Meltzer (ed.) *International Lending and the IMF* (Washington, DC.: American Enterprise Institute), pp. 65–79; and in *The World Economy*, 6, No. 3, pp. 291–303.

Vaubel, Roland (1985) 'The International Organizations and the International Debt Problem: The Next Steps', in Alan Walters (Chairman) *Report of the Technical Committee*, Global Economic Action Institute, New York, pp. 21–33.

Vaubel, Roland (1986) 'A Public Choice Approach to International Organization', *Public Choice*, 51, No. 1, pp. 39–57.

Williamson, John (1980) 'Economic Theory and International Monetary Fund Policies', in Karl Brunner, Allan H. Meltzer (eds) *Monetary Institutions and the Policy Process*, Carnegie-Rochester Conference Series on Public Policy, 13, Amsterdam, pp. 255–78.

Williamson, John (1983) 'The Lending Policies of the International Monetary Fund' in J. Williamson (ed.) *IMF Conditionality* (Cambridge, Mass.: M.I.T. Press), pp. 605–60.

3 Speculative Booms and Crashes*
Robert Shiller

Speculative booms and crashes have been observed throughout history. In the first century Pliny reported a boom in land prices in the vicinity of Rome, a 'sudden advance' in prices which he said was 'much discussed' at the time.[1] There was a boom in the prices in, of all things, tulip bulbs in Holland in 1637, where prices rapidly ascended until one record-setting bulb sold for 5500 guilders or about £25 000 at today's price of gold. This bizarre boom was followed the same year by a dramatic collapse, after which bulbs could not be sold at 10 per cent of their peak price. Then there was the Florida land price boom of the mid-1920s, when people seemed suddenly to conclude that available land in this vacation spot and mecca for retirees was suddenly running out; prices soared. They soon found out that land was not so scarce after all: prices dropped precipitously in 1926. Then of course there was the stock market boom of the 1920s, with prices rising almost five-fold between Summer 1921 and Fall 1929. Following this there was a crash: between 3 September 1929 and 8 July 1932 the Dow Jones Industrial Average lost 84.4 per cent of its real (inflation-corrected) value, and lost 12.8 per cent of its value in one day, 28 October 1929.

Some of these old stories of booms and crashes are so well known as to be part of our popular culture. But it is difficult now to find out just what happened then. For example, Peter Garber [1989] has argued that most of the literature on the 1637 tulip bulb boom derives ultimately from the information in a single anonymous pamphlet written in 1637, and that the author of this pamphlet appears to be trying to use the episode to advance his anti-speculative bias. Even for events as recent as 1929 there is a critical lack of evidence on just what happened.

Fortunately, at least from the standpoint of research opportunities, new speculative booms and crashes are always turning up for us to study. The United States, the United Kingdom, Japan, and other countries have had

---

* This lecture was delivered in November 1989 and first published in booklet form by City University Business School, Dept of Banking and Finance.

their share of spectacular stock market booms and crashes, real estate booms and slumps in the past few years. I have been studying, with several co-authors, some of these booms and crashes for the underlying investor behaviour.

Most academic researchers in economics and finance do not think that investor behaviour during such booms and crashes is a worthwhile research topic, at least judging by the available literature in the scholarly journals. Part of the reason for this is the prominence in academic circles of the efficient-markets hypothesis in finance. This hypothesis asserts that the changes in price of any speculative asset can always be given a sensible justification just in terms of a rational market response to news about fundamentals: future dividends, rents, or interest rates. However, the evidence for this hypothesis has come increasingly into question in recent years.

Once we dispense with our reliance on market efficiency as a theoretical construct, then research on investor behaviour becomes central to understanding these market phenomena. There are two basic approaches to studying speculative booms and crashes. One is experimental economics. Vernon Smith and his colleagues (1989) have conducted economic experiments with subjects in a laboratory setting which sometimes generated speculative booms and crashes. The potential weakness of such experiments is that the experimental setting created by the experimenter is not an adequate representation of the real-world markets we observe. That is why it is important to use as well the other approach to studying booms and crashes: that of observing people who participate in them, as with the research I will discuss here.

I will discuss in this lecture booms in the context of the market for homes and crashes in the context of the stock market.

BOOMS IN THE MARKET FOR HOMES

What appears puzzling to those who experience sudden real-estate booms is often that while the new, higher price of housing, land or other assets may not be unreasonable, given the scarcity of the real estate relative to potential demand for it, the timing of the boom cannot be explained on any rational basis. Suddenly prices start rising. Rational reasons to expect higher prices are often given by people who try to interpret the sudden increases, but these are not rational reasons for a price *change* now.

Karl E. Case (1986) tried to see whether the recent boom in housing prices in Boston, Massachusetts, could be explained in terms of changes in any of the usual demand-or supply-side variables. The price of existing single-family homes in Boston had doubled between 1983 and 1986, a period when the level of prices overall, as measured by the producer price index, increased only 3 per cent. He found no evidence of precipitous changes in Boston in such demand-side or supply-side variables as population growth, employment growth, interest rates (short-term and long-term), construction costs, income growth, tax rates, and the like. He estimated a model of housing prices from ten cities over a ten-year period and found that the model failed to explain more than a fraction of the observed increase in Boston housing prices over this boom period.

There are other puzzles of investor behaviour associated with real estate booms and their aftermath. Why, in the height of a real estate boom, is there often evidence of excess demand? Why do many homes sell for more than the asking price, with buyers scrambling to bid against each other on the first day the home is on the market? Why don't sellers just raise their price enough that the market clears at its normal pace at the asking price? Why, in a postboom housing market, such as we are observing in England today, do we observe prices levelling off rather than crashing as they do in the stock market? Why, in a postboom market, does that volume of sales of homes drop substantially, and homes stay unsold for long periods of time? Why do owners of homes refrain from cutting the asking price of their homes in a down market?

To answer these questions, Karl Case and I hit upon a research plan that involves comparing boom, postboom and unexceptional or control housing market at the same point of time. In mid-1988 many cities in California were experiencing a sharp boom in real-estate values, with price changes from late 1987 to mid-1988 exceeding 20 per cent in many cities. At the very same time, in the Eastern United States, Boston was experiencing a post-boom situation, with home prices actually declining in late 1987, and sales volume of homes sharply reduced. Also, at the same time, Milwaukee, a city in the centre of the country, there was no sign of a boom at all for the past five years; home prices were virtually flat.

Our idea was to send out identical questionnaires to cities in all these markets, questionnaires identical except for the change of the name of the city. By using identical questionnaires, and sending them out at the same time, we know that differences across cities in answers to the questions can be attributed only to differences in the local market for homes and not to differences in the wording or order of questions or to national economic conditions.

We sent out 500 questionnaires to home buyers in May 1988 to each of four cities.[2] These included two boom cities in California, San Francisco and Anaheim, the latter a city near Los Angeles where the boom appeared to be even a little stronger than in Los Angeles itself. They also included Boston, the post-boom city, and Milwaukee, the control city. From the 2000 questionnaires mailed, we received 886 responses.

The most striking difference we observed between the boom cities and the other cities was in expectations people held for *future* price increases in their own city. We asked 'On *average* over the next 10 years, how much do you expect the value of your property to change each year?' In the boom city Anaheim, the average answer was 14.3 per cent, in San Francisco 14.8 per cent. If people understood what they were saying, they were predicting a *quadrupling* of home prices in their city in the next ten years, after price increases had already made these cities among the most expensive in the United States. In contrast, in the post-boom city Boston the answer was only 8.7 per cent, and in the control city Milwaukee only 7.3 per cent.

We asked respondents to indicate whether they agreed with the state-ment: 'housing prices are booming. Unless I buy now, I won't be able to afford a home later.' In Anaheim, 79.5 per cent agreed with this statement, in San Francisco 68.9 per cent agreed, while in Boston only 40.8 per cent agreed and in Milwaukee only 27.8 per cent agreed.

Of course, it is precisely these expectations and fears of being priced out of housing in the future that tend to generate real-estate booms, by bringing more housing demand in, causing further price increases, and then yet more demand.

The expectations of future price increases in boom cities seem, just by their magnitude alone, to be irrational. What reason do people have to expect such future price increases? Are they doing nothing more than extrapolating the boom for another ten years? Now it is true that higher-than-usual price increases in housing do tend to portend slightly higher-than-usual price increases for the near future (Case and Shiller, 1989), but nothing like the expectations our boom city homebuyers showed. Our boom city respondents did not seem to have any cogent reason for these expectations, or any understanding of the causes of the price increases they had already experienced. We asked 'What do you think explains recent changes in home prices in—? What ultimately is behind what is going on? Was there any event (or events) in the last two years that you think changed the trend in housing prices?' In all four cities, interest rate changes were the most commonly cited factor. Yet interest rates are virtu-ally identical throughout the United States, while as I noted above the patterns of price movements are strikingly different across the four cities. These people cannot all be right about the causes of price movements in their cities. In Boston, where housing prices were declining, 25 per cent of the respondents mentioned the stock market crash of 1987, while less than 2 per cent of the respondents in the other cities did. But the stock market crash affected stockholders in all parts of the country, not just Boston.

What is even more remarkable about the answers to these questions is that not a single respondent from our 886 respondents offered any quantitative evidence: any reference at all to any numbers relevant to future supply or demand for housing or to any professional forecast of supply or demand. Instead, we heard most often a lot of clichés or casual observations about the city, observations one might make just by driving around the city.

The picture we get of housing booms is one in which expectations of future price increases fuel greatly increased demand for homes, and therefore further price increases as more people compete for the same housing. People who would not normally wish to live in substantial homes (for example, young unmarried people) feel they must do so if they are to afford such a home in the future, and they thereby push aside some of the other people who might want to live in a substantial home now (for example, families with young children).

There is a great social cost to such misunderstandings. The problem this behaviour creates reminds me of a much smaller, but more immediately apparent, problem that we have all encountered at one time or another in cafeterias in which one must first go through a food line before sitting down to eat. When a cafeteria starts to become crowded, arriving people start to become fearful that they will not find a seat after waiting in line and paying for their food. Some will, before joining the line for food, therefore have a friend sit down at a table to hold it for them, or try to reserve a table by putting coats or other belongings on the table. This behaviour may then serve to create a shortage of tables where none might otherwise have existed if people had just taken their chances to get a table. The social problem that people create by behaving thus is, though smaller, of the same nature as the social problem we observe in the real-estate market.

In the boom cities, a substantial number of homes sold for more than the asking price. In our sample, in Anaheim 6.3 per cent sold for more than asking, in San Francisco 9.8 per cent. (At the same time, most homes, 55.7 per cent in Anaheim and 63.4 per cent in San Francisco, sold below the asking price.) A sale above the asking price typically means that there were a number of offers on the day the home went on the market, and buyers felt that they had to offer more than the asking price in order to stand a chance of making the highest bid.

California newspapers tended to interpret this phenomenon as reflecting some sort of investor madness. The behaviour of those who make these offers is described as 'frenzied' or 'panicky'. We sought to confirm whether these interpretations were shared by market participants. We asked the following question:

In a hot real-estate market, sellers often get more than one offer on the day they list their property. Some are even over the asking price. There are also stories about people waiting in line to make offers. Which is the best explanation?
(a) There is panic buying and price becomes irrelevant.
(b) Asking prices have adjusted slowly or slugglishly to increasing demand.

In Anaheim, 73.3 per cent picked (a), only 26.7 per cent picked (b). In San Francisco, 71.2 per cent picked (a), only 28.8 per cent picked (b). To an economist, (b) is the only sensible answer. Surely price is not irrelevant to buyers. They are carefully making the lowest bid they think they can make to get the home. This kind of bidding war occurs in a minority of homes only because buyers perceive them as underpriced by the seller. But that is not how the majority of market participants themselves interpret the phenomenon!

We asked sellers whether they thought that their home might have sold almost as quickly if they had asked 5 to 10 per cent more for it. Among those who said yes, we asked them to choose among several explanations why they did not ask more. We gave them several possible answers to choose from; we took these answers from what we thought people were telling us in our pre-test interview with home sellers. The most popular explanation, chosen by 32.4 per cent in Anaheim and 27.3 per cent in San Francisco, was 'the property simply wasn't worth that much'. Another choice was 'It wouldn't have been fair to set it that high, given what I paid for it. I was already getting enough for it'. In Anaheim, 16.2 per cent picked this, in San Francisco 22.7 per cent did. Yet another choice was 'I simply made a mistake or got bad advice; I should have asked more.' In Anaheim 21.6 per cent picked this, in San Francisco 18.2 per cent picked this.

We see then that the sales of homes above their asking price reflects nothing more than that a small minority of sellers just do not ask enough for their homes, either because of some sense of intrinsic worth or fairness, or just because of outright mistakes. Such mistakes are more likely to be made in a market where prices are increasing rapidly, and given that *some* minority of people behave this way, one should expect to see homes selling for more than asking in a boom market.

The newspapers and general public do not perceive the homes selling for more than asking in the correct way, and this misperception adds further fuel to the real estate boom. The sense that the market is frenzied or panicky adds to the impressions that prices will continue to go up.

The sense of frenzy in the housing market was certainly present in the boom markets, and, to a lesser extent, in the postboom market as well. We asked respondents whether they agreed with the statement 'there has been a good deal of excitement surrounding the recent housing price changes. I sometimes think that I may have been influenced by it.' In Anaheim, 54.3 per cent and in San Francisco 56.5 per cent agreed, while in Boston 45.3 per cent agreed and in Milwaukee only 21.5 per cent agreed.

In a postboom market we see signs of excess supply rather than of excess demand. In Boston, only 0.5 per cent of our respondents reported paying more than the asking price for their home, and 76.0 per cent paid less than the asking price. Homes tended to stay on the market much longer in Boston than in the other cities. We asked those who sold homes in Boston what they would have done if they were unable to sell their property. Only 4.9 per cent said they would have 'lowered the price till I found a buyer'. We asked them how they arrived at the limit to how far they would lower price, and coded their written answers to this open-ended question. Nearly half, 42.9 per cent, in Boston were coded as saying that the limit was based on what other, similar homes were selling for, while 38.1 per cent were coded as saying that the limit was based on the price of another home that they wanted to buy. With asking prices set in accordance with the prices on the relatively rare sales that took place, there is a built-in downward rigidity in prices. Moreover, homeowners face a sort of coordination problem in a down market: if one wants to sell one home to buy a similar one elsewhere, one cannot lower one's asking price and still expect to buy the other home. If everyone could lower their asking prices at the same time, the market might clear at the lower prices, but no one wants to be the first to lower price. The downward rigidity in home prices is analogous, therefore, to the downward rigidity in wage rates observed by Keynes, who said that 'since there is, as a rule, no means of securing a simultaneous and equal reduction of money wages in all industries, it is in the interest of all workers to resist a reduction in their own particular case.'[3]

Such downward rigidity in asking prices is not strong enough to prevent a sort of crash in housing markets if the decline in demand is strong enough. For example, the median price of existing single family homes recently dropped 24 per cent in two years in Houston, Texas. But to observe really sudden crashes, we have to turn from the housing market to the stock market.

STOCK MARKET CRASHES

Sometimes the things you'd think would be the easiest to explain are actually the hardest. You would think that an event like a stock market crash would be very easy to explain, after it happened. Stock prices are determined by people: the suppliers and demanders of stocks. A stock market crash is a time when many people decide to sell (or would sell if price didn't fall so much). Surely, if very many people had reasons to sell all at once, these reasons should not be difficult to understand, no deep economic research would be needed to find out the cause of the crash. You could just *ask* people why they sold.

Yet the causes of the major stock market crashes in history are often described as completely unknown, and the diversity of theories offered after the crash suggests that analysts are really baffled.

What is particularly puzzling about stock market crashes is that there is typically no discernible trigger for the crash. Why did the crash occur on the day that it did? One would not expect a large number of people to reach the same decision on the same day about anything. Analysts are thus inclined to try to point out some news stories that broke around the time of the crash as the likely trigger for the crash. But their stories often sound of no particular importance.

Consider, for example the stock market crash of 28 October 1929, when the Dow Jones Industrial Average fell 12.8 per cent in a day, setting a record one-day percentage drop in stock market prices, a record that stood until the bigger 1987 crash that I will discuss later. If one reads old newspapers, one finds little news of any apparent import on the day of the 1929 crash, or surrounding days, other than the news of the crash itself. The absence of any news then was so striking that historian Frederic Lewis Allen wrote a famous article entitled 'One Day in History', stressing how ordinary and normal the day of the 1929 stock market peak seemed at the time; it was best described as a nice day for taking walks or visiting relatives. The morning of the crash of 28 October 1928 was little different, the highlight of the news that day seemed to be the latest word from Richard Byrd, who was exploring the Antarctic using dogsleds. It was, if anything, a good day for daydreaming about high adventure.

So why, on 28 October 1929, did so many people get upset at once, what accounts for the sudden decline of stock market value then? You can go back and reread those old newspapers once again, thinking that there *must* have been some bad news. Allan Meltzer (1976) found some news in the *New York Times* on the morning of 28 October 1929 (and which was picked up by the Associated Press and the United News and printed nationally on 29 October, when the market fell dramatically again) that he said he thought was a likely story: news that the Smoot-Hawley Tariff bill was likely to pass. It is true that this was a big tariff bill (the tariffs reached 59 per cent of the average value of imports by 1932), but Rüdiger Dornbusch and Stanley Fischer argued that it cannot be a major cause of the depression then since exports were only about 7 per cent of GNP in 1929, and exports fell only by 1.5 per cent of 1929 GNP between 1929 and 1931. Moreover, a previous large tariff increase, the Fordney–McCumber tariff, had not had much impact on the economy. But the real reason why the news about Smoot-Hawley does not seem adequate is that the news about Smoot-Hawley on the morning of 28 October 1929 really wasn't very dramatic. The story said that Senator Reed had pronounced the tariff bill dead, which provoked denials by Senators Smoot and Borah. The *New York Times* quoted Senator Smoot as saying 'If that is Senator Reed's opinion, I suppose he has a right to express it, but that isn't the view of the Finance Committee.' Senator Borah said, 'My opinion is that the tariff bill is not going to die.' These senators are just contradicting each other; it is hard to imagine how this story could be news that provoked the biggest stock market crash in history. The preceding months' news had featured other pronouncements by prominent people on the likelihood of the passage of the tariff bill. It would seem that the economists were grasping at *anything* to explain the stock market crash. Economists pick out what stories sound of fundamental importance to *them*, but who's to say what is important to the market.

Unfortunately, it appears that no one thought of polling stock market investors in 1989 to see if the news about the Smoot-Hawley tariff was really on their minds on the morning of 28 October 1989. However, there was a bit of a survey research done after another stock market 'crash' that was only half as big. On 3 September 1946, the US stock market fell 6.1 per cent. Most of us have forgotten that episode, but it caused quite a sensation when it happened and spurred a US Securities and Exchange Commission inquiry. The S.E.C. investigators interviewed major buyers and sellers on that day, and asked them for their reasons for buying and selling. They coded the 'major reasons' for selling into 17 categories. The largest category, coded for 43 per cent of interviewees, was 'declining prices on September 3'. No other category came close to being mentioned by 43 per cent of interviewees. The second biggest category was 'Dow Theory', a technical forecasting system. These interviewees would also be described as saying that they were selling in response to past price changes.

It would seem to appear, from the available evidence, that these past crashes are best described as vicious circles, where price declines for some reason fed on themselves: investors react to price declines by selling, causing subsequent price declines and then more selling and so on. But why did they do so on these days and not on other days? Why doesn't every initial price decline start such a downward spiral? In short, what was different about those days?

Academic finance has reacted to these crash episodes by rejecting the notion that price declines can feed on themselves so mechanically, and saying that indeed there must have been some news event that caused the crash. They justify our apparently not knowing what *caused* the crash by saying that the modern efficient markets theory suggests we economists might not know, even after the crash, what caused it.

The efficient markets theory asserts that within minutes of any change in the news situation, the best minds in the world of finance re-evaluate investments, and adjust price rapidly up and down. They do so at the first inkling of a news story, they do not wait until it appears in the newspaper or until they can clearly articulate themselves as to why they have re-evaluated the investment. To wait so long would mean missing out on the opportunity to make profitable trades, which can happen only if they are among the first to act.

Still, any such application of efficient markets theory to explain stock market crashes seems a little far fetched. Let us now turn to the stock market crash of 19 October 1987. The usual description of this crash is that the Dow Jones Industrial Average fell 22.6 per cent between the close on Friday, 16 October and the close on Monday, 19 October, a space of only 3 days. A more telling way to describe the crash is that the Dow fell 15 per cent between 1:30p.m. and 4:00p.m. on October 19, a space of only $2\frac{1}{2}$ hours. Really, no news of any conceivable importance seems to have occurred in that short time period, other than the news of the crash itself. What rational factors could possibly have accounted for such a sudden re-evaluation of fundamental value?

After having tried unsuccessfully to figure out what happened in October 1929 and other crashes, I was thrilled by the research opportunity that another crash offered. I thought that the opportunity presented itself to get more closely into what was on investors' minds on that day.

I sent out questionnaires on the week of the 1987 stock market crash to 2000 wealthy individual investors in the United States and 1000 institutional investors in the United States, asking them about their personal experiences during the crash. I received 605 responses from individual investors and 284 responses from instutional investors.[4]

I asked them to rate on a one-to-seven scale the news stories that were in the newspaper around the time of the crash, a 1 indicating 'completely unimportant' and 7 indicating 'very important'. Of the ten news stories I listed, they chose as the most important the story 'the 200 point drop in the Dow the morning of Monday, October 19.' While other news stories were also granted substantial importance, the news of the crash itself stood as the most important. It is interesting to note that I missed, in my list of ten news stories, one story that many afterwards have claimed is the most likely cause of the crash: the 14 October 1987 news story that tax legislation had been proposed that would make corporate takeovers less likely. This news story was singled out by the Brady Commission appointed by President Reagan to study the crash as the trigger for the crash. On my questionnaire was a space to write in another news story that the respondent thought important. Of 605 individual investors, not a single one wrote in this news story, of 284 institutional investors, only 3 did.

So, what *was* going on that day? I asked some open-ended questions, where the respondents would fill in their own answers. I asked 'Can you remember any specific theory you had about the causes for the price declines October 14–19, 1987?' Respondents hardly ever referred to any news story in their answers; the most common answer was just to say that the market had been overpriced. I asked, immediately following this question, 'Which of the following better describes your theory about the declines: A theory about investor psychology or a theory about fundamentals such as profits or interest rate?' Two-thirds of both individual and institutional investors chose the former, a theory about investor psychology. (A survey of Japanese institutional investors a few months later, Shiller, Kon-ya and Tsutsui [1988] asked them the same question, and three quarters picked the investor psychology.)

I asked, 'Did you think at any point on October 19, 1987 that you had a pretty good idea when a rebound was to occur?' About 30 per cent of both groups said yes. Immediately following this question was an open-ended question: 'If yes, what made you think you knew when a rebound would occur?' The modal answer was something like 'intuition' or 'gut feeling'. Even the institutional investors usually had no clearly stated theory why they thought that they knew when a rebound would occur. This is perhaps what one would expect if investors that day were occupied in trying to guess each others' psychology.

To gauge better the feelings of investors, I asked an explicitly psychological question. I asked whether they had experienced on 19 October 1987 any unusual symptoms of anxiety, specifically 'difficulty concentrating, sweaty palms, tightness in chest, irritability, or rapid pulse'. 20 per cent of individual investors and over 40 per cent of institutional investors said yes.

What seems to have happened on 19 October 1987 was a climax of world attention, like that prompted by such events as Hitler's invasion of Poland, or the assassination of President Kennedy. But the attention generated by the stock market crash was not directly caused by any exogenous event. While other factors, such as portfolio insurance, were part of the story on 19 October, the critical feature of the day may just be that time was, in effect, speeded up on 19 October 1987 due to heightened investor awareness and attention. The heightened attention was a natural consequence of investors' interacting with each other, and was an endogenous social event, just as are many other social movements in human history.

The stock market drop that we saw in October 1989 was different from the 1987 crash in that it seems to have been triggered by a recognisable news event. Just before 3:00 p.m. Eastern Daylight Time on Friday, 13 October 1989, the news broke that the group that sought to acquire the UAL Corporation, the parent of United Airlines, had failed in its $6.75 billion buyout. The group, which included United's pilots' union, UAL executives and British Airways, announced that its banks had advised that the deal could be financed only 'on revised terms'.

When the news broke, the London market was already closed, but the New York Stock Exchange had another hour's trading. The Dow Jones Industrial Average dropped precipitously, closing down 190.58 points, or 6.90 per cent below its close the day before. The drop began sharply within a few minutes of the UAL announcement, so that it is hard to doubt this time that a specific news event was the trigger. The following Monday, 16 October, stocks fell 12.8 per cent in West Germany, and were down about 8 per cent in London, before the US market opened and the London market rallied. (Prices had been down only 1.8 per cent in Tokyo on the Monday, although there were some violent price swings during the day.) The New York Stock Exchange then proceeded to recover half of its Friday losses on Monday.

Now, the UAL news seems to have caused the decline, but it is really unexceptional news. The total value of the buyout, 6.75 billion, is only about two-tenths of 1 per cent of the value of all New York Stock

Exchange, American and over-the-counter issues. The UAL deal would be of course substantially less important as a percentage of the world value of shares. How can news about such a tiny fraction of all shares cause such massive movements in the other share prices? Perhaps one could claim that the news was important for the takeover movement and associated junk-bond market in general, indicating that takeovers of other companies would result in similar problems. But this is not the first bad news about takeovers.

As Michael Harkins, a money-market manager, put it in a national television show, the MacNeil-Lehrer Report, on 13 October, 'Perhaps the strangest thing in this fall's capital markets has been that although we have seen a default almost daily in junk bonds, we continue to see banks sign up for new junk-bond deals. It made no sense. Suddenly people seem to have come to their senses in one hour this afternoon.'

But why should people all come to their senses in one hour? Is this piece of news the straw that broke the bull market's back? But as a description of the behaviour of market participants, the last-straw theory is on the face of it absurd. Even if there were a threshold beyond which a sequence of bad news events becomes significant, we could never expect a large number of people to agree so suddenly on just when the threshold had been reached.

My colleague William Feltus, a pollster, and I decided to try to find out, using telephone survey methods, what market participants were thinking on Friday, 13 October 1989. We acted as quickly as possible, so that memories would be still fresh, and arranged for telephone interviews of market professionals in the United States on Monday and Tuesday, 16 and 17 October. We succeeded in obtaining 101 completed interviews.

The first thing we asked was their interpretation of the stock market drop on Friday. We confirmed that the UAL news played some role in the stock market drop: 37 per cent voluntarily mentioned the UAL deal, and most of them said something related to the takeovers or junk bonds in general. Only 5 per cent mentioned anything about the proposed capital-gains-tax cut. Jude Wanniski wrote in the *Wall Street Journal* (1989) that the stock market drop on 13 October was caused by the news around 2:00 p.m. that the Bush administration had agreed to the reconciliation bill without any assurance from Senate Democrats that a vote on substance on the capital-gains-tax cut would be permitted. None of our respondents seemed to refer to this bit of news. Wanniski is seeking out news that *might* logically have caused the stock market drop, but we have no evidence at all that it had anything to do with the stock market drop.

After asking them what they thought happened, we asked: 'Do you think that what happened on Friday was due more to psychology and emotion or to news about a change in stock market fundamentals?' Only 19 per cent chose the fundamentals, 77 per cent chose the psychology. Even though our price drop seems to have a well-identified trigger, still they think that the price drop is really due to changes in investor psychology.

We then asked: 'Which of the following better represents the view you held last Friday: 1. The UAL news of Friday afternoon will reduce future takeovers, and so the UAL news is a sensible reason for the sudden drop in stock prices; or 2. The UAL news of Friday afternoon should be viewed as a focal point or attention grabber, which prompted investors to express their doubts about the stock market.' 50 per cent of our respondents chose the second option, the focal point, and only 30 per cent picked 1.

Now it should be recognized that if market participants think that investor psychology is the cause of stock market movements, then that is the view that informs their actions, and then, indeed, market psychology *is* the cause of stock price movements. Moreover, if market participants say that the news event that triggered the market decline is merely a focal point, then it *is* just a focal point. The question that still remains is why did they view it as a focal point on this day, why didn't they pick some other bit of bad news about takeovers as the focal point for their actions? At bottom, we want to know what is really different about 13 October 1989 that allowed such a stock market drop to happen?

What will have to rank as the most unusual thing about that date is that it corresponds to the anniversary of the 1987 crash or, more accurately, that it was the anniversary of the Friday before the October 1987 crash. Recall that the 1987 crash occurred on a Monday in October shortly after the stock market had reached a new peak, and following precipitous declines the preceding Friday. The parallel to the 1987 crash was certainly not lost on the news media. For example, Sarah Bartlett, in a front page of the *New York Times* entitled 'Is it 1987 again' on Saturday, 14 October, wrote that 'The parallels are almost eerie ... Here we go again?' But is that what market participants thought?

We asked, 'On Friday, did you think that a replay of the 1987 crash was or was not a real possibility?' 35 per cent said it was a real possibility. We also asked, 'On Friday, did you think that most other investors thought that a replay of the 1987 crash was or was not a real possibility? 41 per cent said yes. while this is a minority, it is a pretty solid minority. We will have to take it as a plausible theory for the stock market drop that it occurred, then, as an anniversary effect of the 1987 crash. People were primed to think that another crash was possible then, and particularly on that date, and so the focal point of the UAL news became a reality. And of course, those who thought a crash was imminent had an incentive to exit the market, thereby creating the risk of the very crash they feared.

CONCLUSION

We have seen that tabulating what market participants are thinking during speculative booms and crashes yields important insights into the causes of these booms and crashes. Those who try to analyse these events almost uniformly fail to try to tabulate what market participants were thinking, and therefore miss some crucial information. Analysts can only speculate as to what participants thought was happening and what they thought would be the likely consequences of their own actions.

Thus, for example, after the stock market drop of 13 October 1989 analysts generally did not offer as an explanation of this event that it was an anniversary effect of the 1987 crash. Such an explanation of the stock market drop is extremely obvious, given the media reporting of the event, yet for an analyst to advance such a theory of the drop would be difficult: the analyst could not martial any more support for this theory of the stock market drop than casual personal observation of the behaviour of other investors. In the absence of any information on what investors are thinking, economists tend to attribute plausible, logical motivations to investors that are not there. We saw this, for example, in the theories that news about capital-gains-tax cut legislation caused the stock market drop of 1989 or that news about anti-takeover legislation caused the stock market crash of 1987.

In the absence of any information on what investors are thinking, economists are likely to miss connections in investors' thinking that are there. Thus, for example, economists miss the fact that home buyers in California incorrectly interpreted news that homes were sold above asking price as evidence of a homebuying frenzy, and as a reason to think that they must buy now if they are ever to buy an affordable home. Thus, economists miss a feedback mechanism that is at work in producing a boom.

The difficulty in uncovering reasons for booms and crashes using survey or interview techniques is that the real reasons for economic behaviour may not be easily or readily expressed by the subjects. This is not a reason to despair of getting more knowledge about these events; it means that we must spend time and care in collecting information. It is probably easier to collect information about people's cognitive processes about economic decisions than it is to get information about the behaviour psychologists traditionally study. Much economic behaviour is likely to be more directly goal-oriented and straightforward than are other life decisions.

Economists should spend more time studying the popular models of the economy and popular theories, even beyond the study of speculative booms and crashes. Only then can we obtain insights into agents' behaviour.

Notes

1. Pliny [1931], Vol. 6, letter 19, p. 487.
2. Names of home buyers are available on public records from the town where the home is located. Most of these are also recent sellers of homes, and usually these other homes are in the same general real-estate market as the home they purchased. Thus, we can learn about behaviour in both the purchase and sale of homes in the city. What is conspicuously missing, however, from our sample are the people who decided not to transact at all during the time period under study.
3. John Maynard Keynes [1936], p. 264.
4. A more complete discussion of these results is in my *Market Volatility* [1989].

References

Case, Karl E. (1986) 'The Market for Single-Family Homes in Boston', *New England Economic Review*, May/June.

Case, Karl E., and Robert J. Shiller (1988) 'The Behaviour of Home Buyers in Boom and Post-Boom Markets', *New England Economic Reivew*, pp. 29–46, November/December.

Case, Karl, E., and Robert J. Shiller (1989) 'The Efficiency of the Market for Single Family Homes', *The American Economic Review*, March.

Dornbush, Rüdiger, and Stanley Fischer (1986) 'The Open Economy: Implications for Monetary and Fiscal Policy', in Robert J. Gordon (ed.) *The American Business Cycle: Continuity and Change* (National Bureau of Economic Research and University of Chicago Press) pp. 459–501.

Garber, Peter M. (1989) 'Who Put the Mania in the Tulipomania?' in *Crashes and Panics in Historical Perspective*, ed. Eugene White (Homewood Ill.: Dow Jones Irwin).

Keynes, John M. (1964) *The General Theory of Employment, Interest and Money* (New York: Harbinger, first published 1936).

Meltzer, Allan H. (1976) 'Monetary and Other Explanations of the Start of the Great Depression', *Journal of Monetary Economics*, 2: pp. 455–71, November.

Pliny (1931) *Letters*, translated by William Melmoth (Cambridge, Mass.: Harvard University Press).

Shiller, Robert J. (1989) *Market Volatility* (Cambridge, Mass.: M.I.T. Press).

Shiller, Robert J., Fumiko Kon-ya, and Yoshiro Tsutsui (1988) 'Investor Behaviour in the October 1987 Stock Market Crash: The Case of Japan', National Bureau of Economic Research, Working Paper No. 2684.

Smith, Vernon L., Gerry L. Suchanek, and Arlington W. Williams (1989) 'Bubbles Crashes and Endogenous Expectations in Experimental Spot Asset Markets', *Econometrica*.

Wanniski, Jude (1989) 'Bradley's Team Gave the Market Its Drubbing', *Wall Street Journal*. 19 October, p. A20.

4 Central Banking Tasks in a European Monetary Union*
Niels Thygesen

INTRODUCTION

Henry Thornton was a perceptive observer of monetary events and a major contributor to the principles of central banking as we know them today. Had the term 'monetary regimes' been known in his times, an important part of his *magnum opus, Paper Credit*, could be put under that heading. He would have had much to say on how to reconcile short-run flexibility with long-run stability, the central task of monetary management, in a national economy as well as in a group of countries trying to develop an appropriate institutional framework for joint management of monetary policy. His ability to distil guidelines from practical experience and to derive inspiration from current events is more than ever necessary as we watch the debate on monetary integration and union in Europe.

The inspiration is not lacking, though his talents may be missing. Within the last few days two events have underlined the momentum of Europe's debate on future arrangements of its monetary affairs. I could not have foreseen the first of them: the resignation of the Prime Minister of the United Kingdom prompted by an intensified debate about the UK attitude to the plans of her EC partners to accelerate the move towards monetary union and a single European currency. The other event has been more predictable for some time. The Committee of Central Bank Governors in the European communities on 27 November forwarded a fairly complete draft of the statutes for a European System of Central Banks to the Finance Ministers. This documents is so far the main input into the Intergovernmental Conference (IGC) on Economic and Monetary Union which starts in Rome on 15 December. Though the draft statutes

---

* This lecture was delivered in November 1990 and published in booklet form by City University Business School, Dept of Banking and Finance. Most of the material in the lecture is based on joint work up to 1991 between Professor Thygesen and Dr Daniel Gros of the Centre for European Policy Studies in Brussels, published in 1991 in *European Monetary Integration – From EMS to EMU* (Longman).

76 *Monetary Economics in the 1990s*

remain confidential, the main points in them have become well known in the public debate in recent weeks, in part through explanations given by the current Chairman of the Committee of Governors, President Pöhl, in London and elsewhere. So this is the right time to discuss and interpret these points, particularly in the country where they are already subject to more intensive and critical scrutiny than anywhere else in Europe.

It is not my task tonight to go through the arguments for or against giving up permanently the use of changes in exchange rates among the currencies likely to participate in a monetary union. I do believe there is a good case for the view that the benefits are likely to outweigh the costs for most, if not all, of the EC member states; that case is set out well, with a number of necessary qualifications, in the EC Commission's recent monumental study *One Market, One Money*.[1] But regardless of the personal preferences of myself, or of those more critical of monetary union, it seems useful to discuss central banking tasks in a monetary union under the assumption of a political decision to have the latter, as indeed repeatedly confirmed by the European Council. Though what follows may sound too assertive for many in the audience, the discussion does not assume that a definitive case for monetary union has been made. It could be read in a less prescriptive perspective, quite fairly advocated by the Governor of the Bank of England in the Delors Committee and subsequently in the Committee of Governors: it is useful to define the responsibilities and functions of a possible future European System of Central Banks and review the implications of various institutional and operation choices. By producing a largely agreed draft of the ESCB statutes, the central bankers have effectively said to the IGC: 'If you decide to have monetary union, this is how we would propose to design the common policy framework.'

It is a consequence of this less prescriptive perspective that more attention is devoted to the final stage than to the transition. Political agreement on the content of the final stage is essential to the proper design of the transition. This explains why the Committee of Governors has chosen to make proposals for the transition only during the course of the IGC. This lecture will follow a similar pattern of emphasis, though I share the concern of pragmatically oriented observers at the present lack of concreteness of the transitional stage.

MANDATE, AUTONOMY AND ACCOUNTABILITY OF THE ESCB[2]

The basic characteristics of a monetary union and its institutional prerequisites are well described already in the Delors Report of 1989.[3] The two main features are (1) the complete liberalization of capital transactions and full integration of banking and other financial markets; and (2) the elimination of margins of fluctuation and the irrevocable locking of exchange rate parties among the participating currencies. Whether a single currency is then introduced or not – and the Delors Report recommends that 'the replacement of national currencies by a single currency should ... take place as soon as possible after the locking of parties' (para. 23) – participating central banks will have to conduct a single monetary policy. The emphasis then shifts decisively from earlier preoccupation with the instruments of relative coordination – that is, interventions, movements of the currency within the EMS grid of bilateral parties and changes in short-term interest differentials – to absolute coordination:[4] the contribution of the joint monetary policy to the overall macroeconomic performance of the union and, in particular, to the control of some measure of inflation in the area as a whole. This is a major simplification, because it makes the familiar tools of analysis of monetary policy in a single, open economy applicable.

The Delors report, though it fell short of providing a full blueprint for how a joint monetary policy could be designed and implemented, did address three main issues for the final stage of monetary union: (1) the mandate for the ESCB; (2) the degree of autonomy of the latter *vis-à-vis* the political authorities at the national and EC levels; and (3) the accountability of the institution, and these three closely interelated issues will be discussed together.

All net benefits from monetary union – the microeconomic benefits to traders and investors arising from the elimination of all exchange-rate related transaction costs and uncertainties, and from the intensified competition in the single market for goods and services outweighing the perceived cost to national authorities of giving up the use of nominal exchange rate changes as an instrument of macroeconomic adjustment – could be more than offset if a deterioration were to occur in the average inflationary performance of the union relative to what would have been observable under a more decentralized system of policy-making. To minimize the risk of an unstable or inflationary monetary policy the Delors Report proposed the following mandate for the ESCB (para. 32):

–   The system would be committed to the objective of price stability;
–   subject to the foregoing, the system should support the general economic policy set at the community level by the competent bodies.

It was not surprising that a committee consisting largely of central bank governors should propose a formulation reminiscent of the classical central bank function of assuring a stable framework for nominal variables. It is more surprising that a mandate nearly identical to the above formulation, viz. (Art. 2 of Draft Statutes):

- – The primary objective of the System shall be to maintain price stability;
- – Without prejudice to the objective of price stability, the System shall support the general economic policy of the Community

has emerged from the recent discussion in the Committee of Governors with clear majority support in the Council of Ministers to back it.

Such a mandate is tougher than that of the Deutsche Bundesbank; Art. 3 of the Bundesbank Act of 1957 defines the main responsibility to be the 'safe guarding of the value of the currency', while Art. 12 stipulates that 'the (Bundes) bank should support the economic policy of the government, but cannot be subjected to instructions by the latter'. This is a more ambiguous formulation. Other EC central banks have mandates far more open to different interpretations, particularly those that have statutes dating from the 1930s and 1940s, when the ambition to integrate central banks fully into the government's decision-making was at a peak.

It would be a mistake to attach exclusive importance to legal texts. Some central banks with little formal autonomy of the government and no special emphasis on price stability in their statutory obligations have nevertheless over an extended period pursued policies – for example, through participation in the EMS – which required such emphasis. Yet it is significant that nearly all EC member states now seem prepared to subscribe to a clear and permanent lexicographical ordering of their preferences with respect to the conduct of their joint monetary policy. Why this conversion to monetary orthodoxy for the prospective ESCB? One might identify three, rather diverse, elements.

The *first* and most basic is a growing recognition in official circles that a high degree of price stability is fully compatible with satisfactory growth in output and employment. This recognition is recent in several of the countries that are prospective participants in an EMU, because slow growth of output and rising unemployment throughout much of the 1980s appeared to be linked to the disinflationary efforts in the EMS. As late as 1988 the Finance Ministers of France and Italy, in memoranda that were part of the debate preceding the launching of the Delors Committee, were openly critical of the implicit weighting of policy objectives in the EMS resulting from a presumed asymmetry of the system: Germany as the centre country, on which other members had aligned themselves through pegging to the Deutsche Mark, was excessively concerned about inflation and 'an engine for growth' in the EMS was absent.[5] The monetary straightjacket of the Bundesbank was seen to prevent desirable macro-economic policies in other EMS countries. While this line of analysis was questionable at the time it was advanced – the growth rate of the German money supply in real terms had been relatively rapid since 1983/4 – the experience from 1986/7 onwards certainly did not bear it out: output and employment picked up in France and Italy as elsewhere in the EC, while inflation rose very moderately. The long hard slog of slow growth since the peak of inflation in 1980 finally appeared to be over.

This change in perception has modified in an important way the context in which the move towards EMU is seen in most of the countries which have participated since the start in the EMS: the sacrifice of giving high priority to low and stable inflation has already largely been made and there is little cost to the real economy in sticking with this objective, given the starting point.

If this first, rather conjunctural, change of perception has been an important element in the conversion to monetary orthodoxy, it is important whether it can be expected to last, as cyclical developments become less favourable as a result of external inflationary shocks and/or pressure on capacity limits in several European economies – and well before the EMU-negotiations and ratification procedures have been completed by 1992. This is not obvious, though initially broadly similar responses to the external shocks of 1990 make it possible to expect that the priority accorded to price stability is more than temporary. That impression is reinforced if the two other causes of the present orthodoxy are taken into account.

The *second* is the recognition in central banks and by governments that a visibly tight monetary regime in the EMU is necessary to impress the financial markets and lock up the gains of low inflationary expectations achieved over the second half of the 1980s. The Delors Report was an effort to outline a regime at least as strict as that which it was to replace. The central banks, but also the governments, have taken the credibility view of an exchange rate system to heart: to achieve the effect of keeping inflationary expectations low it is necessary to adopt visibly 'conservative' principles for monetary policy, as Rogoff (1985) suggested. The Delors Report – and now the draft statutes – therefore leaned over backwards to impress financial markets as well as price and wage setters in the partici-pating economies. The perspective is not merely tactical. Some indicators which inspire monetary discipline in a decentralized system with many national currencies – notably foreign exchange crisis or the fear of such crisis – disappear as national monetary authorities merge into the ESCB. Coordination, or centralization, could indeed become counterproductive unless an overall guideline for overall policy were to become visible. This view, incidentally, should be more compelling for those economists and officials who see the EMS as having already drifted some distance from a stability-oriented, asymmetric system centred on the Bundesbank towards a more symmetric system of quasi-permanently fixed exchange rates in which deviant inflationary behaviour is sanctioned less effectively than before.

The *third* element which I try to identify in the present orthodox position, is a suspicion that with a broader, more 'balanced' mandate for the ESCB, listing several other objectives of macroeconomic policy on a par with price stability, autonomy for the ESCB would quickly become an illusion. The literature on monetary constitutions has paid considerable attention to the importance of central bank autonomy for an effective pursuit of price stability.[6] But it gives less attention to reverse causation: only on the basis of a single-valued objective can there be any effective delegation of the implementation of monetary policy to a central bank. It would be hard to imagine that a European central bank charged with pursuing a number of macoeconomic objectives in some unspecified order could be autonomous; that would imply a competition with the political authorities in weighting the different objectives. That would be a recipe for conflict and lead to continuous involvement by the political authorities in monetary policy. If one wants an autonomous ESCB, that is an argument for a single and simple objective within which the institution can operate and be held accountable for the policy it implements to achieve it.

All three elements have in my interpretation contributed to the present surprisingly widespread agreement on the principles guiding the ESCB: an unequivocal priority for price stability and a high degree of autonomy. But at least as important as any endorsement of these two principles in defining the profile of the institution are the provisions for its operations and the more specific dimensions of its autonomy. I begin with what the ESCB should not do or avoid as best it can; there are two main points.

(1) The ESCB will not be authorised to finance government (or EC) deficits directly. This could take one of two forms: overdraft facilities at the ESCB and/ or purchases of government securities at issue. To suppress formally these two forms of direct deficit financing should be seen as a natural extrapolation of a trend away from monetary financing in the individual member states. Spending power has already been quite effectively

separated from the power to print money. This also applies to Italy since the so-called divorce of Banca d'Italia and the Ministry of the Treasury of 1981.

Would it be desirable to go further by excluding also indirect support from the ESCB to national governments with large deficits and debt? Some observers, for example, Branson (1990), have criticized that the ESCB can undertake open-market operations in national government securities, since such operations could provide a vehicle for favours to individual governments in financial difficulties. It would be safer, according to this view, either to prescribe that operations could take place only in securities with the highest credit rating or to oblige the ESCB to maintain a balanced portfolio. In practice, the problem associated with relatively minor, temporary operations should not be large: problems in the past have arisen mainly when a central bank has been obliged to absorb directly an excess supply of government paper at issue. But monitoring that the ESCB does not conduct its operations so as to smoothe out emerging differences in borrowing costs for national governments due to different perceptions of risk in the markets will be important, since market discipline would otherwise be weakened. (I owe this point to Graham Bishop.)

(2) The ESCB is unlikely to be *obliged* to intervene in third currencies. The political authorities decide on the nature of the exchange-rate regime, and take other formal decisions of exchange-rate policy such as eventual changes in the central rates for third currencies *vis-à-vis* the currency of the union, while the ESCB may intervene, at its discretion, within such a framework. A higher degree of independence in policy execution appears to be intended than that according to either the Federal Reserve or the Bank of Japan; European governments may have noted that public conflicts occasionally arise in the two largest industrial economies between the Ministry of Finance and the central bank over steps to be taken to influence the exchange rate. By moving responsibility for interventions and other policies to influence the external value of the union's currency closer to the ESCB, the Delors Report and the drafters of the central bank statutes have tried to limit the risk of conflicts. However in a global system, where it has become next to impossible for the main actors to modify their respective fiscal policies as a contribution to better macroeconomic coordination, pressure will remain on the central banks to be active in the exchange market in a way that will at times upset temporarily the commitment to price stability. Besides, governments or EC political authorities will at times want to take initiatives on exchange-rate policy with respect to the dollar and the yen or to respond to initiatives taken by

their US or Japanese colleagues. Despite the precautions taken, this is no doubt the area where the greatest risk to the ESCB's autonomy and orientation towards price stability lies. Let us take the current situation in the international economy as an example of what might be in store. Should the prospective EMU-participants refrain from interventions and the monetary easing necessary for preventing further appreciation of their currencies against the US dollar? Or is such appreciation warranted both to dampen inflation in Europe and to facilitate a more rapid reduction in the US external deficit now that a mild US recession is releasing the resources for such a swing? Clearly, the large EC member states do not currently agree fully on this issue; nor would an ESCB, if it were in existence now, be likely to find itself in full accord with a majority opinion in the ECOFIN Council. In the absence of coordination procedures which introduce external considerations in the formulation of budgetary policy, the authorities responsible for the latter – at least in Europe – will be tempted to ask for more international monetary coordination to avoid undesired exchange-rate effects of their policies.

The current situation may be a harbinger of a longer-run dilemma. As EC member states move closer to monetary unification without having endowed themselves with the means to influence their own aggregate budgetary policy, the latter may well on average become more expansionary, as tax rates are lowered and the risks of unpleasant consequences of national budget deficits seem smaller. An EMU does provide more scope for free-riding on one's partners, particularly when budgetary expansion occurs in parallel in several member states. So an emerging EMU could – for very different reasons – be faced with an imbalance in the policy-mix similar to that in the United States in 1981–4 of which Europeans were rightly critical. Expanding national budget deficits and a cautious, stability-oriented monetary policy will for quite some time bring appreciation of the European currencies and pressure will build up for monetary accommodation, not of the deficits directly – because that will not be feasible with the ESCB – but indirectly through purchases of non-EMU currencies. This scenario, of which the shift in the European policy-mix in 1990–1, due largely to German unification, underlines why the real autonomy of the ESCB cannot be regarded as settled through provisions for limiting its participation in the financing of government deficits.

The main argument for some mandatory coordination of national budgetary policies in an EMU – to reinforce whatever financial market discipline and an, in principle, non-accommodating monetary policy will impose – lies in the growing externalities of national budgetary policies as monetary integration advances, and, in particular, in the potential for free-

riding and a bias towards deficits. EMU participants will need to introduce some minimum of coordination outside the monetary area to reduce
those risks and, indeed, to improve their contribution to global policy
coordination. If they do not, one casualty could be the autonomy of the
ESCB.

We turn next to two more formal dimensions of central bank autonomy:
(1) the terms of office of members of the governing bodies, and (2)
financial independence.

(1) It is an important dimension of central bank autonomy that members
of the governing body be given fairly long terms of office and security of
tenure. In most EEC countries the terms of office are 5–8 years, in a few
(Denmark, Italy) of indefinite duration. The draft statutes favour an 8-year
period of office for the ESCB Executive Board members, to be nominated
by the European Council. While harmonization of the national nomination
procedures for the governors of the participating central banks may be
desirable, as their main function shifts to that of being a member of the
ESCB Council, it may not be strictly necessary to assure a high degree of
independence of Council members from their respective national
authorities.

One point on which agreement has unexpectedly emerged in the prep-
arations for the Intergovernmental Conference and which should reinforce
this independence, is that each central bank governor will have one vote,
as will the additional six members nominated to the Executive Board. A
system of weighted voting as in the Council of Ministers – or on the IMF
Executive Board – would have fostered the thinking that the governors
were primarily representing national interests and not equal members of a
collegiate body charged with formulating a common policy. The acceptance of the one-man-one-vote principle should be seen as an important
concession by Germany (to a smaller extent by other large member states)
in return for the mandate to pursue price stability as the primary objective
and the high degree of autonomy embodied in the draft statutes.

Enthusiasm for an admirable new principle should not, however, make
one overlook a potential weakness in the decision-making process. The
members of the Executive Board will be a clear minority in the Council,
and the size of the latter could turn out to be too large for effective
decision-making, particularly if membership in the EC and in EMU
expands, as it seems likely to do in the next decade or two, potentially to
even twice the present number of member states. Certainly in this eventu-
ality, but more likely well before, either thought must be given to a system
of constituencies (as in the IMF) where smaller countries merge into one
voting area, possibly with rotation inside such a group as to who exercises

the voting right, or nearly all authority may have to pass to the Board. It is worth noting that the Bundesbank, now faced with an enlargement of its already sizeable Council through the accession of the five Länder of the former German Democratic Republic, is discussing how the number of decision-makers could be reduced to assure efficiency.

(2) Financial independence in the sense of determining salary structure and audit system is a non-negligible part of central bank autonomy, as one might infer from observation of the Federal Reserve System which is subject to externally imposed ceilings on remuneration and to government audit. This is thought to be one reason why the Fed has occasionally experienced difficulties in retaining Board members and top staff. The founders of the ESCB appear well aware of such dangers.

Autonomy in conducting policy will be essential to the proper functioning of the ESCB. However, the general public and the domestic political environment in the member states that contribute to the pooling of monetary sovereignty will no doubt be more anxious to see in what ways the ESCB will be made accountable to European political authorities for its performance. This will be of particular interest to UK opinion which is used to regular political debate on monetary policy with an intensity and a degree of detail which is today hardly to be found in any other EC member state.

Accountability should be seen as an obligation of the ESCB, to explain publicly how it views the European economy and how it justifies its own actions in the light of its general mandate. The president of the ESCB would appear in the European Parliament to present an Annual Report and more regularly before a specialized committee, on the pattern of the Chairman of the Fed's appearance before Congressional Committees. The President would also report to the European Council on the occasion of the Annual Report and he would have the right to participate in meetings of the ECOFIN Council. Conversely, the Presidents of that Council and of the EC Commission would have the right to be represented in meetings of the ESCB Council without voting.

These proposed procedures should be sufficient to assure that the ESCB will not be functioning in a political vacuum – the risk of that being in any case limited given the input into decision-making by the national central bank governors. Accountability should, in addition, be tightly linked to the general mandate for the ESCB: to aim for price stability.

To make monitoring of the performance of the ESCB easier, the bank may have to make the price objective more specific than is the national practice where the emphasis is typically on one or more monetary aggregates. Interpretation of aggregate monetary data will initially be particularly tricky. Preliminary research, for example, in Kremers and Lane (1990), does suggest that narrow money for the group of EMS participants has in the past been at least as stably related to aggregate nominal income as is the case for the comparable relationship in any individual country. Yet there is a case for targeting a price objective directly rather than indirectly via a monetary series. The former procedure is suggested both by the stronger emphasis in the ESCB mandate on price stability and by the uncertainty about the properties of the collective demand for money.

The literature on monetary constitutions, see for example Friedman (1962), typically discusses four main ways by which approximate monetary stability for a group of countries could be achieved. Disregarding a non-institutional approach through competition between national currencies, favoured within the EC only by the UK authorities, they are: (1) a commodity standard; (2) a constitutional rule on price stability; (3) an autonomous central bank with safeguards against obligations that could undermine its anti-inflationary commitments; and (4) a rule for the joint money supply. The above discussion of the mandate, autonomy and accountability emphasizes (2) and (3) as the central elements for the ESCB. Though (1) has recently been re-proposed for the EMU in Walters (1990), and commodity-price trends play a supplementary role as an indicator in evaluating monetary policy in the United States, they appear too far removed from monetary policy to be central to policy formulation. It was argued above that (4), a joint money supply rule, would be difficult to apply, at least in the early stages of EMU, because of uncertainties surrounding the collective demand for money. But a combination of a constitutional rule through the commitment to price stability and strong provisions for autonomy could give the ESCB a clear role and one that could be relatively easy to monitor, hence facilitating accountability.

UNRESOLVED ISSUES: INSTRUMENTS, DECENTRALIZATION AND TRANSITION[7]

There is little discussion in the Delors Report or in subsequent elaborations in official papers of the instruments to be assigned to the ESCB – but such relative silence is also a feature of most national legislation on central banks. Indeed, if it had been, such legislation would have had to be modified regularly to reflect the evolution of new instruments. The past 20 to 25 years have seen a gradual, but cumulatively significant shift from administrative methods such as credit ceilings and interest rate regulation towards market-oriented instruments. Money market interest rates and repurchase agreements for government securities currently dominate as short-term instruments of money control in the EMS countries and elsewhere in the industrial countries (see Kneeshaw and van den Bergh, 1989; and Batten *et al.*, 1990). The ESCB is likely to continue this trend towards reliance on market-related instruments, though the draft statutes leave open the possibility that variable reserve requirements will also be used in influencing credit and money creation.

While decision-making in the ESCB has to be vested centrally, that is, in the Council with the necessary operational delegation to the Executive Board, it is an appealing thought – in line with the emphasis on subsidiarity which figures prominently in other EC policy areas – that implementation of the jointly decided policy could be decentralized to the individual participating central banks. Why build up a full-scale new operational capacity at the centre (at the Board) when the necessary expertise and resources exist at the national level? Do not large Federal systems operate well with only policy-making, analysis and monitoring at the centre – with the Federal Reserve Board in Washington as a prime example of experience in the application of subsidiarity?

Decentralization and delegation of operations have much to recommend them in particular areas where national expertise is essential (even in a monetary union) and they could be the general practice in the longer run – provided the centralization of decision-making and of monitoring of its implementation are sufficiently strong from the centre. That is the case in the United States, where the ultimate authority of the Board is unambiguous, not only because it has a *de facto* dominant position on the FOMC, but also because the Federal Reserve Act has assigned some important policy instruments directly to the Board (discount rate changes and variations in reserve requirements).[8]

In Germany the Direktorium may have a potentially weaker position in the decision-making, but all significant policy operations are centralized in Frankfurt which makes up for any deficiency. Neither of the two large Federal Central banks therefore provides direct guidance as to whether decentralization of operations can be combined with a Board/Direktorium as relatively weak as might be expected for the ESCB, at least initially. A situation might develop akin to the first two decades after the start of the Federal Reserve in which the Board was unable on some occasions to assert authority among the more firmly established regional banks. This proved to be a recipe for indecisiveness and required major reforms in the 1930s. Although the lessons of that early experience have no doubt been taken into account in preparing the ESCB statutes, further thought could still be given to the risk that the Board is left with too little to do, being squeezed on one side by a Council which absorbs all major policy-making functions and on the other side by the participating national central banks anxious to preserve as many operational tasks as possible. Some assignment of operational tasks and/or of instruments directly to the Board may be advisable, and this is reinforced by transitional considerations (see below).

In some important functions the involvement of the national central banks is indispensable. Relations with financial institutions outside the market-place could with advantage be through the national central bank which has easier access to information than does the ESCB Board. If there is to be ESCB participation in prudential supervision, as seems desirable to improve financial stability and to coordinate with a lender-of-last-resort function, this could hardly be achieved in a centralized way. Some discretion within pre-specified limits may in that case be left with the individual participating central bank.

In the area of instruments and operational procedures reflections are clearly at a more preliminary stage than with respect to the general mandate and the balance between operational autonomy and accountability. There is a gap between the relative precision of some of the institutional prescriptions and the vagueness of the outline of how a joint monetary policy would be implemented.

The draft statues may have gone as far as is practically possible *a priori* in outlining working relationships that will only become clear when experience has been gained. The formula of centralization of policy-making and decentralization in execution is appealing in reconciling the two main considerations of wide participation in decisions and operational efficiency. Some doubt may be legitimate whether the former has been given too much emphasis relative to the latter. These concerns seem to be accentuated when seen as a guidepost during the transition – stage two – which the European Council committed itself to starting on 1 January 1994. The conclusions of the Presidency on that occasion stipulated several conditions to be met for stage two to begin, in particular ratification of the Treaty changes required to implement the final stage. Unless the United Kingdom decides not to ratify, it does seem likely that the IGC will produce a result sufficiently specific for this condition to be met, and stage two with the launching of the ESCB would then be barely 3 years away. What would be the content of stage two?

A majority of countries have maintained that monetary authority, including the right to initiate a realignment, should remain in national hands in stage two. This attitude may be consistent with the view that monetary authority is indivisible – hence why it should, in principle, be centralized in the ESCB in the final stage. But, taken at face value, the attitude makes it difficult to conceive of a stage two which is visibly tighter and more credible than stage one and leaves a meaningful, not purely supplementary, role for the new ESCB. A stage two which did not in substance go beyond what is achievable in stage one may not be worthwhile. How does one break out of this impasse except by stressing that stage two is meant to be a short transition to a well-defined final stage, the procedures of which should be rehearsed as closely as possible?

Most of the proposals made so far for stage two by individual central banks implicitly reject the rigid logic of indivisible authority for monetary policy. Definitive pooling of part of foreign exchange reserves, as favoured by France and Spain, would imply both some centralization of decision-making and an operational capacity for the Board in stage two. A system of reserve requirements on domestic money creation by the participating central banks (or by commercial banks) as proposed by Italy,[9] would require a joint decision in the Council. Issue of a thirteenth currency foreshadowing a future joint monetary standard, as foreseen in the hard ecu proposal of the United Kingdom, would require vesting some discretionary power in the new institution, while operations with private market participants could be decentralized.

If these approaches all prove unfeasible because they imply a genuine transfer of part of national monetary authority not yet acceptable in stage two – despite agreement on (and ratification of) Treaty changes which show clearly how such transferred authority is to be handled in the ESCB in a not-distant future – it may be preferable to use stage two for remedying a potential longer run defect of the design for the ESCB, viz. the emphasis on a maximum degree of operational decentralization and delegation. The set-up in stage two of a joint operational facility at the new institution for implementing foreign exchange and open market operations, but without any transfer of authority, would give valuable experience and present a common appearance of the participating central banks in the markets. A proposal to this effect was outlined in Professor Lamfalussy's annex to the Delors Report. It would at the same time obviate the inherent operational weakness of the Board which may be unavoidable, if the latter comes into being with operational functions only at the start of the final stage.

The second stage might further be used for preparing more specifically those tasks of central banking which will unavoidably become a responsibility of the Board in the final stage, notably relating to the ECU. With the conclusions of the Rome European Council affirming the objective of having the ecu as the single currency in the final stage and of the need to strengthen its definition in the transition – in September 1993 when a revision is due shortly after the start of stage two? – an obvious task for the ESCB will be to develop through its Board the clearing and payments system for the ecu. The reinforced ecu has a potential role during stage two in relation to all three of the proposals referred to above: as a medium of intervention against third currencies, as a unit for the management of a reserve requirement system and as a transactions unit in the private sector. Operational involvement in the development of these roles – in addition to monitoring them – on the part of the Board would help to give the ESCB a substantive activity at the centre in stage two and to avoid handicapping the Board relative to the participating national central banks in preparing for management of the single currency.

It is currently unclear whether agreement can be reached at the IGC on the substance of stage two and unlikely that the ESCB will have as full an agenda as outlined above. That is a source of concern because, as already hinted at, stage two might not then be preferable to an extension of stage one. Recent academic research has underlined the risks of instability in both a prolonged stage one and weak stage two (see Dornbusch, 1991; and Giovannini, 1990). Officials would not put their concerns in the stark terms of academic papers, but many share them, particularly in countries such as Belgium, France and Italy which favour an early move to the final stage.

Is there an alternative, less gradualist scenario? There might be, once the substantial degree of agreement which already exists with respect to the final stage, and in particular on the provisions for the joint monetary policy, becomes clear during the IGC. It will become increasingly difficult, at least in those countries that have participated in the EMS for 12 years, to justify to their respective public opinion that they can on the one hand advocate a system for joint policy-making in an EMU and on the other hand propose that its implementation be delayed for a number of years. These positions are not easy to reconcile; and the difficulties of achieving that will be increased by the perception that Germany may over the next few years be more favourably disposed towards an integrated, even a federal, Europe than can be expected in the longer term when unification with the former GDR has been completed. Then the option of developing its individual potential of becoming Europe's main power and global spokesman may look more attractive than it apparently does now.

The proposed Treaty changes put before the IGC by the EC Commission take the desirability of moving to the final stage of EMU after the shortest possible transition into account. According to this proposal, a qualified majority of eight member states may, once progress in market integration and in economic and monetary convergence has been deemed sufficient by the European Council for moving to the final stage, decide to implement full EMU amongst them (Art. 109 F-G). The evaluation has to be made within 3 years of the start of stage two, but it could be made well before then. Such a challenge to the gradualist strategy is bound to be strongly resisted by some member states initially, but it may look more widely acceptable towards the end of the IGC than it does today. Then the subject of this 1990 Henry Thornton lecture would have proved more topical than even I could have imagined in preparing it.

Notes

1. EC Commission (1990) 'One Market, One Money', *European Economy* No. 44, Brussels, October.
2. An earlier version of this section is Thygesen (1990).
3. Delors, J. *et al.* (1989) *Report on Economic and Monetary Union in the European Community* (Luxembourg: Office of Publications of the European Community) August.
4. The terminology of relative and absolute coordination to denote efforts to influence differences between countries, respectively the aggregate thrust of policies, is borrowed from Currie, Holtham and Hughes-Hallett (1989).
5. Memorandum of Treasury Minister G. Amato to the ECOFIN Council, February 1988.
6. See, for example, Neumann (1991).
7. The issue of decentralization is discussed more fully in Thygesen (1991).
8. For an assessment of this division of responsibility see notably Louis, J.V., 'Annexe sur Le Federal Reserve System', in Louis (1989).
9. See Ciampi (1989).

References

Batten, D.S. *et al.* (1990) 'The Conduct of Monetary Policy in the Major Industrial Countries', *IMF Occasional Paper* 70, International Monetary Fund, Washington D.C.

Branson, W.H. (1990) 'Financial Market Integration, Macroeconomic Policy and the EMS', in C. Bliss and J. Braga de Macedo (eds) *Unity with Diversity in the European Economy: The Community's Southern Frontier* (Cambridge University Press).

Ciampi, C.A. (1989) 'An Operational Framework for an Integrated Monetary Policy in Europe', Annexe to Delors Report.

Currie, D., G. Holtham and A Hughes-Hallett (1989) 'When does Coordination Pay?', in R. Bryant *et al.* (eds) *Macroeconomic Policies in an Interdependent World* (Washington D.C.: International Monetary Fund).

Delors, J. *et al.* (1989) *Report on Economic and Monetary Union in the European Community* (Delors Report) (Luxembourg: Office of Publication of the European Communities).

Dornbusch, R. (1991) 'Problems of European Monetary Integration', in A. Giovannini and C. Mayer (eds) *European Financial Integration* (Cambridge: Cambridge University Press).

European Economy (1990) 'One Market, One Money: An Evaluation of the Potential Benefits and Costs of Forming an Economic and Monetary Union', *European Economy*, Vol. 44, Commission of the European Communities, Brussels.

European Economy (1991) 'The Economics of EMU', Special Issue (Brussels: Commission of the European Communities) (forthcoming).

Friedman, M. (1962) 'Should There Be an Independent Monetary Authority?', in L. Yeager (ed.) *In Search of a Monetary Constitution*, ed. Lealand B. Yeager, (Harvard University Press).

Giovannini, A. (1990) 'The Transition to EMU', *Princeton Essays in International Finance*, No. 178.

Kneeshaw, J.T. and P. Van den Bergh (1989) 'Changes in Central Bank Money – Market Operating Procedures in the 1980's', *BIS Economic Papers*, No. 23 (Basle: Bank for International Settlements).

Kremers, T. and T. Lane (1990) 'Economic and Monetary Integration and the Aggregate Demand for Money in the EMS', IMF Research Department, WP/90/ 23 (Washington, D.C.: International Monetary Fund).

Louis, J.V. (1989) *Vers Un Système Européen de Banques Centrales* (Etudes Européennes, Université de Bruxelles).

Neumann, M. (1990) 'Central Bank Independence as a Prerequisite of Price Stability', in European Economy (1991).

Rogoff, K. (1985) 'Can International Monetary Policy Cooperation be Counterproductive?', *Journal of International Economics*, Vol. 18.

Thygesen, N. (1989) 'A European Central Banking System – Some Analytical and Operational Considerations', Annexe to Delors Report.

Thygesen, N. (1990) 'Monetary Management in a Monetary Union', *European Economic Review*, Papers and Proceedings, Lisbon Congress.

Thygesen, N. (1991) 'The Relations between the European System of Central Banks and the National Central Banks, in Committee for Monetary Union in Europe', *EMU – The Political Dimension* (Paris: Crédit National).

Walters, A.A. (1990) *Sterling in Danger, The Economic Consequences of Pegged Exchange Rates* (London: Fontana/Collins).

5 Wage and Price Stickiness in Macroeconomics: Historical Perspective*

David Laidler

INTRODUCTION

There is more to the history of macroeconomics than a series of bilateral conflicts between competing schools of thought, but such debates have been a significant part of the story. Most recently the competing schools have worn the labels 'New-classical' and 'New-Keynesian', and the major issue between them has been the role of money wage- and price-stickiness in generating those more or less regular fluctuations in economic activity which we refer to as 'the business cycle'. For New-classicals, output and employment fluctuations are either responses to shocks to tastes and technology, or to unanticipated shifts in aggregate demand, typically stemming from money supply changes. In either cases though, prices give signals to which quantities respond, and variations in real magnitudes take place precisely because prices change. New-Keynesians emphasise demand-side shocks but, in their view, quantities vary, not because prices vary, but because they do not.

Now, as I have argued elsewhere (Laidler, 1982, Ch. 3), the above-mentioned characteristic of New-classical economics implies a view of the economy in which Say's Law holds true at each and every moment; and just as surely, in New-Keynesian analysis, that Law – that there cannot exist a state of generalised excess demand or supply for all goods and

---

* This lecture was delivered in November 1991 and published in booklet form by City University Business School, Dept of Banking and Finance. It draws upon a broader study of the development of macroeconomics which Professor Laidler has been carrying out with the financial aid of the Lynde and Harry Bradley Foundation, whose support is gratefully acknowledged. Professor Laidler is indebted to Mr Toni Gravelle for assistance in the research on which this lecture is based, to Tom Humphrey, John Swithin, Geoffrey Wood and members of the University of Western Ontario, Economic History/History of Economic Thought Workshop, the Economics Dept seminar of Kwansei Gakuin University, as well as the York University History of Economic Thought Workshop for many helpful comments.

services (excepting money) – may be violated for periods of time long enough to matter. Given that 'everybody' knows Say's Law to have been the centreprice of 'Classical' economics, and the denial of its universal validity to have been one of the key characteristics of 'Keynesian' econ-omics, it would seem at first sight that modern schools of thought have been well named. In this view, the recent renewal of interest in the price stickiness postulates on the part of certain erstwhile exponents of New-classical economics (for example, Lucas, 1989; King 1990) either signals a reaffirmation that Keynesian economics' alleged reliance on wage sticki-ness did after all represent an important intellectual advance, and that an intriguing attempt to revive older ways of thinking has, in the end, failed; or it is a sign that macroeconomists are taking an 'easy' option by using a postulate from which it is trivially obvious that fluctuations in real vari-ables can be predicted. In this lecture, I shall argue that either view repre-sents a gross distortion of the historical record.

I shall show: that from the very outset, Classical and Neo-classical economists took money wage, and sometimes price, stickiness for granted, though their relationship to Say's Law, and their potential importance for understanding the cycle, were not recognised until the final quarter of the nineteenth century; that *The General Theory*, far from placing additional emphasis on the phenomenon, downgraded its significance, and that Keynes treated money wage stickiness, and therefore price stickiness, as facts of life which had to be taken account of in analysing the causes and cures of unemployment, while disputing the Neo-classical view that they were, in and of themselves, an important cause of unemployment; that Haberler (1939), Pigou (1943, 1947) and Patinkin (1948, 1956) extended and clarified certain aspects of Keynes's treatment of the analytic role of wage-price flexibility; that by the time the Phillips Curve came upon the scene, ideas about secular money wage stickiness, perhaps descended from Marshall, had come to play a key role in macroeconomics and under-lay the idea that inflation was largely a matter of exogenous 'wage-push'; and that, in the ensuing debate, what was characterized as 'wage-price flexibility' would, from the later perspective of New-classical economics, better be termed 'wage-price stickiness'.

This lecture's implications for the interpretation of modern macro-economics can, therefore, be summarized as follows. If the criterion is the treatment of money wage and price flexibility, then New-classical economics is new, but it is surely not Classical; and New-Keynesian economics is neither new nor distinctively Keynesian. Moreover, there is nothing inherently 'easy' about understanding the effects of wage and price stickiness. If it is now trivially obvious that their presence in an economy implies that real variables will fluctuate, this is only because economics has taken about 250 years to work out how such effects are brought about.

WAGE-PRICE STICKINESS IN CLASSICAL ECONOMICS

By 'Classical Economics' I mean that body of economic thought which begins with Cantillon and Hume, ends with Mill, who died in 1873, and in addition to them includes among the most distinguished contributors to its monetary analysis Adam Smith, David Ricardo and of course, Henry Thornton. I shall apply the adjective 'Neo-classical' to the economics of Marshall, Pigou, Wicksell and their contemporaries, though, confusingly, it was this later body of doctrine that Keynes had in mind when he launched his assault on 'Classical' economics. The main focus of Classical economics as I define it here was, on the real side, growth, distribution and allocation; and on the monetary side, the price level, the balance of payments and the exchange rate, banking and central banking. The business cycle is conspicuously absent from the above list. Although Classical economists from Henry Thornton (1802) onwards were well aware of, and wrote extensively about, financial crises, recognition that such crises were but one phase in a repetitive pattern of economic fluctuations came towards the end of the Classical period – roughly speaking during the two middle quarters of the nineteenth century; and understanding that such fluctuations involved real magnitudes such as output and employment as well as financial variables came even later. Even for those Classical economists who discussed it explicitly, the cycle was the 'credit cycle', not the 'trade', or 'business' cycle.

It is hardly surprising that *explicit* statements, to the effect that sticky money wages were crucial in transforming fluctuations in what we would now call aggregate demand into fluctuations in real income and employment, are few and far between in the Classical literature; but they can be found. The best known of them is in Thornton's (1802) *Paper Credit* (p. 118):

> But a fall [in prices] arising from temporary distress, will be attended probably with no correspondent fall in the rate of wages; for the fall of price, the distress, will be understood to be temporary, and the rate of wages, we know, is not so variable as the price of goods. There is reason, therefore, to fear that the unnatural and extraordinarily low price arising from some sort of distress of which we now speak, would occasion much discouragement of the fabrication of manufactures.

These words occur in a striking passage in which Thornton distinguishes between permanent and transitory shocks, suggests that transactions costs make wages sticky in the face of the latter, and attributes output and employment effects to this fact. It clearly describes a mechanism tailor-made for inclusion in a model of the cycle, and indeed in the 1980s, Brunner, Cukierman and Meltzer (1983) did just that.[1] But that is not how Thornton deployed it. Rather, the above quotation arises in the context of his discussion of the appropriateness of the Bank of England meeting downward pressure on the then-floating sterling exchange rate with a monetary contraction; and its argument is used to defend the claim that, in the face of a temporary deficit, caused say by a poor harvest, such contraction would be both unwise and perhaps even counter-productive. The disruption to output that it would create would, according to Thornton, simply compound the difficulties created by the initial shock, which left to themselves would in any event be temporary.

This argument of Thornton's was criticised by Ricardo, who regarded *any* balance of payments deficit or exchange depreciation, permanent or transitory, as *prima facie* evidence of an excess money supply, and hence requiring its reduction. Thornton seems, in due course, to have accepted this criticism.[2] In 1810, he was an important contributor to the *Bullion Report* (see Cannan, 1919) which, among other things, criticised the Bank of England for failing to contract its issues when the 1808 French blockade of North Germany (surely a transitory shock) drove down the exchange rate, and recommended a speedy restoration of gold convertibility at the parity ruling in 1797 when convertibility had been suspended, a measure which in 1810 would have required an immediate and significant cut in money prices and wages. Thornton, then, was no prototype 'Keynesian' economist, old or new, and yet it would be a mistake to infer from the foregoing account that Classical economists were usually inclined to reject the wage-price stickiness postulate. On the contrary, in certain contexts they appear to have taken it for granted, albeit without being entirely self-conscious and explicit about doing so, and therefore without drawing out its full implications for the economy's functioning.

As early as 1752 Hume, perhaps building upon the foundations laid by Cantillon (1734) (though there is no explicit evidence that Hume was aware of his predecessor's work), had set out the basic framework of Classical monetary theory. In a well-known and much quoted passage dealing with what we would now call the transmission mechanism, whereby a change in the quantity of money affects the level of prices, he noted:

though the high price of commodities be a necessary consequence of the increase of gold and silver, yet it follows not immediately upon that increase ... At first no alteration is perceived; by degrees the price rises, first of one commodity, then of another; till the whole at last reaches a just proportion with a new quantity of specie which is in the Kingdom. In my opinion, it is only in this interval or intermediate situation, between the acquisition of money and rise of prices, that the increase of gold and silver is favourable to industry ... we shall find, that it must first quicken the diligence of every individual, before it increases the price of labour.

(p. 293)

Furthermore:

this interval is as pernicious to industry when gold and silver are diminishing, as it is advantageous when metals are increasing. The workman has not the same employment ... though he pays the same price for everything in the market. The farmer cannot dispose of his corn and cattle, though he must pay the same rent to his landlord. The poverty and beggary, and sloth, which must ensue are easily foreseen.

(p. 296)

These passages tell us that time elapses between a monetary impulse and the response of money wages and/or prices, and that in the interim, quantities move instead. Such a non-instantaneous response is precisely what we nowadays mean by 'stickiness'; and this idea of Hume's in due course entered the Classical mainstream.[3]

Adam Smith, being concerned in the monetary analysis contained in the *Wealth of Nations* (1776) with the long-run beneficial effects on an economy's capital stock of replacing commodity money with paper, did not discuss short-run adjustment problems; but Ricardo, universally regarded as the epitome of Classical orthodoxy in matters of monetary theory, and who seems to have persuaded Thornton to abandon a policy position that hinged on the postulate of wage stickiness in the face of a temporary disturbance, nevertheless did. His 1816 'Proposal for an Economical and Secure Currency' urged the creation of a monetary system based, not on gold coin but on paper convertible on demand into bullion, albeit at the 1797 parity, and he defended this proposal on two grounds. First it would economise on precious metals and hence, as Smith had argued, permit the country to enjoy a larger capital stock; and second it would minimise the demand for gold and therefore the amount of price deflation needed to restore sterling to its 1797 parity.[4] This second argument was completely in the spirit of Ricardo's view that there was a limit to the speed with which nominal prices could be forced downwards, as implied, for example, in his observation (1810–11):

> The remedy which I propose for all the evils in our currency, is that the Bank [of England] should gradually decrease the amount of their notes until ... the prices of gold and silver bullion shall be brought down to their mint price ... its sudden limitation would occasion so much ruin and distress ... If gradually done, little inconvenience would be felt.
>
> (p. 96)

The Humean idea that money wages and prices did not adjust instantaneously to the money supply, so that monetary changes had real short-term consequences, is also expressed in several passages in Mill's *Principles*, but not when he discussed the credit cycle. However an apparently separate phenomenon, which Mill did describe in the context of the cycle, also requires a failure of prices to move sufficiently quickly to keep markets cleared if it is to occur. I refer to his analysis, first presented in an 1829 essay (not published until 1844) but also incorporated into the *Principles*, of how a general glut of commodities can occur at the crisis phase of what he called the credit cycle as a complement to an excess demand for money. The essential insight underlying this analysis is captured in the following quotations from these two sources.

> But those who have, at periods such as we have described, affirmed that there was an excess of all commodities, never pretended that money was one of those commodities; they held that there was not an excess, but a deficiency of the circulating medium. What they called a general superabundance, was not a superabundance of commodities relatively to commodities, but ... relatively to money ... the result is, that all commodities fall in price, or become unsaleable.
>
> (1844, pp. 71–2)

> At such times there is really an excess of all commodities above the money demand...
>
> (1871, p. 574)

Now Mill most assuredly did not postulate price *rigidity* here; on the contrary, falling commodity prices were of the very essence of a financial crisis as far as he was concerned, but the fact remains that in an economy in which prices were sufficiently malleable to maintain supply equal to demand in all markets, the temporary excess demand for money and matching glut of commodities described in the foregoing passages could not arise.

The point of all this is not that Classical economics had a well worked-out view of how the economy functioned, in which postulates about money wage and price stickiness played a central and clearly defined role. Neither the fragments of the Classical literature which I have quoted, nor anything else in it of which I am aware, could support such a claim. However, the nominal stickiness idea did make frequent appearances in that literature, inasmuch as that certain ideas universally agreed to have been central to Classical monetary theory, specifically those about the short-run non-neutrality of money, do not make sense unless we interpret their exponents as having taken it for granted that money wages and prices fail to move fast enough to keep markets continuously cleared. And the same may be said of the much less frequent references to the possibility of a general glut of commodities arising during a financial crisis. The inter-connectedness of these phenomena, and their relationship to cyclical fluctuations, was not, however, to be fully worked out until the 1960s. Neo-classical economists began this process; Keynes contributed to it, but it needed Haberler, Pigou and Patinkin, not to mention Phelps and Friedman, to complete it.

NEO-CLASSICAL CONTRIBUTIONS

The passages of Mill referred to above are well known as early, though far from complete, descriptions of the real balance effect at work. As Becker and Baumol (1954) later documented, such descriptions became rather common in the literature of Neo-classical economics as the nineteenth century drew to a close. Sometimes they dealt with falling and sometimes with rising prices, and the following much-quoted passage from Wicksell (1915) is notable for clarity and incisiveness, but not uniqueness:

A general rise in prices is ... only conceivable on the supposition that the general demand has for some reason become, or is expected to become, greater than the supply. This may sound paradoxical because we have accustomed ourselves, with J.B. Say, to regard goods themselves as reciprocally constituting and limiting the demand for each other. And indeed *ultimately* they do so; here, however, we are concerned with precisely what occurs, *in the first place*, with the middle link

in the final exchange of one good against another, which is formed by
the demand of money for goods and the supply of goods against money.
(p. 159, italics in original)

This passage displays a clear and explicit understanding that, for a change
in the quantity of money to affect the price level, it must first create a disequilibrium situation in which Say's law does not hold, that is to say, a
state of affairs in which markets are not cleared. It is paradoxical, therefore, that neither Wicksell, nor Irving Fisher, who was every bit as clear
about these matters (see 1911, pp. 153–4), did not, in their pre-World War
I writings, go on to associate such a failure of markets to clear with the
occurrence of output and employment variations, even in the case of
monetary contraction.

When Wicksell analysed his celebrated cumulative inflationary process
in the case of a 'pure credit' economy, in which there could not exist an
excess supply of 'money' – in his vocabulary synonymous with 'currency'
– for the simple reason that money did not exist, he did so in terms of a
model which the labour and output markets cleared, sequentially rather
than simultaneously to be sure, but cleared nevertheless. Though the
model in question contained a sticky price, this was the nominal rate of
interest, not the money wage or money price level; and the failure of the
capital market to function smoothly had its real effect on the distribution
of profits between entrepreneurs and capitalists, not on the overall levels
of employment and output. Similarly, Fisher (1911, Ch. 4), whose cycle
theory depended on interest rate stickiness and a failure of the loans
market to remain in equilibrium following an initial shock, explicitly
referred to the cycle as a phenomenon of rising and falling prices, not
rising and falling output.[5] Neither Wicksell nor Fisher even raised the
question of how a condition of general excess demand or supply of goods
might affect the output and labour demand decisions of producers, let
alone attempted an answer to it.

One important strand of Neo-classical economics that developed at
Cambridge *was* self-conscious about money wage stickiness however, and
did attempt to investigate its consequences for income and employment.
The focus here, however, was not the real balance effect, but the consequences for real wages of the interaction of flexible prices and sticky
money wages. In 1879 Alfred and Mary Marshall gave an account of the
cycle, which closely followed that of Mill, but extended it with the
comment, 'The connexion [sic] between a fall in prices and a suspension
of industry requires to be further worked out' (p. 155). Their solution to
this problem was as follows:

It ... very seldom happens ... that the expenses which a manufacturer has to pay out fall as much in proportion as the price which he gets for his goods. For when prices are rising, the rise in the price of the finished commodity is generally more rapid than that in the price of the raw material, always more rapid that in the price of labour; and when prices are falling, the fall in the price of the finished commodity is generally more rapid than that in the price of the raw material, always more rapid than that in the price of labour.

(p. 156)

Money wage stickiness is invoked here as an apparently self-evident fact of life, and not as a tentative hypothesis in need of theoretical defence or empirical justification. It is hard to believe that the Marshalls thought their observations concerning its existence controversial, and no evidence of which I am aware in the subsequent literature suggests that anyone else found it so. And indeed, if we turn to that slightly earlier classic of empirical monetary economics, Jevons' 'Serious Fall in the Value of Gold ...' (1863), we find the following:

In a large proportion of cases, the salaries of clerks, officials, and other employés, or the wages of servants and labourers, will remain unchanged for long periods of time by want of attention to the changed value of gold, or the general dislike to altering or discussing an agreement once made ... the salary or wage will be raised after the lapse of a certain time.

(p. 85)

Money illusion and the costs of contracting are here invoked by Jevons, and the context of the discussion makes it clear that he was self-consciously aware of both phenomena. He discussed strikes as a manifestation of the former, and the main thrust of the pamphlet from which the above quotation is taken was to demonstrate, with the use of newly developed price indices, that stability in the purchasing power of money, widely taken for granted among his contemporaries, ought not to be. And once introduced into the literature, these ideas stayed there. They were deployed, for example, by Pigou in his 1913 book on *Unemployment*, a work aimed not at academics, but like others in the Home University Library series in which it was published, at a lay readership.

All in all, I think it is safe to conclude that money wage stickiness was a phenomenon widely taken for granted in Britain in the late nineteenth and early twentieth centuries, and that the Marshalls' originality lay, not so much in postulating it, but in recognizing its potential relevance to the explanation of output and employment fluctuations as integral features of the cycle. It was to become a staple, though not always central, ingredient of British discussions of these matters for the next century. Hawtrey, Robertson, Pigou, Hayek, and Robbins, among others, all at various times cited money wage stickiness as one of the reasons why the downswing of the cycle brought with it not merely falling prices, but falling output and employment too.[6]

However, until the development of multiplier-accelerator theory, which did not begin until the late 1930s, cycle theorists concentrated on explaining the boom and crisis phases of the cycle; downswing and slump were regarded as the inevitable aftermath of these and seldom analysed with as much care: Marshall's evidence to the Indian Currency Committee of 1899 is typical of this sort of treatment.

> a sudden fall of prices, presses hardly on business enterprise of all kinds. It is likely to make many employers fail, and generally interrupt industry ... Such a fall of prices is an almost unmixed injury to the employee as it is to the employer. Such a fall of prices ... is nearly always, if not always, the result of a previous inflation of prices and launching of frail enterprises by fraudulent or incompetent people who have floated into prosperity at the cost of others on the top of the wave of rising prices.
>
> (1926, p. 285)

Hence, though sticky money wages were much cited by British Neoclassical economists and blamed by them for cyclical unemployment, the explanation offered as to why seldom got beyond that initially offered by the Marshalls in 1879, namely that the interaction of flexible output prices with sticky money wages induced a perverse countercyclical movement into the time path of real wages. One exception here is Hawtrey, who as early as 1913 not only discussed the effects of money wage stickiness on the behaviour of real wages, but also (1913, p. 65) pointed out that stickiness of money wages would prevent money prices falling as fast as they otherwise might. This latter mechanism is of course crucial to ensuring that the consequent effect on real balances works only slowly on the demand for output. Hawtrey was aware of this connection, but his appreciation of its implications was far from complete. The matter did attract more attention later, as we shall see, but not until *The General Theory* had shifted the centre of attention from supply side to demand side considerations.

Marshall also discussed secular, as opposed to cyclical, money-wage stickiness on a number of occasions. His evidence to both the Gold and Silver Commission of 1888–9 and the Indian Currency Committee of 1899 (reprinted in Marshall, 1926) on the relative merits of a secularly rising, stable, or falling price level, saw him citing as an advantage of the last of these the fact that it would induce a long-term increase in real wages; nor did Marshall discuss any adverse effects on employment in this context. His discussions of the cyclical and secular consequences of wage stickiness were thus, in strict logic, inconsistent. I conjecture that we should reconcile them by attributing to Marshall the view that relatively small and slow-moving secular price-level-induced changes in real wages would go unnoticed by participants in the labour market, as more violent cyclical fluctuations would not. Marshall did, after all, warn readers of his *Principles* that, with regard to the labour market;

> It is ... important to insist that we do not assume for members of any industrial group to be endowed with more ability and forethought, or to be governed by motives other than those which are in fact normal to, and would be attributed by every well-informed person to, the members of that group.
>
> (8th ed., p. 448)

Whatever his reasons for holding it, however, Marshall's idea that the secular time path of money wages could (perhaps within limits) be treated as given and independent of that of prices, was later to become important.

WAGE STICKINESS AND THE THEORY OF EMPLOYMENT

The discussions of money wage and price stickiness dealt with in the preceding section of this paper were unsatisfactory by modern standards, and indeed perfunctory by contemporary standards too. It was only as the 1920s progressed that, in Britain at least, economists began to conclude that large-scale unemployment presented theoretical problems worth analysing in their own right, rather than being simply an inevitable and unfortunate, but nevertheless temporary, consequence of war-time and immediate post-war inflationary booms.[7] To many British economists, unemployment in the inter-war years appeared to be a secular phenomenon, not in the modern sense of requiring analysis in the context of a model of economic growth, but in a looser sense, which has no exact parallel in our current vocabulary, of persisting for longer than a single cycle and therefore requiring tools over and above those provided by cycle theory for its understanding. That is why, for example, Pigou regarded his 1933 *Theory of Unemployment* as a complement to his 1927 *Industrial Fluctuations*, rather than as being in any way a substitute for the earlier work. And as unemployment was discussed more frequently, so was too high a real wage level induced by money-wage stickiness as its cause, and policies designed to bring about wage flexibility as its cure. In Britain the importance of analysing the interaction of money wages, real wages and employment was enhanced by the price deflation required by the 1925 restoration of the gold convertibility of sterling at the 1914 parity. Virtually all contemporary commentators on this measure, supporters as well as opponents, agreed that the key to its success would lie in securing money wage cuts and that this would be a painful process; disagreement about its wisdom hinged on judgements about just how difficult this would be, and on whether the restoration of the old parity would bring enough benefits to justify the hardship it would inevitably cause.[8]

Pigou's 1933 *Theory of Unemployment* provides the fullest account of what Keynes was, in the *General Theory*, to call the 'Classical' (but which this paper would call Neo-classical) theory of unemployment. Keynes was correct to single this book out for discussion 1936, though he was also brutally unfair in the account he gave of its content.[9] Pigou deployed a standard Marshallian apparatus in which, with a given capital stock, the interaction of the supply and demand functions for labour determine equilibrium employment and the real wage. Unemployment, as Pigou used the word, can only arise in such a framework if the real wage is above its equilibrium level. Pigou was explicit that wage bargaining was proximately about money wages, but the analytic tools he utilised forced him to treat real, rather than money, wage stickiness as the basic phenomenon in need of explanation. Though he still pointed out that the money-illusion induced money wage stickiness of which he had made much in his earlier (1913, p. 115 et seq.) discussion of cyclical unemployment exacerbated real wage stickiness, Pigou did not, in 1933, think that this was by any means the whole story. Furthermore, the question about the effects of a cut in real wages which he addressed was not *whether* such a policy would influence employment – he took it for granted that it would – but *how large* that influence would be. As to cuts in *money* wages as a cure for unemployment, the main question Pigou addressed was how big an effect on *real* wages, and hence on the demand for labour, they would have.

Keynes accused Pigou (1936, Ch. 19, Appendix) of implicitly and unwittingly assuming full employment throughout his analysis; but this charge was unfair. On the contrary, Pigou was careful and explicit about avoiding this particular trap. He considered the possibility that a cut in money wages would lead to an equiproportional fall in prices, and leave the real wage, and therefore, according to his model, output and employment unchanged, and he rejected it on the grounds that, to obtain an equiproportional fall in prices, one would have to *begin* by assuming constant output and employment.

> The conclusion we have reached ... describes what would happen if money wage-rates were reduced *and if the quantity of employment remained unaltered.* The idea sometimes entertained that, by means of it, we can prove that the quantity of employment, and therewith the real rate of wages, *will* remain unaltered is completely fallacious. The answer is assumed before the argument has begun.
>
> (p. 101, italics in original)

In Pigou's view, the effect of a cut in money wages on money prices would depend on the degree of openness of the economy and on the operation of the monetary system. He argued explicitly, for example, that, in the limiting case of a small price taking open economy, the price level would be given exogenously, so that a money wage cut would bring about an equiproportional real wage cut. In the polar opposite limiting case of a closed economy, he made the operating assumption that the monetary authorities would act so as to maintain the level of money income constant. On that assumption a fall in the price level would have to be offset by an increase in output. Therefore, the price fall in question would be less than proportional to that in money wages, the real wage would be reduced, and the quantity of labour demanded would increase. In all cases, whether the economy was open or closed, it was on the supply-side response triggered by the effect on real wages of a cut in money wages that Pigou concentrated. As an empirical matter, he believed that the effect of a money wage cut on employment would be significant in contemporary Britain.

> in times of deep depression, after an interval not less than the period of production of the generality of wage-goods and export goods, an all round cut of 10 per cent in money rates of wages would lead, *other things being equal*, to a more than 10 per cent expansion in the aggregate volume of labour demanded, and so, apart from unfilled vacancies, in the volume of employment.
>
> (p. 106, italics in original)

Logically speaking, Pigou's assumption, in the closed economy case, that money income was held constant by the monetary authorities produces a limiting 'vertical LM-curve' version of a by-now-rather-standard, indeed old-fashioned, macro model, whose more general form can capture all the demand side influences of a money wage cut to which Keynes later pointed – those operating 'on the propensity to consume for the community as a whole, or on the schedule of the marginal efficiency of capital, or on the rate of interest' (1936, p. 262). This was not apparent in 1933 or indeed in 1936, however. Keynes believed his treatment of aggregate demand to be quite different from any that used the quantity theory, rather than, as we now understand, a more general formulation of the same analysis.[10] Though hindsight enables us to see that the effect of a price level fall on the quantity of real balances must underlie Pigou's 1933 deployment of the quantity theory to close the demand side of his system, this was not apparent to anyone in 1936, least of all Pigou, who did not incorporate such effects into his analysis until his 1938 response to Kaldor's 1937 criticisms. In this exchange, Kaldor argued, correctly, that Pigou had earlier overemphasized the significance of money wage cuts for the real wage, and correspondingly underemphasized their influence on the price level and hence on the real quantity of money; and Pigou accepted both points.

Keynes' major contribution to the theory of unemployment was to shift the centre of attention from the supply to the demand side of the aggregate economy. He accepted and paid attention to the same demand curve for labour as a function of the real wage which Pigou had analysed in excruciating detail – but his treatment of the economy's supply side was almost as perfunctory as had been Pigou's of the demand side. What principally mattered for Keynes was not what a cut in money wages would do to real wages, but rather what indirect effect its influence on prices would subsequently have on aggregate demand; and since he believed this effect to be minor and unreliable he did not attach great importance to money wage stickiness as a cause of low real income and employment. For Pigou (before 1938) as for other Neo-classical economists, money wage cuts of sufficient magnitude were a sure cure for unemployment, whose principal cause was too high a level of real wages. For Keynes, they would be of dubious benefit in dealing with a problem at whose heart lay a deficiency of aggregate demand.

A 'policy of wage flexibility' had serious drawbacks in Keynes' view:

It is ... on the effect of a falling wage- and price-level on the demand for money that those who believe in the self-adjusting quality of the economic system must rest the weight of their argument ... if the quantity of money is virtually fixed, it is evident that its quantity in terms of wage units can be indefinitely increased by a sufficient reduction in money-wages...

We can ... theoretically at least, produce precisely the same effects on the rate of interest by reducing wages, whilst leaving the quantity of money unchanged, that we can produce by increasing the quantity of money whilst leaving the level of wages unchanged ... Just as a moderate increase in the quantity of money may exert an inadequate influence over the long-term rate of interest, whilst an immoderate increase may offset its other advantages by its disturbing effect on confidence; so a moderate reduction in money-wages may prove inadequate, whilst an immoderate reduction might shatter confidence even if it were practicable.

There is, therefore, no ground for the belief that a flexible wage policy is capable of maintaining a state of continuous full employment; ... the economic system cannot be made self-adjusting along these lines.

(pp. 266–7)

Besides,

To suppose that a flexible wage policy is a right and proper adjunct of a system which on the whole is one of *laissez-faire*, is the opposite of the truth. It is only in a highly authoritarian society, where sudden, substantial, all-round changes could be decreed that a flexible wage policy could function with success.

(p. 269)

Hence, Keynes did not recommend such a policy. Far better, he thought, to concentrate on increasing aggregate demand by other means, and to rely on a rising price level to induce the real wage fall that would permit the economy's supply side to respond.

Whether Keynes assumed money-wage stickiness or not is sometimes debated. On this evidence, he took it for granted as a fact of life – that is why wage flexibility was termed 'a policy', involving the taking of measures to overcome a property of the labour market. But surely the question is of minor relevance to understanding Keynes' intended contribution. In the first eighteen chapters of *The General Theory*, he held money wages constant, not because he thought that the assumption was crucial to his results, but because, as he explained in Chapter, nineteen, he thought that money wage fluctuations were a factor that complicated his analysis without changing its basic characteristics. And one implication of his analysis was that money wage fluctuations mainly affected employment indirectly, through prices and thence aggregate demand, rather than directly through the real wage.

When Haberler (1939), Pigou (1943, 1947), and Patinkin (1948, 1956) came to reassert the *analytic* correctness of the proposition that, in the absence of complete money wage *rigidity*, a market economy tends to converge on a full employment equilibrium (a proposition usually termed 'Classical'), they did not also reassert the central importance of real wage behaviour on the economy's supply side for its validity. Rather, they took up and elaborated on Keynes's transmission mechanism which worked through aggregate demand. 'Keynes had conceded the possibility of falling money wages, and hence prices, driving down the rate of interest. To this channel, Haberler and Pigou added a direct wealth effect working through the changing real value of nominal assets; while Patinkin (1948) synthesized these mechanisms, and later (1956) refined the relevant analysis by investigating the micro foundations of the real-balance effect.[11] Classical economics had, as we have seen, developed the analysis of the latter effect, but its clearest exponents, Wicksell and Fisher, had not associated cash balance mechanics with variations in income and employment. It required Keynes' explicit application of aggregate demand analysis to the problem of unemployment to enable this all-important link to be made. As Patinkin (1948) put it,

> Although both Pigou [1943 and 1947] and the 'classics' stress the importance of 'price flexibility', they mean by this term completely different things ... The classical school holds that the existence of long-run unemployment is *prima facie* evidence of rigid wages. The only way to eliminate unemployment is, then, by reducing *real* wages ... Pigou now [that is, 1943 and 1947] recognizes that changing the relative price of labour is not enough, and that the absolute price level itself must vary.
>
> (p. 265, italics in original)

This analysis nevertheless seemed to many, at the time of its publication, to be profoundly anti-Keynesian, even though its exponents were careful to avoid claims of any policy significance for this analysis. Thus Pigou (1947):

> the puzzles we have been considering ... are academic exercises, of some slight use for clarifying thought, but with very little chance of ever being posed on the chequer board of actual life.
>
> (p. 251)

and Patinkin (1948):

> The conclusions of this paper can be summarised as follows: in a static
> world with a constant stock of money, price flexibility assures full
> employment ... But in the real dynamic world in which we live, price
> flexibility with a constant stock of money might generate full employ-
> ment only after a long period; or might even lead to a deflationary spiral
> of continuous unemployment. On either of these grounds, a full employ-
> ment policy based on a constant stock of money and price flexibility
> does not seem to be very promising.
>
> (pp. 277–8)

But the fact remained that Keynes had claimed to have created a theory
of unemployment *equilibrium*. He had also, in Chapter 19, of the *General
Theory*, denied that money wage flexibility would inexorably lead to full
employment, and he based this claim on theoretical, not empirical arguments. Thus, Keynes' position was to deny any overriding importance to
wage stickiness in determining the way in which the economy functioned;
and the exponents of what we now know as the 'Neo-classical Synthesis'
gave a much more important role to the phenomenon. Even so – following
Pigou and Patinkin – those exponents denied that their analysis of this
matter was policy relevant, precisely because of an empirical judgement to
the effect that money wages were, if not rigid, then certainly sticky enough
to render the working of the economy's self-correcting mechanisms
unacceptably slow.

THE PHILLIPS CURVE AND AFTER

The adjustment mechanism underlying the real balance effect has the
money wage rate falling in the presence of high unemployment. It is small
step, but a distinct one nevertheless, from this observation to the proposition that the rate of change of the money wage rate is an inverse function
of the unemployment rate. Perhaps not entirely coincidentally, Pigou had
presented a time series chart showing just such an inverse relationship in
Industrial Fluctuations (1927, p. 215), but it was not until the work of
Brown (1955), Phillips (1958) and Lipsey (1960) that the so-called
'Phillips Curve' attracted much attention. Phillips, and with more elab-
orate analysis Lipsey, presented the Phillips Curve as a by-product of a
standard supply and demand stability experiment applied to the labour
market, with unemployment standing as a proxy variable for the excess

demand for labour; but before Phelps (1967) and Friedman (1968) offered their well-known extension of his analysis – based on the simple observation that the supply and demand for labour determine the real, not the money, wage – the construct was controversial for another reason, which we must now discuss.

We have seen earlier that Marshall had treated money wage stickiness as a secular, as well as a cyclical, phenomenon in the 1880s and 1890s. In the 1930s a version of this hypothesis again became current. The very fact that such commentators as Pigou (1933) and Keynes (1936) treated unemployment as a long-term problem, significant beyond the confines of the cycle, and discussed money wage stickiness in this context, is evidence of this. And some writers were quite explicit about the matter. For example, Myrdal (1931), in discussing the appropriate price level behaviour for the authorities to aim at, usually made the assumption that 'the prices of the basic factors of production are the principal sticky prices ... practically, this means an assumption that wages are relatively sticky prices.' (p. 139).[12] He also found it instructive to analyse the policy problems posed to a monetary authority in the limiting case where the presence of one-sided monopoly in the labour market ensured that 'the workers would not become unemployed as a result of their monopolistic wage increase' so that 'a general process of rising prices accompanies [a self-generating movement caused by monopolistic activity of the sticky and therefore dominant prices]' (p. 148). In such circumstances, according to Myrdal, the appropriate aim for monetary policy would be to '*adapt the flexible prices to the sticky ones*' (p. 133, italics in original).

By the post-war period, the idea of a secularly sticky money wage to whose time path policy should be adapted had evolved into the notion that the time path of the variable in question was institutionally (perhaps politically) determined. In 1955, for example, Sir John Hicks argued as follows:[13]

> But the world we now live in is one in which the monetary system has become relatively elastic, so that it can accommodate itself to changes in wages, rather than the other way about ... It is hardly an exaggeration to say that instead of being on a Gold Standard, we are on a Labour Standard.
>
> (p. 196)

In some versions of this kind of argument, the behaviour of wages was quite independent of market forces; and more generally, the view that inflation was mainly a phenomenon of 'wage-push' became dominant in Britain, and very popular elsewhere.

The Phillips curve had it that, unless the unemployment rate was at some equilibrium level determined by structural and frictional forces, money wages would move in a fashion calculated to restore that equilibrium (see Figure 5.1, p. 118). Hence it ran counter to the secularly sticky money wage hypotheses, and seemed, at the time, to be supported by a great deal of empirical evidence too. However, the mainstream response to this challenge was not to abandon the idea that the time path of money wages was independent of market forces, but to concede, as indeed had Hicks, that the pressure of demand could modify the extent to which institutionally conditioned secular money wage behaviour would assert itself. The views expressed by the *Radcliffe Report* (1959) are quite representative:

> It is sometimes argued that the rate of rise of wage rates is very closely related with the percentage of unemployment. But it has also been argued to us with no less authority and force that over a significant range of variations in the demand for labour there is a 'band of indeterminacy' within which the precise rate at which wage rates and prices rise depends upon institutional factors which ... have little or no connection with the pressure of demand ... All that can be assessed as agreed opinion is that, as the fullness of full employment rises, the risk of accentuating a rise of prices increases.

> (p. 21)

This is not the place for a long digression into debates about institutionally determined 'cost-push' inflation, and the role of the Phillips curve therein. What matters for the topic at hand is simply that 'cost-push' advocates sometimes argued that the money wage rate's time path was at least insensitive, and at most utterly impervious, to market forces; while on the other side, those who believed in the Phillips curve argued that it would always move in response to excess demand or supply in the labour market, as proxied by the unemployment rate, in a manner summarized by that curve. Debate was, therefore, between those who believed money wages to be essentially rigid, and those who thought of them as being merely sticky. The possibility of money wages being sufficiently flexible as to keep the labour market perpetually cleared was never raised, let alone discussed.

As I remarked earlier, Phillips's and Lipsey's theoretical underpinnings for the Phillips curve were soon challenged by Phelps and Friedman, who noted that the relevant price in the labour market was the real, not the money wage. As Friedman put it

Phillips' analysis of the relation between unemployment and wage change is ... an important and original contribution. But, unfortunately, it contains a basic defect – the failure to distinguish between *nominal* wages and *real* wages ... Implicity, Phillips wrote his article for a world in which everyone anticipated that nominal prices would be stable.

(p. 102, italics in original)

Now theoretical analysis of the influence of the price level on real aggregate demand, such as that of Haberler, Pigou and Patinkin, was invariably carried out in terms of a model in which the nominal money supply was held constant and in which therefore such an assumption about agents' anticipations was reasonable. But in the early 1960s the Phillips curve had begun to be treated as a policy relevant structural relationship whose form was independent of the conduct of monetary policy; and by the early 1970s, it had ceased to exist as an empirical phenomenon.

For those who would soon come to be labelled Monetarists, the expectations-augmented Phillips Curve of Phelps and Friedman provided a ready-made response to this new empirical evidence; but for British Monetarists, at least, the addition of expected inflation to its right-hand side, so that there existed a family of curves in wage inflation – unemployment space, one for every value of the expected rate of price inflation (see Figure 5.2, p. 118), did not mean that it had ceased to characterise a labour market which could be out of equilibrium in the short run; and out of equilibrium not just in the sense that the actual price level could differ from that expected or perceived by those involved in wage bargaining, but also, crucially, because given expected and actual values of money wages and prices, the supply and demand for labour could differ from one another. My own 1971 account of the matter went as follows:

If the excess demand for labour is inversely related to the level of unemployment and positively related to the rate of change of the *real* wage, then ... there will exist a stable inverse relationship between the rate of change of *real* wages and the level of unemployment ... to get to the Phillips curve we must introduce the expected rate of price inflation into our model.

We need the expected rate of inflation and not its actual current rate because individual wage bargains are struck at discrete intervals and, for any particular bargain, it is not the current price level that matters in determining the real wage that is being aimed at but the level of prices that is expected to rule over the period for which the bargain is being struck.

(pp. 79–80, italics in original)

In treating the short-run Phillips Curve as describing disequilibrium wage adjustment, this analysis, for which I make no claim of originality, was much like that of American Keynesians such as Robert Solow (1969) and James Tobin (1973). Differences of opinion here were about whether expectations of price level behaviour held by participants in the labour market would, in conditions of mild inflation, ever fully adjust to reality; and hence about whether the long run Phillips Curve was vertical (as it has been drawn in Figure 5.2), or merely 'steep'. Ironically, in their belief that the long-run curve still had a negative slope, American Keynesians were perhaps truer intellectual descendants of Marshall than were their Monetarist contemporaries (which is not to say that they were right). In the 1880s and 1890s Marshall had, as we have seen, argued that secularly falling prices would leave money wages unaffected and, in the long run, produce a permanent increase in real wages. This aspect of the monetarist debate was, on the whole, settled in favour of those who denied the existence of any long-run inflation – unemployment trade-off, and during the 1970s macroeconomists found newer, and to that extent at least more interesting, matters to argue about.

At first the major novelty of New-classical economics seemed to lie in its deployment of John Muth's (1961) rational expectations hypothesis to replace the error learning mechanism in models of inflation – unemployment interaction: who after all could resist the idea that rational agents would make 'full' use of 'all available' information? It is by now recognized, however, that its adoption of the assumption that all markets are continuously cleared by flexible prices, and its reconciliation of this assumption with the existence of variations in real variables such as income and employment (neither of which steps logically depended upon assuming rational expectations), represented far more profound analytic innovations; and yet the innovations in question slipped into the literature almost unnoticed. It was a simple matter to include the expected price level as a variable in an aggregate supply curve of a type that Marshall, Pigou, or indeed Keynes, would have understood, and, by simple algebraic manipulation, to produce a relationship apparently identical to a conventional-expectations-augmented Phillips curve. This much was implied by Friedman's ambiguous analysis (1968), and was shown explicitly by a number of contributors to the so-called 'Phelps Volume' (Phelps et al., 1970).[14]

Once the possibility had been broached that the expectations-augmented Phillips curve was a particular transformation of an aggregate supply curve, and hence of a demand function for labour depending on the real wage, the way was open to explain the values of output, employment, wages and prices as the solutions to the equations characterizing a simple general equilibrium model. To take this apparently purely technical step, however, was to make a very important substantive assumption as well, namely that money wages and prices could always move freely to keep all markets cleared; though I strongly suspect that this radical departure from earlier ways of doing macroeconomics owed more to the unselfconscious application to a new set of problems of standard analytic techniques, involving formulating an economic model as a set of simultaneous equations and deriving its predictions as those equations' solutions, than it did to any conscious attempt to create a revolution in economic thought.

The analytic techniques were, of course, those of Walrasian general equilibrium analysis, which by the 1970s had largely driven Marshallian partial equilibrium tools out of microeconomic theory, and it is instructive to consider Walras' own opinion of the empirical relevance of the idea of general economic equilibrium. As is readily apparent from the following passage, Walras (1874) shared the views of his contemporaries on the relative stickiness of input prices. Hence, he regarded a state of general equilibrium in which supply equals demand in each market as defining a hypothetical benchmark around which the economy fluctuates, and not a condition which holds at each and every moment. Indeed, in expressing this view at such an early date, he anticipated some aspects of the Marshalls' analysis of the cyclical significance of money wage stickiness discussed earlier.

the market is like a lake agitated by the wind, where the water is incessantly seeking its level without ever reaching it. But whereas there are days when the surface of the lake is almost smooth, there never is a day when effective demand for products and services equals their effective supply .... It ... frequently does happen in the real world, that ... the selling price will remain for long periods of time above cost of production ... while under other circumstances a fall in price ... will suddenly bring the selling price below cost of production and force the entrepreneurs to reverse their production policies. For, just as a lake is, at times, stirred to its very depth by a storm, so also the market is sometimes thrown into violent confusion by *crises*, which are sudden and general disturbances of equilibrium.

(pp. 380–1, italics in original)

Now it is important to distinguish between 'good' economics, and 'correct' (better say 'not-yet-refuted') economics. The former predicts much from little, and the latter, in addition, finds that what it predicts seems to occur. In these terms, New-classical economics was most assuredly good economics. The trouble was (and is) that its distinguishing predictions were inconsistent with the facts and that, as Karl Brunner (1989) made abundantly clear, a good deal of the problem stemmed from its refusal to postulate money wage and price stickiness. Its exponents have, therefore, either turned to 'real' business cycle theory, which relies on applying the theoretically flawed concept of an aggregate production function to the very problem area, namely the cycle, where its flaws are most likely to prove misleading, and/or have begun to re-introduce the idea of money-wage-price stickiness into their models, sometimes (for example, King, 1990) trying to find a foundation for the phenomenon in maximising behaviour, and sometimes (for example, Lucas, 1989) taking its *existence* for granted, but seeking to model the *extent* to which prices move when they are free to do so. If New-classical and New-Keynesian analysis do indeed merge, as now seems quite likely, the postulate of wage-price stickiness will once again have become uncontroversial, though our understanding of it will also, it is hoped, have been advanced yet further.

SUMMARY AND CONCLUSION

What, then, are we to make of this story? Certainly I do not wish to leave my audience with the impression that, in the matter of wage-price stickiness, it was, 'all in Marshall' (or 'all in Thornton' for that matter). Economics does, on balance, make progress. I have shown that the idea that money wages and prices are sticky has a long history, but I have, I hope, also shown that our understanding of the significance of the phenomenon has systematically deepened over time.

In Classical and Neo-classical economics the twin roles of money-wage stickiness, in creating real wage stickiness and in slowing down the real balance effect, were treated as separate and distinct; and as far as the theory of employment was concerned, the former took precedence. Keynes shifted the emphasis of the theory of employment to aggregate demand, and showed how output and employment changes could be viewed as equilibrating movements. He also provided a framework in which the crucial role of wage stickiness in slowing down price-level changes, and hence the operation of the real balance effect, could find its proper place alongside the analysis of real wage changes in that theory.

But it was Haberler, Pigou and Patinkin who made us completely aware of this; and it was not until Friedman and Phelps had incorporated expectations about price-level behaviour into the Phillips curve that this line of analysis was fully and generally worked out.

A more extreme version of the wage-stickiness doctrine has also had a rather lengthy history. Marshall sometimes argued as if he believed that the secular time path of real wages would be influenced by that of money prices and hence implied that the time path of money wages was, at least within limits, independent of market forces. In the 1930s the idea that money wages were the prices least susceptible to market forces, so that monetary policy would be wise to accommodate itself to their path, became current. British 'Keynesians' economics of the post-war period developed this hypothesis, and had it that money wages were institutional or political, rather than economic, variables; while the more moderate American 'Keynesianism' postulated the existence of a permanent inflation – unemployment trade off, even after allowing for expectational effects.

The point that I would particularly stress here is that, throughout the history of macroeconomics until the early 1970s, debate was always between advocates of greater or lesser stickiness. Until the 1970s no one used such a phrase as 'wage and/or price flexibility' to characterise continually clearing markets such as are found in so-called, as we can now see misleadingly, New-classical models, for the simple reason that no school of macroeconomic thought entertained the possibility that markets always cleared. The 'new' macroeconomics of the 1970s and 1980s was, then, new indeed. If however it is nowadays 'easy' to turn to wage and price stickiness as an explanation of fluctuations in real income and employment, that is surely, as I have tried to show, because we have 250 years of work on just this question to draw upon, and not because the issues it raises are in any sense intellectually trivial. Hence the revival of interest in wage and price stickiness that is now taking place among 'New-classical' macroeconomists, and their apparent willingness to take up what we can now see is an equally misleadingly labelled 'New-Keynesian' line of research, is in no sense a symptom of intellectual laziness. It simply represents a return to a line of investigation which began in the mid-eighteenth century and has more than proved its value in the intervening years.

Notes

1. These authors were aware of Thornton's discussion of the issue, but their own understanding of the significance of the permanent transitory distinction for the matter of price stickiness antedated their discovery that Thornton had anticipated them. I am indebted to Allan Meltzer for discussion of this point.

2. Thomas Humphrey (1990) provides an insightful comparison of the views of Thornton and Ricardo on this matter, arguing correctly that Ricardo's position hinges upon his attaching considerably less weight than Thornton to the possibility of short-term wage stickiness. Nevertheless, Ricardo did not consistently ignore the potentially disruptive effects of falling prices for real variables, as Samuel Hollander (1979) in particular has stressed. See also below pages 98–9 and footnote 4.

3. The fact that Hume is explicit about quantity changes preceding those in prices makes it difficult to interpret his insights as prefiguring those of Lucas (1972). The temporary output and employment effects which occur in New-classical models in response to monetary shocks arise because agents misperceive the price changes which those monetary shocks engender. Nevertheless, Hume's discussion of this matter is more a description of a series of events than it is an explanation of why those events occur in the order they do, so one should not be dogmatic here.

4. Ricardo, however, did not regard money wage stickiness as being as important a phenomenon as did Malthus, who accorded it a central role in creating the depression which followed the end of the Napoleonic wars. For Ricardo it was sudden deflation, and not deflation in general, which would have adverse consequences. Malthus, of course, was far from being an orthodox Classical economist in his treatment of these issues. On all this see Hollander (1979, pp. 523 *et seq.*). Note that some commentators, for example, Humphrey (1990), are unwilling to grant that Ricardo placed as much importance on nominal wage and price stickiness as Hollander finds in his work. This disagreement is probably best resolved by recognising that Ricardo was not always consistent in his treatment of this question. Compare note 2 above.

5. See Fisher (1911, p. 70). Note that Wicksell and Fisher offered differing explanations of interest rate stickiness. For Wicksell, banks would have no incentive to raise (lower) rates until they experienced a drain (influx) of reserves. For Fisher, the sluggishness of interest rates stemmed from a slowness on the part of lenders to adjust their expectations of inflation.

6. See, for example, Hawtrey (1913, pp. 41 *et seq.*), Robertson (1915, p. 215) Pigou (1913, pp. 75–6), Hayek (1935, pp. 106, 160), and Robbins (1934, pp. 60–1). It is nevertheless worth pointing out that the references to wage stickiness in Hayek's *Prices and Production* occur only in the second, 1935, edition of that book, and that Robbins treats the phenomenon as being of post-war origin, caused, among other things, by overly generous unemployment benefits. The Austrian cycle theory of Hayek and Robbins was old fashioned for its time in treating the boom and crisis phase of the cycle in great detail, and discussing downswing and trough, with their associated unemployment, in a cursory fashion.

7. The emphasis here should be on the adjective theoretical. An extensive, but largely descriptive, literature dealing with unemployment existed even before World War 1. The very fact that Pigou (1913), already cited, was intended for the general reader attests to the social and political importance that attached to unemployment; but in 1913 Pigou, like other writers on the topic (for example, Beveridge, 1909), wrote as if unemployment was a by-product of various frictions (of which money wage stickiness was but one

example) that should be taken account of when standard economic theory was applied to the real world, rather than a fact requiring standard theory itself to be re-examined.

8.   On this reading, Keynes' famous 1926 essay, 'The Economic Consequences of Mr. Churchill', far from prefiguring the *General Theory*, represents a straightforward combination of orthodox Neo-classical theory and pessimistic judgement about the degree of money wage flexibility to be expected in the British economy.

9.   See Keynes (1936) *Appendix* to Ch. 19.

10.   See (1936) pp. 295–98.

11.   Indeed, Patinkin (1956) developed the analysis of a labour market 'off' its demand curve which, combined with certain insights of Robert Clower (1965) by Barro and Grossman (1976) and Malinvaud (1977), would eventually establish the complete irrelevance of the level of real wages to 'Keynesian' unemployment. The adjective 'Keynesian' is here used in the sense of Malinvaud (1977), to refer to the unemployment which can occur in a simple general equilibrium model if the price level is arbitrarily set at a level that is too high, given the quantity of nominal money, to produce a level of aggregate demand sufficient to absorb the volume of output which firms would be willing and able to supply, were nominal prices free to vary. In such a situation the level of employment is given by the 'effective' demand for labour, which is not a function of the real wage, and unemployment can occur if the level of real wages is at, or even below, that which would rule in full employment equilibrium. Barro and Grossman (1976) Chs. 1–3 provide the most accessible account of the analysis that produces that conclusion.

12.   I have not investigated with any thoroughness the question of whether Myrdal and subsequent contributors to the idea of money wages being largely institutionally determined were explicitly influenced by Marshall's discussion of the matter. Though *Monetary Equilibrium* does contain references to Marshall, these are invariably general in nature, and none specifically refer to his views on the behaviour of wages. That is why I here talk only of the idea of secular money-wage stickiness again becoming current.

13.   Though Hicks (1955) does not cite Myrdal but rather takes as his starting point some 1929 remarks of Sir Henry Clay on the role of 'ethical standards of "fair" and "living" wages [etc.]' in ensuring that 'the process of general wage-changes has, we may say, been constitutionalised', he was nevertheless a careful reader of *Monetary Equilibrium*, having reviewed its German translation for *Economica* in 1934 (reprinted as Ch. 4 of Hicks 1982). In that review, moreover, he drew explicit attention to Myrdal's treatment of wage-price stickiness.

14.   As I have argued in Laidler (1990), selective reading of Friedman's presidential address can be used to support either the view that he interpreted the Phillips curve as a disequilibrium wage adjustment relationship, but thought it needed supplementing with an expected inflation variable, or the view that even at this stage he re-interpreted it as an aggregate supply curve. In the Phelps volume too, both interpretations of the Phillips curve are to be found in different essays, without anyone drawing attention to the profound issues

which hinge on this matter. The expectations-augmented Phillips Curve in price inflation $(p - p_{-1})$ and output (y) space

$$(p - p_{-1}) = fy + (p - p_{-1})^e$$

may be derived from the aggregate supply curve

$$y = 1/f(p - p^e)$$

by inverting the later, subtracting p_{-1} from each side and noting that

$$p^e - p_{-1} \equiv (p - p_{-1})^e.$$

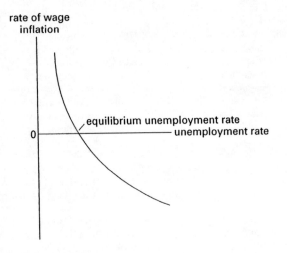

Figure 5.1   The Phillips Curve

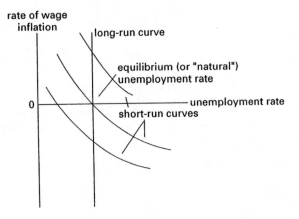

Figure 5.2   A Vertical Long-Run Phillips Curve and Representative Short-Run Curves

References

Barro, R.J. and Grossman, H.H. (1976) *Money, Employment and Inflation* (Cambridge: Cambridge University Press).

Becker, G. and Baumol, W. (1952) 'The classical monetary theory: the outcome of the discussion', *Economica* NS 19 (November), pp. 355–76.

Beveridge, W. (1909) *Unemployment, a Problem of Industry* (London: Longman).

Brown, A.J. (1955) *The Great Inflation* (London: Oxford University Press).

Brunner, K. (1989) 'The disarray in macroeconomics', in Capie, F. and Wood, G.E. (eds) *Monetary Economics in the 1980s* (London: Macmillan).

Brunner, K., Cuckierman, A. and Meltzer, A.H. (1983) 'Money and economic activity, inventories and business cycles', *Journal of Monetary Economics* 11, 281–319.

Cannan, E. (1919) *The Paper Pound 1797–1821 (The Bullion Report of 1810)* (London: P.S. King and Son).

Cantillon, R. (1734) *Essai sur la nature du commerce en général* (Ed. with English tr., H. Higgs, 1931) (London: Macmillan).

Clower, R.W. (1965) 'The Keynesian counter-revolution – a reappraisal' in Hahn, F.H. and Brechling, F.R.P. (eds) *The Theory of Interest Rates* (London: Macmillan).

Committee on the Working of the Monetary System (1959) *Report (The Radcliffe Report)* (London: HMSO).

Fisher, I. (1911) *The Purchasing Power of Money* (New York: Macmillan).

Friedman, M. (1968) 'The role of monetary policy', *American Economic Review*, reprinted (1969) in Friedman, M. *The Optimum Quantity of Money* (London: Macmillan).

Haberler, G. (1939) *Prosperity and Depression, 2nd Revised Edition* (Geneva: League of Nations, 6th Ed. [1964] New York and Cambridge, Mass.: Harvard University Press).

Hawtrey, R. (1913) *Good and Bad Trade* (London: Constable).

Hayek, F.A. von (1935) *Prices and Production* (2nd. ed.) (London: Routledge and Kegan Paul).

Hicks, J.R. (1955) 'Inflation and the wage-structure', *Economic Journal*, reprinted as Ch. 16 of Hicks (1982).

Hicks, J.R. (1982) *Money, Interest and Wages: Collected Essays in Economic Theory vol. 11* (Cambridge, Mass.: Harvard University Press).

Hollander, S. (1979) *The Economics of David Ricardo* (Toronto: University of Toronto Press).

Hume, D. (1752), 'Of money', in *Essays Moral, Political and Literary*, reprinted 1963 (London: Oxford University Press).

Humphrey, T. (1990) 'Ricardo versus Thornton on the Appropriate Monetary Response to Supply Shocks', *Federal Reserve Bank of Richmond, Economic Review*, 76/6 (November/December) pp. 18–24.

Jevons, W.S. (1863) 'A serious fall in the value of gold ascertained and its social effects set forth', reprinted 1884 in *Investigations in Currency and Finance* (ed. H.S. Foxwell) (London: Macmillan).

Kaldor, N. (1937) 'Prof. Pigou on money wages in relation to unemployment', *Economic Journal 47* (December) pp. 745–53.

Keynes, J.M. (1926) 'The economic consequences of Mr. Churchill', reprinted in *Essays in Persuasion* 1931 (London: Macmillan).

Keynes, J.M. (1936) *The General Theory of Employment Interest and Money* (London: Macmillan).

King, R.G. (1990) 'Money and business cycles', University of Rochester (mimeo).

Laidler, D. (1971) 'The Phillips curve, expectations and incomes policy', in Johnson, H.G. and Nobay, A.R. (eds) *The Current Inflation* (London: Macmillan).

Laidler, D. (1982) 'On Say's law, money and the business cycle', Ch. 3 of *Monetarist Perspectives* (Deddington: Philip Allan).

Laidler, D. (1990) 'The legacy of the monetarist controversy', *Federal Reserve Bank of St. Louis Quarterly Review*.

Lipsey, R.G. (1957) 'The relationship between unemployment and the rate of change of money wage rates in the United Kingdom 1862–1957', *Economica* NS 27, pp. 1–37.

Lucas, R.E., Jr. (1972) 'Expectations and the neutrality of money', *Journal of Economic Theory* 4 (2) pp. 103–24.

Lucas, R.E., Jr. (1990) 'The effects of monetary shocks when prices are set in advance', University of Chicago (mimeo).

Lutz, F. and Mints, L. (eds) (1952) *Readings in Monetary Theory* (London: Allen and Unwin).

Malinvaud, E. (1977) *The Theory of Unemployment Reconsidered* (Oxford: Basil Blackwell).

Marshall, A. (1890) *Principles of Economics*, 8th ed. (1920) (London: Macmillan).

Marshall, A. and Marshall, M.P. (1879) *Economics of Industry* (London: Macmillan).

Marshall, A. (1926) *The Official Papers of Alfred Marshall* (ed. J.M. Keynes) (London: Macmillan).

Mill, J.S. (1844) 'On the influence of consumption upon production', in *Essays on Some Unsettled Questions in Political Economy*, 2nd ed. (1874) (London, reprinted 1967, New York: Augustus Kelley).

Mill, J.S. (1848) *Principles of Political Economy, with Some of Their Applications to Social Philosophy* 7th ed. 1871, reprinted (ed. J.M. Robson) 1965 (Toronto: University of Toronto Press).

Muth, J.F. (1961) 'Rational expectations and the theory of price movements', *Econometrica* 29 (May) pp. 315–35.

Myrdal, G. (1931) *Monetary Equilibrium*, English tr. with minor emendations 1939 (London: W. Hodge).

Patinkin, D. (1948) 'Price flexibility and full employment', *American Economic Review*, reprinted with amendments in Lutz and Mints (eds) (1952).

Patinkin, D. (1956) *Money, Interest and Prices* (New York: Harper and Row).

Phelps, E.S. (1967) 'Phillips curves, expectations of inflation, and optimal unemployment over time', *Economica* NS. 34 (August) pp. 254–81.

Phelps, E.S. et al. (1970) *Microeconomic Foundations of Income and Employment Theory* (New York: W.W. Norton).

Phillips, A.W. (1958) 'The relation between unemployment and the rate of change of money wage rates in the United Kingdom', *Economica*, NS, 25 (November) pp. 283–99.

Pigou, A.C. (1913) *Unemployment* (London: Williams and Norgate).

Pigou, A.C. (1927) *Industrial Fluctuations* (London: Macmillan).

Pigou, A.C. (1933) *The Theory of Unemployment* (London: Macmillan).

Pigou, A.C. (1938) 'Money wages in relation to unemployment', *Economic Journal* 48 (March) pp. 134–8.

Pigou, A.C. (1943) 'The classical stationary state', *Economic Journal* 53 (June) pp. 343–51.

Pigou, A.C. (1947) 'Economic progress in a stable environment', *Economica*, reprinted in Lutz and Mints (eds) (1952).

Ricardo, D. (1810–11) 'The high price of gold bullion, a proof of the depreciation of bank notes', reprinted in Vol. III of *Works and Correspondence of David Ricardo*, ed. P. Sraffa, 1951 (Cambridge: Cambridge University Press for the Royal Economic Society).

Ricardo, D. (1816) 'A proposal for an economical and secure currency', reprinted in Vol. IV of *Works....*

Robbins, L.C. (1934) *The Great Depression* (London: Macmillan).

Robertson, D.H. (1915) *A Study of Industrial Fluctuations*, reprinted 1948 (London: LSE).

Smith, A. (1776) *An Enquiry into the Nature and Causes of the Wealth of Nations* (London: reprinted 1976, ed. Campbell, R.H., Skinner, A.S. and Todd, W.B.; Oxford: Clarendon Press).

Solow, R.M. (1969) *Price Expectations and the Behaviour of the Price Level* (Manchester: Manchester University Press).

Thornton, H. (1802) *An Enquiry into the Nature and Effects of the Paper Credit of Great Britain* (London: reprinted 1939, ed. F.A. von Hayek, George Allen and Unwin; reprinted 1962, New York: Augustus Kelley).

Tobin, J. (1972) 'Inflation and unemployment', *American Economic Review* 62 (March) pp. 1–18.

Walras, L. (1874) *Elements d'économie politique pure*, English translation by W. Jaffé from the 1926 definitive edition, 1954 (Homewood Ill.: Richard Irwin).

Wicksell, K. (1915) *Lectures in Political Economy Vol. II* (2nd Swedish ed.), English translation by E. Claassen, 1935 (London: Routledge and Kegan Paul).

6 The Lender of Last Resort: Pushing the Doctrine Too Far?*

Charles P. Kindleberger

I perhaps owe my readers an apology for referring once again to the doctrine of lender of last resort. The late Fred Hirsch brought the subject to the forefront of discussion with a brilliant paper half a generation ago (Hirsch, 1977). Hugh Rockoff discussed it earlier in this series honouring Henry Thornton (1986). Governor Carlo Ciampi of the Bank of Italy lectured on the subject in his own country in February of this year (Ciampi, 1992). The issue has been pursued in at least two of my books (1986, Chs. ix, x; 1993, *passim*, but especially pp. 277–83 of the 1984 edition). On this occasion, however, my purpose is not to defend the doctrine in the face of monetarists who believe that the money supply should be fixed, or grow at a fixed rate, rather than be allowed to expand in periods of widespread illiquidity and distress. That issue, to my mind, has been settled in favour of a lender of last resort in financial crisis. Rather, I suggest that the world may have pushed the doctrine too far with deposit insurance for commercial banks and thrifts, the rescue from bankruptcy of such bodies as New York City, some corporations such as Penn Central, Lockheed and Chrysler Corporation, banks 'too big to fail' even though their deposits exceed insured limits by wide margins, brokerage houses that loaned to such a commodity speculator as Bunker Hunt, who tried to corner the world silver market in the early 1980s. Even now in Japan, government money is called upon to make whole an institution owned by a rich bank, the troubles of which were caused by fraud rather than mistakes (*The Economist*, 1992, p. 105). Many high-minded principles suffer from entropy or decay over time, and the lender of last resort may be one of them.

The doctrine was first enunciated by Sir Francis Baring and Henry Thornton at the end of the eighteenth century apropos of a series of recent financial crises, especially that of 1793. It was formulated more precisely by Walter Bagehot, at age 22 in 1848, written following the 1847 suspension of the Bank Act of 1844. To quote that paper:

---

* This lecture was delivered on 11 November 1992 at City University, London.

It can be a great defect of a purely metallic circulation that the quantity of it cannot be readily suited to any sudden demand ... Now as paper money can be supplied in unlimited quantities, however sudden the demand may be, it does not appear to us that there is any objection on principle to sudden issues of paper money to meet sudden and large extensions of demand ... This power of issuing notes is one excessively liable to abuse ... It should only be used in rare and exceptional cases ... when the fact of an extensive *sudden* demand is proved.

(Bagehot, 1848 [1978], IX, p. 267, emphasis in original)

The constant repetition of the word 'sudden', and its emphasis in one instance, makes clear that Bagehot at an early age was thinking in terms of what is now known as rational expectations which makes special allowance for 'unanticipated events'. It is also of some mild interest that Bagehot in *Lombard Street* ascribes the origin of the idea of a lender of last resort to David Ricardo. However modest on his part, the notion seems far-fetched (1873 [1978], p. 75).

I should perhaps mention in passing T.S. Ashton's view that the Bank of England and the Exchequer recognized well before economists laid down rules for treatment of crises that the remedy was for an emergency issue of some form of paper which bankers, merchants and the general public would accept 'until men regained trust in one another', and that the Bank of England was already a lender of last resort in the eighteenth century (1959, pp. 110–2). In *Lombard Street*, written in response to the Overend, Gurney failure of 1866, Bagehot refined the concept of a lender of last resort, calling for the central bank to lend freely at a penalty rate, freely since limited lending on earlier occasions in the eighteenth century had increased the panic, and at a penalty rate to fend off merely pre-cautionary borrowers who were not in dire straits.

In 1793, the Bank of England stated its invariable practice of discounting only two-months commercial paper on two first-class London names (Clapham, 1945, I, p. 261). Crisis by crisis the rules were breached as loans were made on important but not first-class names, on mortgages, a coal mine, a West Indian plantation, copper works, to three American banks in Liverpool whose initial requests had been refused (Clapham, 1945, I, II, *passim*). As panic and bank runs built up because of an absence of rescuers on the horizon, central banks and governments everywhere found it necessary to rescue themselves and provide the sought-for cash, or make ready to do so, which usually relieved the situation by itself. Often when one institution promised not to save banks from the consequences of imprudent speculation or lending, when the crash arrived it preserved its dignity by finding another means, for example the Bank of England in 1826 when Lord Liverpool at the Treasury had sworn not to relieve a liquidity crisis through issuing Exchequer bills, and banking guarantees of Barings liabilities in 1890 when Lord Lidderdale of the Bank of England judged that rescues by the Bank were becoming so usual that the market counted on them.

As an aside, I may mention that in writing *Manias, Panics and Crashes*, I came across a remark that in some crisis the Bank's lending had not been 'over nice'. I seemed to have lost the reference, and so gave none (1978 (1989), p. 196). For some purpose undisclosed to me, my colleague, Stanley Fischer, asked where I had gotten the statement, and I diligently searched my notebooks but to no avail. He then turned to his friend Mervyn King, Executive Director of the Bank of England, where research revealed that the characterization had been cited by W.C.T. King in his *History of the London Discount Market* (1936). I had accurately remembered the phrase, but failed to note its provenance. Its origin was from the testimony of Jeremiah Harman, director of the Bank between 1794 and 1827, governor in 1817 and 1818, before the 1832 Parliamentary Committee of Secrecy on the Bank of England. The evidence dealt with the Bank's response to the crisis of 1825, with the expression furnished in an answer to the question in para. 2217 – in case any of you share Professor Fischer's curiosity.

In an episode foreshadowing the United States troubles of the 1980s and 1990s, the Bank of England yielded to the pleas of the three American 'W' banks – Wiggins, Wildes and Wilson – but failed in the effort to save them, and succeeded in liquidating the assets taken over only 14 years later (Clapham, 1945, II, p. 157).

After World War I, the Bank of England undertook a wider policy of intervention in industry, along with banking, that Sayers called 'out of character' (1978, I, p. 314). The problems lay particularly in steel, which had experienced a boom immediately after the war, when it appeared that German industry would be out of action for a time. The Bank started with a private customer of the Newcastle branch, Armstrong Whitworth, the overdraft for which had been increased in 1918. The company then plunged. By 1925 it was clear that it had made a great many bad investments, and the Bank of England loaned it £2.7 million on the construction of a newsprint plant in Newfoundland. In the end, the Bank lost only £200 000 capital, and £300 000 in foregone interest on these operations. In 1928 Vickers Armstrong was formed and received a five-year guarantee of its profit, which cost the bank £1 million over five years. Further complex operations in steel took more and more of the Bank's and Governor Norman's time, especially after the Hatry crisis of September 1929. In this, and in its dealings in cotton textiles, the Bank tried to keep its activities secret, partly so as not to encourage the Labour Party to involve the rescue operations in politics (Tolliday, 1987, esp. ch. viii).

Rescue in cotton textiles was necessitated by the troubles of the Williams Deacon Bank, a London clearing institution with its head office in Manchester, and with, at the end of 1928, advances of £3 770 000 to 40 cotton companies. The Bank first guaranteed these advances up to £1 million. In an interesting exercise in what is now called 'conditionality', to preserve secrecy, the Bank allowed Williams Deacon to maintain its dividend, but not to raise it, and required it to reduce its dividend if any other clearing bank were to do so (Sayers, 1976, I, p. 285). When in 1929 the Royal Bank of Scotland took Williams Deacon over, the Bank of England added a sweetener to the deal by throwing in its own Burlington Gardens branch in west London. Sayers explains that the Bank had, on the one hand, lost interest in its own profits from private business, and sought to divert public attention away from the real reason for the merger (ibid., pp. 285–6). All in all, the Bank's net loss was £3.2 million, most of which was written off early.

I shift from London to Italy by an easy transition without getting into the 1974 'life boat' operation in favour of the fringe banks. Along with steel and cotton, the Bank in 1929 led a rescue of the Banca-Italo Britannica, owned and controlled by a British holding company, in which London clearing banks and a British insurance company were involved, along with some Roman and Milanese banks. Banca-Italo Britannica was operated in Italy where it suffered from the 1926 deflation, some bad investments, a certain amount of malfeasance in the accounts, plus the tightening of interest rates in the Wall Street boom that started in March 1928. Sayers said that the Banca-Italo was widely regarded as a British responsibility, despite its Italian management. As it began to fail, the Bank of England and the three London clearing banks put up most of the funds to keep it going for a while before it was ultimately wound up. The Bank of England's loss of £250 000 – its entire contribution to the rescue – is stated to have been 'the cost of saving London from threatened shame' (ibid., pp. 259–62).

Secret rescue, or as the Italians call them 'salvage', operations, had been under way for a quarter century as the Bank of Italy took over bad assets of leading banks in financial crises of 1907, 1921, 1926 and 1930. When the full fury of the 1929 depression broke, the Italian government formed the Istituto Riconstruzione Italiana (IRI), to take over these assets from the Bank of Italy in exchange for government bonds, with the thought that they would be worked off over time. IRI was patterned to some extent after the 1931 Reconstruction Finance Corporation (RFC) in the United States, established to make advances to banks and business with liquidity problems, but handicapped by a Democratic party requirement in subsequent legislation that loans to banks be made public. This last requirement effectively barred its use for banks which would, by borrowing, announce that their condition was shaky. Substantial loans were made to industry. When the war came, the RFC was converted into the Defense Plant Corporation (DPC) to simplify the provision of credit to the defence industry as compared to reliance on the capital market or commercial banks. In due course, with strong recovery during and after the war, the RFC/DPC were able to liquidate all these investments, as companies with profits paid off their loans or bought plant to enable debtors to do so. This was a successful workout without a trace of scandal. IRI on the other hand was reorganized. The collection of financial and industrial assets was converted into ownership, and IRI operated the companies concerned, largely because of the difficulty of privatization – to use a current neologism – given a weak Italian capital market and the absence of large wartime corporate profits.

Success in working out bad loans and investments, in contrast to writing them off, depends on one or more of several felicitous circumstances: rapid and strong recovery of the economy and asset prices; a buoyant capital market such as that prevailing in the United States in the postwar 'golden years'; buyers willing to take over failed banks, minus government write-offs. In this last connection, valuations placed on 'good' and 'bad' assets in a financial crisis may not hold up over the long run. The cautionary tale is that of the 1929 threatened failure of the Bodencreditanstalt in Austria, rescued by being taken over by the Creditanstalt, which itself collapsed in May 1931, largely as a consequence of the turning bad of the good assets it had acquired from the Bodencredit.

A conservative view of banking is that assets should always be 'market to market', and that a bank should be closed down and liquidated if its capital is impaired. I confess I do not understand the reasoning of young Henry Thornton, the nephew, in closing down Pole, Thornton & Company in the crisis of 1825 because while solvent he was concerned that if he borrowed a second time to gain liquidity, as all the directors of the Bank of England were willing that he should, he feared that it would be taken from him by the country banks for which Pole, Thornton served as London correspondent (Ashton and Sayers, eds, 1953, ch. vii, esp. pp. 102–4). The doctrine of marking to market, however, leaves little room for work-outs. It fails, moreover, to recognize the distinction between a mutual fund and a bank, or the functions of banks in issuing liabilities that are used as money. If all loans and investments were traded in efficient markets, assets could be marked to market at appropriate intervals, but unless there were a very large amount of capital, liabilities would have to change correspondingly and could no longer serve as money, which has a fixed price. On the asset side, moreover, cash and investments can be valued regularly, but loans cannot. Securitization of mortgages, credit-card liabilities, and in Britain export credits, changes the balance between assets that can be valued regularly, and those – loans – that cannot.

One must be careful, too, to insist that the markets in which assets are priced are efficient. At the outbreak of the crisis in Third World debt, a few economists insisted that there were market valuations for some of these loans, such as Mexican bonds. But these quotations were largely nominal, and an attempt to sell a substantial quantity would have quickly disclosed their illiquidity. The same is true of many assets which bulk large in balance sheets, even of central banks. Gold is the classic example. Once the United States closed the gold window in 1968, the metal became a commodity and no longer represented money. The liquidity of asset markets is infinitely graded from short-term government bills at one extreme – although in some financial crises, it has been claimed that even they cannot be sold at any, meaning any normal, price – and the junkiest of junk bonds at the other. But as Charles Goodhart (1986) and Albert Wojnilower (1992) assert, there is a difference in kind, as well as in degree, between investments saleable in a market, and loans based upon a relationship with a borrower. The latter are not marked to market except in the doleful circumstances of bankruptcy proceedings that have advanced some distance.

Perhaps the largest step in the progressive breakdown of the pure doctrine of the lender of last resort came with the adoption in the United States of deposit insurance. Its origin in the 1933 depression was in what is now called, somewhat ponderously, asymmetric information, the difference in sophistication between individuals of wealth and substantial corporations, and the ordinary householder and small business. The former were thought to be able to judge the solvency of a bank, the latter unable. A limit initially set at $5000 per depositor was thought adequate to divide the two groups. With inflation after World War II, rather than any extension of financial ignorance, the figure was progressively raised, first to $10 000, then $20 000, $40 000 and finally to $100 000. I am told that the $100 000 limit was agreed upon in a Congressional conference committee

as a compromise between the House and Senate conferees, one set of
which had brought in a bill raising the limit from $40 000 to $50 000, the
other from $40 000 to $60 000.

All was quiet during the golden years to 1973, with deposit insurance
coming to the rescue of the few banks in trouble. Difficulties were still
minimal in the middle 1970s until the second sharp rise in the price of oil
in 1979 that threatened inflation. Banks had been forbidden to pay more
than 5 1/2 per cent on time deposits under Federal Reserve regulation Q.
When interest rates rose sharply in 1979 to 1981 widespread disintermediation took place as sophisticated depositors withdrew time and saving
deposits from banks to redeposit them in new money funds which paid
higher returns because they were unburdened by ceilings. It is a matter of
some cynical interest that savings banks in poor parts of cities or poor
regions of the country were not disintermediated because their depositors
were not conscious of the opportunity to increase their return on idle cash
from 5 1/2 per cent to 10 per cent or more.

Disintermediation was particularly hurtful to the thrift institutions –
savings banks, saving and loan associations and credit unions – which
were limited to a few assets, largely long-term fixed-interest mortages.
Squeezed between the high rates they had to pay to replace the withdrawn
deposits and low fixed-interest income, the industry pleaded with the
Congress to remove limits on which they could pay depositors, and for
permission to make wider and riskier investments. There was also a shift
to the adjustable-rate mortgage, but too late to produce substantial change.
Deregulation, however, occurred simultaneously with the development of
the so-called 'junk bond', one below investment grade because of the
lesser coverage of interest paid by normal income. The consequence was
that a wide number of thrift institutions started to pay high rates of interest
to attract deposits, and to invest in high-paying risky investments to earn
the necessary returns. A further development which increased the ultimate
burden to be borne by the Federal Deposit Insurance Corporation (FDIC)
and its thrift analogue, the Federal Savings and Loan Corporation (FSLIC,
pronounced like a patent medicine, Fislick) was the spontaneous development of a new business of deposit brokering. Substantial deposit amounts
would be broken up by these brokers into amounts of less than $100 000,
and parcelled out among a number of high-interest paying banks, almost
certainly weak, in order to qualify for deposit insurance. This was adverse
selection with a vengeance. In retrospect, raising the insurance limit from
$10 000 or $20 000 per deposit was a mistake as the transactions cost of
placing, say, $5 million among 500 or 250 banks might not have been
worth while as compared with 50.

As interest rates paid on deposits rose, and investments became riskier, the ethics of old-fashioned banking wore thin, and a number of bankers slipped into unseemly ways, buying Rembrandts with bank money to decorate their offices, yachts to entertain their boards of directors, and possibly their deposit brokers, hiring salesmen to persuade unsophisticated depositors to switch out of insured deposits into the bank's uninsured (junk) debentures, this to bolster the banks' capital/deposit ratios. Hundreds of such bankers are currently on trial or in jail in the United States.

The ostensible purpose of deposit insurance was to protect the unsophisticated depositor from the odd failure of an individual bank. At a deeper level, the rationale was to prevent bank runs that might spread to other banks and other localities and thus threaten the safety of the banking system as a whole. It was this purpose, in my judgement, that led to the progressive raising of the insured-deposit limit. It was clearly the motive for saving the Continental Illinois which had bought a great many oil loans from the high-flying Penn Square Bank of Oklahoma, close to the top of the oil market. With its high interest rates, the Continental Illinois had attracted a lot of Japanese depositors, with large amounts of money, who may or may not have been sophisticated. To avoid a precipitous run and a foreign-exchange crisis, the Continental Illinois was rescued without limit with respect to deposit size, and the doctrine that some banks are too big to fail was born or resurrected. In the same vein, the Federal Reserve System urged the New York banks to rescue J.S. Bache and Company, a brokerage house, not a bank, which had advanced hundreds of millions of dollars to Bunker Hunt when he was trying, unsuccessfully, to corner the world silver market, loans which he was unable to repay on schedule.

There are two types of bank runs, one by public depositors, the outsiders, the second by other banks which become suspicious of an adventurous bank, perhaps a newcomer trying to push its way into the market; after a time they refuse to accept its paper, or exchange contracts, or to lend it federal funds. This was the fate of the Franklin National Bank in 1974, when other New York banks first approached the Federal Reserve Bank of New York to warn it that the Franklin National was on a dangerous course, and, when the Federal Reserve seemed to take no steps to correct the situation, finally stopped dealing with it (Spero, 1980).

A recent book on financial crises has some curious remarks about depositor runs. It suggests that the depositors who lead such a movement – called 'sequentially-served depositors' – are helpful insofar as they monitor the performance of banks (Calomiris and Gorton, 1991, p. 120). One wonders whether they would say the same of those who start panics in theatre fires. The authors call this source of bank runs 'asymmetric information' – some depositors and presumably bank officials know more than others and contrast it with a separate theory based on 'random withdrawals', such as used to occur in the United States in the nineteenth century when bank credit was strained each fall by the necessity to finance the seasonal movement of crops off the farm. Asymmetric information is measured in another paper in the same volume (Mishkin, 1991) by the spread in yields between high-quality assets like treasury bills and commercial paper of equal maturity, or between government or triple A bonds and B bonds, both of which spreads widened in financial crisis. Another term for this phenomenon is a 'flight to quality', as sophisticated investors shift assets to higher grade (and lower yield) assets as the banking system moves into distress as it approaches crisis.

In the United States monitoring of bank performance may have been left to a limited extent to sequentially-served depositors, but legally was assigned to government regulators whose performance in the 1980s left much to be desired. In one view the problem lay in the duplication of bank examinations by the staffs of the Comptroller of the Currency in the US Treasury, the Federal Reserve System, and state bank commissions, plus to some extent the personnel of the FDIC and FSLIC. 'Shared responsibility', said Ludwig Bamberger, a prominent German banker a century ago, 'is no responsibility'. Edward Kane, who is more cynical than I deem is warranted, believes that the multiple layers of examination led to bureaucratic competition in deregulation (Kane, 1987). Nor have the legal and accounting professions covered themselves with glory in a number of isolated cases where representatives of each have blessed transactions that later have proved to be some distance below the standards of professional probity. Lenders of last resort in my country have brought suit against lawyers and accountants in these circumstances, but have no chance of recovering any sizeable part of the losses from malfeasance. The same problem cropped up last spring in Japan when Toyo Shinkin, an Osaka-based credit union, forged certificates of deposit and ended up with bad debts of ¥252 billion. After trying first to push the loss on the creditors, and then on the Sanwa Bank group that owned Toyo Shinkin, both of which resisted, the Ministry of Finance laid the burden on the official Industrial Bank of Japan, an instance of public money used to make good losses from criminal fraud rather than imprudent lending, although the line between the two, in this age, is sometimes hard to draw (*The Economist*, 1992, p. 105).

Choosing between work-out or write-off presents an agonizing problem for banks in distress, but equally so for the lender of last resort.

Sometimes, of course, a bank will embark on one course, and then choose or be obliged to change, as Citicorp did in the spring of 1987 after five years of attempted workout, when it wrote off more than $1 1/2 billions of its Third World sovereign debt. Even more perplexing is the task of the Resolution Trust Corporation (RTC), charged with disposing of the assets taken over by the FDIC and FSLIC from banks that are closed, merged, or bailed out. Substantial cyclical recovery might float some of the boats that look wrecked. On the other hand, the longer the RTC waits the more its losses mount because of accumulating interest. Other questions are whether to sell off the odds and sods of hotels, office buildings, shopping malls, banking quarters, residential housing, golf courses and the like, at wholesale or retail, and if retail, through regular market channels of brokers or by auction. A decision has been made that the government, that is, the taxpayer, bears the loss, now or in the future as debt is paid off, rather than the bank depositor and the holder of bank shares, as in 1930 to 1933.

I came late to at least a partial understanding of the issues through reading a short time ago Homer Hoyt's book, *One Hundred Years of Land Values in Chicago*, written in 1933. Hoyt has more detail on the separate sections of that city that grew at various rates during the century in question than interests me, but he is superb on the question of real-estate bubbles and their bursting. (Parenthetically I learned about the book when I made up a list of 50 books to be read for enjoyment and instruction by retired bankers, only to have Moses Abramovitz ask why I left off Hoyt.) Hoyt pointed out that stock-market booms often spread to real estate, especially in growing cities, but that their respective down-side behaviour differs. In a stock-market collapse, the shakeout of leveraged speculators is wound up in a matter of months. At the time of the crash speculators in real estate who had been infected by the euphoria in shares congratulate themselves that they are financed by term loans, rather than day-to-day money, and have real instead of paper assets. In the five crashes in Chicago to 1933, and again in 1987, however, it was not possible to evade the liquidation process in real estate. Interest on real-estate loans stayed high, along with taxes on the property. Lenders became shy about renewing or extending loans. Buyers suddenly saw the advantage of waiting, rather than carrying out previous intentions. Rents fell as new speculative buildings came on the market, and their owners had difficulty in selling them or finding tenants. When old leases in existing buildings ran out existing tenants bargained rents down. Instead of liquidation coming to completion in less than a year, it stretched to four, five or even more years with devastating effects on owners and lenders, especially banks. It was this experience that produced the FDIC and later FSLIC. Those of you who watched the Olympia and York story unfold in Canada, New York and Canary Wharf will understand the prescience of Homer Hoyt, writing sixty years ago.

Despite widespread opinion to the contrary, it was not the decline in the money supply that produced the depression of 1929 to 1933, but the reverse. Ben Bernanke was correct when he wrote in 1983 that tight money could lead to depression otherwise than through the money supply. The analysis applied well to the stock-market crash of 1987 which made banks leery of lending, and produced a delayed but sharp collapse in real estate, bursting the bubble of the 1980s. In 1929, however – at least in my opinion – the effect was felt immediately on commodity prices, as banks in trouble because of illiquid brokers' loans rationed credit to commodity brokers, who were thus unable to clear commodity markets of goods shipped to New York on commission at anything close to prevailing prices. This effect could not recur in 1987 because imported commodities in the United States are bought in the exporting country, not sold on arrival in New York. The major impact in the 1929 depression of falling commodity prices in the first few weeks after the stock-market crash has been questioned lately by Barry Eichengreen who observes that the same mechanism did not operate in London where brokers' loans were much less substantial than in New York. The reasoning seems not to take into account that if prices of internationally traded goods fall in one market they fall in all (1992, p. 230).

As lender of last resort, the Resolution Trust Corporation seems still, at the time of writing, to be experimenting with how to handle the disposal of its ragbag of assets. With only a few assets of modest value, at any one time, the Bank of England could work off its acquisitions slowly and secretly, covering losses by annual modest charges against profits. In the United States today, the problem is far too substantial to admit of such a relatively happy solution. To sell in large batches runs the risk of awarding profits to wealthy capitalists so large as to give rise to an echo of the scandals that contributed to the lamentable problem.

A precedent exists in Italian history when, just after unification in 1860 in which the new kingdom acquired substantial debts from the constituent kingdoms, duchies and principalities, it seized church lands and a number of large estates. To convert these into cash, it created a private concern, the *Società Anonina per la Vendita dei Beni del Regno* (Corporation for the Sale of Assets of the Kingdom) to sell the collection of 'church properties, iron mines on the island of Elba, forests, mineral springs, arsenals, some irrigation canals and common lands, especially sea swamps and mountain tops', administered from 1860 to 1882, with an estimated total value of 1928 million lire (then approximately $400 million [Clough, 1964, pp. 47–54, quotation from p. 49]). Similar disposal problems for which I lack sources with details, were the seizure of church lands and buildings by Henry VIII in Britain, of church and noble lands in France in the revolution, and another large-scale confiscation in Spain in the early nineteenth century. In no case, I gather, was the operation accomplished neatly and without steps forward and back. The problem forcibly dumped in the lap of the RTC will equally become, in the inelegant American expression, 'a can of worms'.

The central question is who bears the burden of this ill-advised investment and thievery. The list of candidates is substantial:

- the investors and malefactors themselves;
- their creditors;
- bank owners, through the decline in their shares, or their worthlessness, assuming limited liability, leaving aside double liability, such as obtained in many states before 1929, or the unlimited liability, that afflicted the Glasgow tobacco lords who lost their estates in 1772 in the failure of the Ayr bank;
- depositors when banks failed without deposit insurance, or were covered only to a limit, except in those cases where the limit was ignored to prevent a run;
- the central bank, although where central-bank profits above statutory amounts accrue to the government, and the losses do not reduce profits below this amount, the loss falls on the state;
- the state through many possible channels: directly in the case of institutions like the RTC, either the original write-off, or an ultimate one; through tax losses where the losses of depositors, investors, banks and others are written off against other taxable income; through the forgiveness of foreign loans through such arrangements as the Paris club.
- the country as a whole if bad investments lead to bank runs, collapse and depression;
- debt holders of all kinds if the debts acquired by the state in fending off financial crisis are shrugged off through inflation.

Inflation is an unlikely indirect effect of bad investments, though it could occur if a lender of last resort operated with such a lavish hand, failing to shrink the money supply after first enlarging it, that spending got out of hand.

Now that the lender-of-last-resort function has shifted from a rare and infrequent expedient, held under tight control, to one undertaken readily, perhaps too readily, and even light-heartedly, it is well to bear in mind that it has strong features of redistributing income and wealth. Ambiguity as to whether investors or their banks will be saved or not has much to recommend it in order to reduce moral hazard and make nominal caretakers take real care. As in *Candide*, it is well from time to time to cut off the head of a general (let a substantial bank collapse) to 'encourage the others'.

One appropriate set of losers when a bank fails through ineptitude or worse is the officers, who should lose not only their jobs and the value of their shares but also any options to buy more at low prices, should the bank and its shares ultimately recover. At the time of the salvage of the Continental Illinois, I was offended that while the responsible officers were sacked, they left by the terms of their employment contracts with golden parachutes in amounts which, in a few cases, exceeded one or two million dollars. When on one occasion at a meeting I expressed this indignation, a lawyer present said that such amounts were inconsequential solace for the lawsuits to which the officers would submit for years ahead. Even so.

The redistribution effects evoke an aspect of last-resort lending and its entropy that I have not stressed, that is, the political dimensions. Recall that Governor Norman wanted to keep his activities in steel and textiles secret so as not to let the Labour Party become involved in the decision-making. Lender-of-last-resort help for Austria and Germany in May and June 1931 aborted when France made them conditional on Austria giving up the Zoll-Union with Germany, and on Germany abandoning the construction of the *Panzerkreuzer* (pocket battleship). Japan is holding back in efforts to carry the Commonwealth of Independent States through the current crisis because of the Kurile Islands. In the United States, voting new funds for the FDIC, the FSLIC and RTC is embroiled in party politics, which is why the money is voted in spoonsful rather than in an effective dollop, evoking a reminder of Bagehot's 'freely'. There are strong political arguments against entrusting last-resort operations to independent bodies which might play favourites, and discriminate against outsiders in favour of the Establishment. But financial crises often call for decisive and immediate action that central banks are capable of producing, and deliberative political bodies, including such international organizations as the International Monetary Fund, may not be able to deliver.

A sharp observer of financial economics in the United States, Albert M. Wojnilower, senior advisor of First Boston Asset Management, suggested some years ago, at the start of the banking crises, that since the United States government had to make good in one way or another most of the losses from exuberant and misguided investment in booms and/or bubbles, there might be merit in converting parts of the government into a monopoly bank, making loans and investments, and issuing money, hoping for positive returns and/or seigniorage, but ready to absorb unpreventable losses. Ricardo in 1824 proposed a similar idea that all bank notes be issued by the government (Fetter, 1980, p. 109). It is remotely possible that this was the origin of Bagehot's view in *Lombard Street* that Ricardo, rather than Henry Thornton and Sir Francis Baring, first formulated the last-resort doctrine (1873 [1978], p. 75).

Rather than move to having government take over the financial system, including banking, I would prefer to try to stuff the genie back in the bottle, reduce the last-resort function to a weapon of rare and occasional use, buttressed by better and more responsible bankers, lawyers and accountants, stricter bank examinations and occasional isolated bank failure. I fear this is a counsel of perfection. Communication today is so far-ranging and instantaneous, innovation so institutionalized, emulation so dominant and independence of thought so rare, that booms and busts are a continuous threat and require that government maintain constant alert to damp down the first and fend off the second. This may be merely the pessimism of advanced years. I fervently hope so.

References

Ashton, T.S. (1959) *Economic Fluctuations in England, 1700–1800* (Oxford: Clarendon Press).

Bagehot, Walter (1848 [1978]) 'The Currency Monopoly', in Norman St. John-Stevas (ed.) *The Collected Works of Walter Bagehot* (London: *The Economist*) Vol. ix, pp. 235–75.

Bagehot, Walter (1873 [1978]) *Lombard Street*, in Norman St. John-Stevas (ed.) *The Collected Works of Walter Bagehot* (London: *The Economist*) Vol. ix, pp. 48–233.

Calomiris, Charles W., and Gary Gordon (1991) 'The Origins of Banking Panics: Models, Facts and Bank Regulations', in R. Glenn Hubbard (ed.) *Financial Markets and Financial History* (Chicago: University of Chicago Press) pp. 109–73.

Ciampi, Carlo A. (1992) 'Lending of Last Resort', in Banca d'Italia, *Economic Bulletin*, No. 14 (February) pp. 63–9.

Clapham, Sir John (1945) *The Bank of England: A History* (Cambridge: Cambridge University Press) 2 vols.

Clough, Shepherd B. (1964) *The Economic History of Modern Italy* (New York: Columbia University Press).

(The) Economist (1992), Vol. 323, no. 7758, May 9 to 15.

Eichengreen, Barry (1992) *Golden Fetters: The Gold Standard and the Great Depression, 1919–1939* (New York and Oxford: Oxford University Press).

Fetter, Frank W. (1980) *The Economist in Parliament: 1780–1868* (Durham, N.C.: Duke University Press).

Goodhart, Charles (1972 [1986]) *The Business of Banking, 1891–1914*, 2nd ed. (Aldershot: Gower).

Hirsch, Fred (1977) 'The Bagehot Problem', *The Manchester School of Economics and Social Studies*, Vol. 45 (September) pp. 241–57.

Hoyt, Homer (1933) *A Hundred Years of Land Values in Chicago: The Relationship of the Growth of Chicago to the Rise in Its land Values, 1830–1933* (Chicago: University of Chicago Press).

Kane, Edward J. (1989) *The S&L Insurance Mess: How Did it Happen?* (Washington, D.C.: Urban Institute Press).

Kindleberger, Charles P. (1973 [1986]) *The World in Depression, 1929–1939*, rev. ed. (Berkeley: University of California Press).

Kindleberger, Charles P. (1978 [1989]) *Manias, Panics and Crashes: A History of Financial Crises*, rev. ed. (New York: Basic Books).

Kindleberger, Charles P. (1984 [1993]) *A Financial History of Western Europe* (New York: Oxford University Press).

King, W.C.T. (1946) *A History of the London Discount Market* (London: Routledge).

Mishkin, Frederic S. (1991) 'Asymmetric Information and Financial Crises', in R. Glenn Hubbard (ed.) *Financial Markets and Financial Crises* (Chicago and London: University of Chicago Press) pp. 69–108.

Rockoff, Hugh (1986) 'Walter Bagehot and the Theory of Central Banking', in Forrest Capie and Geoffrey Wood (eds) *Financial Crises and the World Banking System* (London: Macmillan) pp. 160–80.

Sayers, Richard S. (1976) *The Bank of England, 1891–1914*, 3 vols (Cambridge: Cambridge University Press).

Spero, Joan Edelman (1980) *The Failure of the Franklin National Bank: Challenge to the International Banking System* (New York: Columbia University Press).

Thornton, Marianne (1825 [1953]) 'The Crisis of 1825: Letters from a Young Lady', in T.S. Ashton and R.S. Sayers (eds.) *Papers in English Monetary History* (Oxford: Clarendon Press) pp. 96–108.

Tolliday, Steven (1987) *Business, Banking and Politics: The Case of British Steel, 1918–1939* (Cambridge, Mass.: Harvard University Press).

Wojnilower, Albert M. (1990) 'Financial Institutions Cannot Compete', pamphlet (New York: First Boston Management Corporation).

Wojnilower, Albert M. (1992) 'Markets and Relationships', pamphlet (New York: First Boston Management Corporation).

7 The Conduct of Monetary Policy in an Open Economy*

Helmut Schlesinger

A lecture on the 'Conduct of Monetary Policy in an Open Economy' is easily linked to the ideas of Henry Thornton who contributed significantly to the theory of money of his time, even though the underlying conditions have changed at the end of the twentieth century.

A responsible monetary policy cannot today ignore the implications and repercussions of the openness and interdependence of national economies. The construct of ideas of a closed economy cannot serve as a guide for a monetary policymaker. Nevertheless, over the years and decades, and also internationally, there have been quite different views on the subject. As is often the case, it is evident here, too, that currently prevailing basic (economic) views cannot be assessed in isolation from the historical context.

Now, what does the openness of an economy mean specifically? First of all, it means the openness of the goods and financial markets to other countries, that is, giving other countries access to the national markets. In this respect, Germany has to some extent set the pace in Europe. In 1959, ten years after the currency reform, it opened its capital market to foreign countries and soon largely liberalised cross-border movements of money and capital. In the goods and services markets protectionist tendencies – excluding agriculture – have been taboo for a long time. A share of exports in GNP in excess of 35 per cent and the significance of foreign investors in the German capital market, as well as the role played by the D-Mark as an international investment, reserve, issue and intervention currency do not allow any but a liberal-minded attitude today.

For a monetary policy geared to the principles of a market economy trends in the financial markets, that is, the globalisation and internationalisation of the financial system, are of paramount importance. Basing monetary analyses on what is known as an 'insular economy', as was still often done as late as the sixties, would now lead to misjudgements from the very outset.

---

* This lecture was delivered on 15 November 1993 at City University, London.

Let there be no misunderstanding: despite, or especially because of, the international integration of financial and goods markets, any successful monetary policy invariably begins at home. I am speaking only for myself, but you would certainly not be wrong if you assume that my views are based on more than forty years of work in the Bundesbank. This view is also in line with the legal mandate given to the Deutsche Bundesbank: safeguarding price stability is the primary objective of German monetary policy.

These convictions are likely to have gained international acceptance as well. Otherwise it would not be conceivable that safeguarding price stability has been made the priority objective of the European Central Bank in the Maastricht Treaty. A currency which has a stable value at home makes it easier to meet international obligations and to take the international context into adequate account. In the light of growing global economic integration, closer international coordination in the monetary field is of course useful in encouraging internationally consistent policies. It reaches its limits, however, whenever the problems it is expected to solve were created nationally, because, say, no safeguards were provided against excessive government deficits or because monetary policy has been lax. I shall deal with this in more detail later on.

In Germany, the Deutsche Bundesbank has tried since the mid-seventies to facilitate the fulfilment of its task by announcing monetary targets (since 1988 for the money stock M3). The Bundesbank has focused its policy, which is geared to medium-term objectives, explicitly on the proven link between monetary growth and price trends. A prerequisite for this has been met in Germany in that monetary relations – that between the money stock and prices, demand for money, the trend in the velocity of circulation – are comparatively stable. Internal and external studies (compare OECD, BIS) suggest that these have continued to exist even after German unification.

Countries, such as yours, which seek to attain the objective of stability direct seem to do so not because they consider such an approach to be basically superior to a strategy of intermediate targets, but rather because they are unable to define an appropriate intermediate target. Mervyn King, the Executive Director and Chief Economist of the Bank of England, noted, for instance, that

> the Bundesbank's approach is usually contrasted … with the UK experience, in which the emphasis on monetary targets was significantly reduced during the 1980s. But this change in emphasis was in no way a reflection of any lack of commitment to price stability. Rather it

reflected the instability in velocity which arose from the liberalisation of our financial markets at the beginning of the decade. This disrupted the relationships which had previously obtained between money and inflation, and afflicted policymakers in the same way that constantly-sounding car alarms afflict innocent passers-by.[1]

(By the way, the instability of velocity was also a concern of Henry Thornton, nearly 200 years ago.)

It would be too much to analyse the reasons, to ask what should be done to restore a reliable link between the money stock and price trends. Basically, every definition of the money stock has its strong and weak points. The openness of an economy poses particular problems in this connection, as the absence of capital controls allows money to be transferred easily from the domestic financial centre to countries abroad. Thus, for some years now, the Bundesbank has additionally monitored the growth of 'M3 extended', which also includes assets held in the Euro-DM-market. The growth of M3 extended tends to outpace that of traditional M3.

The Bundesbank, of course, also takes other indicators into account which might provide information on the future trend in prices. These include not least the exchange rate of the Deutsche Mark. It would be an illusion to believe it to be possible to safeguard the value of money at home and, at the same time, to ignore the exchange rate trend of one's own currency. A monetary policy which is geared to an ultimate goal which does not take account both of external ties between goods markets and of international price links would soon lose confidence and credibility.

The Bundesbank has succeeded, despite adverse external factors since German unification, in maintaining confidence in the D-Mark. As the D-Mark plays a major role as a reserve and international investment currency – it accounts for 15 to 20 per cent of total international assets, and hence for far more than would correspond to Germany's weight in the world economy – particular attention must be paid to this fact. Non-resident's heavy investment in D-Mark was one of the reasons why long-term interest rates in Germany have dropped to historical lows. The yield on domestic bonds outstanding, for instance, is now below 6 per cent.

As has already been noted, any good monetary policy invariably begins at home. But its effects and the transmission mechanisms differ in an open economy, depending on whether the country concerned has a system of fixed or floating exchange rates. German monetary policymakers must take both systems into account, because the D-Mark floats against major partner currencies (US dollar, Japanese yen, Swiss franc, pound sterling), but is integrated into a regional fixed-rate system in the EMS. The two systems have various advantages and drawbacks.

The collapse of the Bretton Woods system in the early seventies, and the transition to floating exchange rates in 1973, provided the Bundesbank with some additional degree of freedom in the implementation of its policy. Floating exchange rates basically allow each country to pursue an independent monetary policy to realise its national objectives. In such a system it is easier to control the domestic money stock and to carry out monetary targeting as there is no need for forced purchases of foreign exchange to maintain a particular exchange rate.

On the other hand, there may be a high degree of volatility, or even an 'overshooting', of the exchange rate. Rapid exchange rate changes, in conjunction with the rather slow adjustment of the real economy, may create conflicts between domestic and external requirements. In this connection, I need remind you only of the relationship between the D-Mark and the US dollar in the late seventies and in the eighties, or of the movements of the meanwhile freely floating pound sterling and Italian lira against the ERM currencies. The chances of exchange rate management under this system are limited to the extent that monetary policy is conducted primarily with national objectives in mind.

In the past, the volatility just mentioned made it seem desirable to strengthen international monetary policy coordination and cooperation. In a global context, this is done in a loose form through cooperation between the G-7 countries. In western Europe, this was the reason for the establishment of the European Monetary System with fixed but adjustable exchange rates.

From the very outset, the rationale behind the EMS was to create a 'zone of stability'. This meant not only, wherever possible, to stabilise the exchange rates between participating currencies, but also to ensure the highest possible degree of price stability in each economy. This noble goal, however, must be set against the constraints such an exchange rate system imposes on a country.

In a fixed-rate system there is only limited scope for the pursuit of a national monetary policy, at least if there is only little willingness to accept realignments. During the Bretton Woods system responsibility for stability over time focused on a specific currency (US dollar). This currency played the part of a monetary anchor and, when the anchor failed, the system broke down (1973).

In the EMS, this role has come to be played by the D-Mark. Acting as some kind of 'market leader', the Bundesbank thus determines the global thrust of monetary policy in the ERM. This was evident from the movement of money market rates in ERM partner countries. While they need not be above the level of German rates in each country, their changes largely shadow those in money market rates in Germany. Depending on the risk premium included in the exchange rate of individual currencies, rates will be higher or lower. The anchor role played by the D-Mark is not god-given, but it reflects the confidence won over an extended period of time in the markets.

The limits to the European fixed-rate system are particularly striking whenever real exchange rates diverge or asymmetric shocks occur. If prices in one country rise faster than in another for some time, while nominal exchange rates remain unchanged, an exchange rate system with fixed exchange rates will become very vulnerable to speculative capital movements. The viability of the EMS depends on a willingness to effect realignments whenever divergent national underlying conditions – lack of convergence (in respect of inflation rates, economic conditions, interest rate level, choice of exchange rate on joining the ERM) – make this seem imperative.

The years 1987 to 1992 were marked by a failure to realign central rates despite declining convergence; this deficiency was the main factor triggering the EMS crisis that began in September 1992. In these circumstances the risk of speculation on a depreciation of weak currencies is relatively minor. On the other hand, the potential profit to be realised if central rates are realigned, or a currency leaves the ERM, is large, while the risk of loss is small. What is involved here is fairly riskless one-way speculation.

During the crises of autumn/winter 1992 and mid-1993, the foreign exchange reserves of the Bundesbank, the central bank of the country receiving the influx, were boosted enormously, while those of countries registering outflows diminished. Purchases of foreign exchange in support of EMS currencies made by the German central bank in September 1992, and the D-Mark sales by EMS partner central banks it financed, alone amounted to over DM 92 billion. This came down to a virtual doubling of monetary reserves against the level at the end of August 1992, and entailed a sharp increase in the liquidity of the domestic banking system, providing it with a multiple of the central bank money required for the year as a whole. And support operations in July 1993 added another DM 60 billion to the Bundesbank's external assets. Support in such an order of magnitude calls for the influx to be ended by a realignment, notwithstanding the text of the Treaty according to which they must be continued in 'unlimited' amounts.

Neutralising these liquidity effects posed an exceptional challenge for the Bundesbank. Although the Bundesbank mops up sizeable amounts of liquidity through short-term operations in the money market, these measures allow the Bundesbank to absorb only the liquidity effects of exchange market intervention within an acceptable length of time. The impact on the money stock, by contrast, cannot be controlled as easily.

In the course of September 1992, for example, the money stock M3 expanded at a seasonally adjusted annual rate of 27 per cent. Past experience has shown that there is a time-lag before a reversal in external payment flows leads to a normalisation of the growth of the money stock and that this occurs only if the realignment (or withdrawal from the ERM) is considered to be adequate.

During the last ERM crisis – in July 1993 – there was no realignment but rather a widening of the margins of fluctuation from 2.25 to 15 per cent instead. The only exception is the bilateral exchange rate between the D-Mark and the Dutch guilder, where the old margins were retained, as is feasible given largely parallel developments in the underlying conditions. The transition to wider margins introduces floating exchange rates within the limits mentioned. This helped to overcome the crisis of confidence and to stabilise the system without abandoning it. This also increased the room for manoeuvre for the pursuit of an autonomous national economic policy. At the same time, this pragmatic step took account of the differences in economic performance while maintaining the European integration process. The future of the ERM, and the EMS as a whole, is likely to depend not least on whether economic trends among the participating countries converge to an adequate degree. This demands action not only on the part of monetary policymakers, even though they play a particularly significant role.

In a given exchange rate system, monetary policymakers are faced with different conceptual solutions depending on the size of the country concerned. For small countries, the obvious approach is to peg the exchange rate to the currency of a major country, or to the ECU. This applies explicitly (in the case of Austria and Estonia, for instance) to exchange rates *vis-à-vis* the D-Mark, but in fact also to the Netherlands and a number of other neighbours.

In this connection, Switzerland is a special case. Despite its comparatively small size, Switzerland pursues a monetary policy geared toward national targets, in a system of floating exchange rates. The exchange rate, however, above all that *vis-à-vis* the D-Mark, is considered to be of importance for some monetary policy decisions, but not decisive. On the basis of sound financial conditions and the international reputation of the

Swiss franc, the Swiss National Bank has been able successfully to pursue a policy of safeguarding price stability. And this success is attributable not least to the bank's autonomy in taking monetary policy decisions.

Larger countries, by contrast, could more easily opt for a national monetary policy in the narrow sense; in a system of fixed exchange rates, however, this freedom is limited. Moreover, these countries have a greater responsibility, as their action has implications for other countries. In a global setting of an increasingly free movement of goods, sharp exchange rate fluctuations may also influence trade flows more strongly (lira, US-dollar *vis-à-vis* yen), and may lead to a new misallocation of resources.

The greater openness and increased international integration was also accompanied by a certain adjustment and convergence of the monetary policy instruments available to economies geared to market principles. Specifically, the question for the Bundesbank, and other central banks, is how the desired money market conditions can be achieved most efficiently. Control procedures have generally become more flexible, and there has been an international convergence of the methods used. In retrospect, it would seem that this was mainly ascribable to the innovative powers of the financial markets, which have made repercussions of exchange market developments and international interest rate movements more and more important. As a result, monetary policymakers were able to rely ever-less on their traditional courses of action, such as the active use of discount and lombard policies or variations in minimum reserve ratios (which have a strong signalling effect). Instead, open market policy with all its variants has come to the fore.

While the specific events which gradually led in this direction differed from country to country, the ultimate outcome has been fairly similar. The emphasis of monetary policy action, for instance, is now on open market operations under repurchase agreements, on what are known as securities repurchase agreements. In Germany, over two-thirds of central bank money requirements are met by means of this instrument. These transactions enable the money market rate to be adjusted gradually and flexibly. Open market policy in Germany today features a large number of variants (for example, fixed-rate and variable-rate tenders, different maturities), so that operations can be designed to meet any situation. Official central bank rates – in the German case, the discount rate (for trade bills) and the lombard rate (for 1-day credit) – have, by contrast, come to be used increasingly as supporting instruments, while the international public still attaches an (overly) great weight to them.

The minimum reserve cuts (especially those for time deposits) in recent years and the extension of the scope for issuing liquidity paper which was first used in March 1993, were due mainly to international considerations. The latter have the advantage that, among other things, they can also be used to influence non-banks and their liquidity position direct. This can be helpful, in particular, in the event of heavy inflows of funds in the wake of currency unrest which one wishes to neutralise as directly and comprehensively as possible.

My remarks were intended to show you that, today, no central bank is capable of decoupling or insulating itself from international influences and developments. This held true of the decades in which I worked in the Bundesbank, and no doubt also applies today. New challenges have now been added. Under the Treaty on European Union, which came into effect on 1 November 1993, the exchange rates between the currencies of those countries which meet the entry criteria for the third stage will be fixed irrevocably as from 1999, at the latest (the introduction of a European currency will mark the end of this development). There will then be room for only a single monetary policy for the economies which participate in EMU. It will then be the responsibility of the European Central Bank System to take decisions for its member countries.

In the now-impending second stage, which is to begin on January 1, 1994, monetary policy cooperation is to be strengthened. The Treaty provides for the coordination of the monetary policies of the Member States with the aim of ensuring price stability. However, the individual national central banks will continue to be responsible. This also implies that the D-Mark will retain its anchor role for the time being. In the EMI statute the Maastricht Treaty also provides that the EMI shall 'normally be consulted by the national monetary authorities before they take decisions on the course of monetary policy in the context of the common framework for *ex ante* coordination' (Article 4.1). It will be interesting to see how this will agree with the national sovereignty of monetary policy decisions likewise provided for in the Treaty.

For transition to Stage 3, it will be essential to insist on the strict compliance with the convergence criteria rather than the time schedule. Ahead of the transition, agreement on the monetary policy strategy and the monetary policy instruments available to the European Central Bank will also be necessary. The concept of monetary targeting would be even more advisable for EMU than for a single country like Germany. And as far as the instruments level is concerned, there is probably agreement that open-market policy should be at the centre. The introduction of minimum reserve requirements for all money-creating institutions is in my opinion also to be recommended – especially for a new currency, a new credit system, a new central bank.

Our experience has shown that flexibility and continuity are required to implement an anti-inflationary policy. All that has happened internationally should not make us forget that domestic stability must have first priority for the central bank, both on the national and (in future) on the European plane. As long as one's own house is kept in order, formal co-ordination efforts are easier but also less important. Internationally, there is now no longer any disagreement about this basic orientation. To put it in the words John Maynard Keynes, the great British National Economist, used in 1920:

> There is no subtler, no surer means of overturning the existing basis of society than to debauch the currency. The process engages all the hidden forces of economic law on the side of destruction and does it in a manner which not one man in a million can diagnose.[2]

And this holds true not only in a national, but also and especially in an international context.

Notes

1. King, Mervyn (1993) 'The Bundesbank: a view from the Bank of England', *Quarterly Bulletin*, Bank of England, Vol. 33, pp. 269–74.
2. John Maynard Keynes (1920) *The Economic Consequences of Peace* (London: Macmillan Press).

8 The Triumph of Paper Credit

Michael Mussa*

It is always a pleasure to return to London, where I spent fifteen happy months associated with the International Monetary Research Programme in 1975–6. Those were eventful days in Britain's postwar economic history – in a manner that is relevant to the subject of this lecture. In 1975, the inflation rate in the United Kingdom hit an historic peak of 25 per cent.

Henry Thornton, whom this lecture commemorates, would have well understood the underlying cause of that high inflation rate and of the generally high inflation rates of the 1970s. As a practical man, he might well have recognized that events such as surges in world oil prices played an important role in the annual pattern of inflation; but at a more fundamental level, he would have emphasized the underlying monetary causes of general price inflation. Henry Thornton's great book, *An Enquiry into the Nature and Effects of Paper Credit in Great Britain*, provides a persuasive analysis of how the expansion of the supply of money, under an inconvertible paper standard, brings about a general increase in the level of prices – or, as they referred to this phenomenon two centuries ago, 'a high price of bullion'.

At that time, the link between excessive money creation and inflation was not as well understood as it is today. Indeed, in replying to enquiries from the Parliamentary Select Committee on the High Price of Gold Bullion, the Bank of England relied on the 'real bills doctrine' to deny that its actions had anything at all to do with the problem. Walter Bagehot later described these replies as 'answers almost classical by their nonsense'. Fortunately, now in its three hundredth year of life, and with the benefit of another 185 years of experience since its encounters with Henry Thornton, the Bank of England has learned better; it now clearly recognizes the fundamental responsibility of monetary policy to control inflation – and Her Majesty's Treasury agrees.

* The views expressed in this paper are those of the author and do not represent the views of the International Monetary Fund. This lecture was delivered at City University, London on 10 November 1994.

146

I have titled my lecture this evening, 'The Triumph of Paper Credit'. In one vital respect, Henry Thornton's analytical contributions to monetary economics are far more significant today than when he published them in 1802. Back then, a monetary standard based on inconvertible paper money was an anomaly, an aberration, a temporary expedient to be employed only in times of national crisis. The norm, the standard of sound money, was a currency based on gold, silver or bi-metallism. Now gold and silver are gone from monetary systems all around the world; and everywhere paper money is the accepted norm.

What difference does this fundamental – and I believe permanent – shift in the character of our monetary systems really make? This is the main issue that I plan to address. I do not promise novel answers. In academia, great value is properly placed on new ideas, even if they are often quite bad ideas. In a bureaucracy, especially an international bureaucracy, it is generally better and safer to repeat old truths – in the hope that they really are truths. As a former academic who is now an international bureaucrat, I shall attempt not to be too novel – nor, I hope, too boring.

Concerning the implications of the 'Triumph of Paper Credit', there are five main points to my thesis. Let me set them out and then attempt to defend them.

First, with the demise of metallic monetary standards and the widespread acceptance of discretionary paper standards during the past fifty years, there has been a fundamental change in the long-run behaviour of the general level of prices. Metallic monetary systems compelled stability of the general level of prices over the longer term, with periods of general price inflation offset by periods of general price deflation, and conversely. In contrast, under the modern, discretionary paper standards, deflation is no longer observed, and the general price level exhibits an inexorable upward trend.

Second, modern monetary standards that have taken over from the old metallic standards may usefully be described as 'discretionary paper standards' under which national monetary policies are sequentially adjusted to achieve a variety of generally worthy objectives.[1] Maintenance of a generally low inflation rate is usually one of these worthy objectives (except in high inflation countries where the exigencies of government finance dictate otherwise); but monetary policy is not effectively constrained by the objective of price level stability in the long run. This raises the key issue of what determines the nominal anchor for modern monetary systems in the longer term.

Third, price deflation, which often occurred and was broadly accepted under metallic monetary standards, simply does not appear to be politically feasible under discretionary paper standards. All things considered, this may not be bad. But, without the capacity to move the price level down, after it has gone up, long-term stability of the level of prices – as it existed under metallic standards – cannot be sustained. We should not necessarily be sad about this; but we must recognize that it is an important constraint on the type of nominal anchor that may be established in modern monetary systems.

Fourth, while price deflation is no longer observed and no longer acceptable, the public does appear to accept the necessity of disinflation when the inflation rate has risen above levels regarded as tolerable. The public also appears to accept, perhaps somewhat grudgingly, that disinflation generally has some short-term costs for economic activity and employment. This provides the basis for a 'floating anchor' for national monetary policy; that is, for a commitment for monetary policy to keep the longer-run inflation rate at a low (but positive) level. The trend toward lower rates of inflation in the industrial countries in recent years, together with the apparent willingness to endure the costs necessary to establish this trend, suggests reason for optimism that low long-term rates of inflation will become the established monetary standard.

Fifth, turning from national monetary systems to the international monetary system, I will argue that the old system of metallic monetary standards at the national level naturally supported a system of fixed exchange rates at the international level. In contrast, the triumph of paper credit at the national level strengthens the case for concluding that a system of floating exchange rates among the major national currencies will continue to prevail in the modern monetary era.

In developing these main points, I do not intend to be particularly rigorous. There will be no equations or derivations, and no complex data analyses or statistical tests. It is not that I object to these modern scientific methods for others; I simply do not believe in applying them to my own pet ideas. Instead, I shall rely on a few facts and figures and a good deal of potted history. Monetary economics is a field where an understanding and appreciation of history is arguably more important than a lot of high-powered mathematical and statistical analysis. It is also certainly a field where an understanding of the political dimension is critical; and I shall make repeated reference to the importance of political constraints. On the other hand, monetary economics is the pre-eminent field for economic crackpots; and you always want to be aware of the danger that you may be listening to one.

PRICE STABILITY UNDER THE METALLIC MONARCHS

Until sometime in the present century, national monetary systems were predominantly based on some form of metallic standard. The value of the monetary unit was defined in terms of a specified amount of some metal, most commonly gold or silver or, under bimetallic systems, by a combination of the two. Typically, part of the circulating medium of exchange was also 'full bodied' metallic coin whose monetary value was determined (except for the small minting fee of 'seigniorage') by the weight of bullion contained in the coin. Paper currency in the form of bank notes and bank deposits often formed a larger part of what we would now call the 'money supply' in such systems; but the value of paper money was regulated by the maintenance of its convertibility into the metallic standard.

The Gold Standard that prevailed in the United Kingdom from the end of the Napoleonic Wars to World War I is generally cited as the premier example of a monetary system based on a metallic standard. After 1870, the gold standard became the common monetary standard for most of the industrial world, although some countries such as Mexico and China remained on silver standards well into the present century. Before 1870, however, the gold standard was not predominant; France and much of continental Europe was on a bimetallic standard. Under the French bimetallism, the ratio of the value of gold to silver was set at 15.5 units of silver equivalent to 1 unit of gold. As gold bullion in world markets was worth slightly more than 15.5 times the equivalent weight of silver bullion, by Gresham's law gold largely disappeared from monetary use in France and silver was the predominant monetary standard prior to the Franco–Prussian War.

The United States was also on a bimetallic standard prior to the US Civil War. Under the US standard, however, the equal value ratio for silver to gold was set at 15 to 1 prior to 1834 and then raised to 16 to 1. At the time of the change in the ratio, the world relative price of gold for an equal weight of silver was just above 15.5 to 1 (the French ratio). Accordingly, by Gresham's law, the increase in the monetary value of gold (and reduction in the monetary value of silver) led the United States to shift from a *de facto* silver standard to a *de facto* gold standard in the twenty-five years before the Civil War.[2] Downward pressure on the world relative price of gold after the California gold discoveries reinforced this shift. During the Civil War, the issue of large amounts of 'greenbacks' by the Union government forced the abandonment of the metallic standard and generated sufficient inflation to raise the general price level by about a factor of two. After the war was won by the Union, it was decided to restore the metallic standard. In 1875, Congress passed an Act to re-establish the pre-war gold parity on 1 January 1879.[3]

Although there was the later agitation over silver, the resumption of a metallic monetary standard after the US Civil War was not a particularly controversial issue. As in the United Kingdom after the Napoleonic Wars and after World War I, there was general acceptance that re-establishment of the pre-war metallic standard was to be expected as part of the natural order. By 1873, there had already been a good deal of price deflation in the United States, and more would come, both before the resumption of the gold standard in 1879 and in subsequent years. This price deflation did not come without significant short-term economic pain; but that too was accepted, although not without complaint, as part of the system.

By the mid-1880s, the general price level in the United States had been pushed back to the level prevailing before the Civil War. Price deflation, however, did not stop here. As more countries adopted the gold standard, as the demand for money rose with levels of activity in gold-standard countries, and with the gold supply rising generally less rapidly than demand at a constant price level, moderate price deflation was the norm toward the end of the nineteenth century. In the United States, this situation was exacerbated by the agitation over silver which caused nervousness about the maintenance of the standard and contributed to deflationary pressures that were particularly acute in the economic downturn of the mid-1890s. Indeed, in 1896 the general price level in the United States fell to its lowest level in history. Subsequently, advances in the extraction of gold from low grade ores began to expand the supply of monetary gold and contribute to modest worldwide inflation in the period up to World War I.

The phenomenon of the long-run stability of the price level under the metallic monetary standards is illustrated in the two panels of Figure 8.1 for the United Kingdom and for the United States. Similar behaviour was also observed in other countries that maintained metallic standards for long periods. The long-run stability of prices lasted until the inter-war period when the price level began the long uninterrupted climb that we will discuss shortly. For the present, however, it is relevant to note that long-run stability of the price level over periods of several decades did not preclude substantial shorter-term movements in the price level over periods of a decade or longer.[4] This pattern of very long-run stability of the price level, maintained by offsetting periods of inflation and deflation, was a key characteristic of metallic monetary standards.

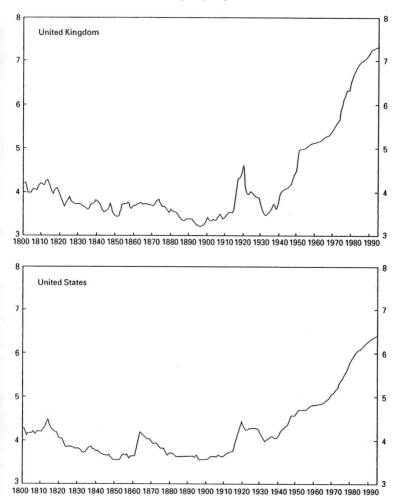

Figure 8.1   Long Price Level Histories: United Kingdom and United States
(logarithm price level, 1950 = ln(100))

From a broader economic perspective, the period of dominance of metallic monetary standards was much like a bed of roses – it had flowers, but also thorns.[5] In order to sustain metallic standards, it was occasionally necessary to subject the economy to bouts of price deflation. This was especially the case when countries left the standard temporarily, usually because of war, and then sought to re-establish it. History records that deflations were often periods of considerable economic pain. Adjusting for the massive economic changes that have occurred during the past century, including the structural shift to less cyclically sensitive industries, it is difficult to know whether occasional deflation under the old monetary regime was actually a great deal more painful than occasional disinflation in the modern era.[6] There should be no illusion, however, that metallic monetary standards were free of serious economic difficulties.

Moreover, it should be stressed that while longer-term price stability was an important consequence of metallic monetary standards, it was probably not the basic reason for the widespread public support of these standards. In the United States, for example, few people probably knew or cared that the general price level tended to return to roughly the same level at intervals of fifty years or so. Nevertheless, there was widespread popular demand for 'sound money' in a form that people could readily understand – namely, in the form of adherence to a metallic monetary standard. In contrast, a purely paper money standard, without convertibility of paper money into something physically valuable, was not easy to understand or accept.[7]

When a country temporarily left its metallic standard because of some emergency, and significant inflation occurred under the paper standard employed during the emergency, there was usually a popular demand to get back to 'sound money' after the emergency was past.[8] This would normally require a painful deflation; but this was tolerated, even desired, in the interests of sound money. The objective, however, was not to restore the general level of prices to what it had been before the emergency. Indeed, before this century, there was no well-defined notion of the general level of prices, and there were no broad-based indices to measure the general price level that captured the public attention. Rather, under the old regime, the public wanted a monetary standard where they could literally see and feel the metal that they believed gave value to money; and where they could (individually if not collectively) convert paper claims denominated in metallic units into the hard metal itself. Deflation was not accepted to maintain or restore the value of money in terms of some non-existent price index, but it was accepted to maintain or restore the metallic value of the currency. Specifically, in Britain after the Napoleonic Wars, the objective was not to go back to the price level of 1790, but rather to go back to the old gold parity of sterling. The same was true after World War I in the United Kingdom and, in the United States, after the Civil War.

Thus, longer-term stability of the price level was an important side-effect of a metallic monetary standard, but was not the primary rationale for the maintenance of such a standard. This point, I believe, is especially important in the modern era of the triumph of paper credit because it reveals the key problem of fixing the longer-term orientation of monetary policy – finding something upon which to focus the popular demand for a money of reasonably stable value.

THE DEATH OF DEFLATION

Metallic monetary standards no longer function on a significant scale anywhere in the world economy. The last tenuous link between gold and actually functioning monetary systems was not finally eliminated until the early 1970s, when the United States government formally withdrew its commitment to convert dollars into gold for official payments. Nostalgia for the monetary rigours of the gold standard lives on in some quarters; but, practically speaking, the gold standard and other metallic monetary standards departed from the hearts, minds, and pockets of most mortals well before the early 1970s.

When, exactly, the age of metallic money really ended is somewhat difficult to say. The question is rather like when, precisely, did the Russian monk Rasputin actually die? Even for quite determined assassins, Rasputin proved difficult to kill. He was poisoned, stabbed, shot, cut up into pieces, burned to ashes, and blasted through a canon. Surely, at the end of that process, Rasputin was scientifically dead – at normal levels of statistical confidence. But when, exactly, Rasputin died – that remains somewhat of a mystery.

From Figure 8.1, it is clear that since sometime in the inter-war period there has been a dramatic change in the long-run behaviour of the price level. Since this time, the price level has exhibited a persistent upward trend and a very large cumulative upward movement. Indeed, the logarithmic scale of these charts somewhat conceals the magnitude of the change. In the United States, the general price level is up by about a factor of 7 or 8 since the 1930s. In the United Kingdom, the price level is up by about a factor of 20 or 30 in this period. Other industrial countries have experienced similar, in some cases even more dramatic, changes in the long-run behaviour of their price levels. The observed change is not like the temporary inflations that have afflicted some countries; it is a fundamental change in the longer term behaviour of the price level that has no historical precedent. This change in the long-run behaviour of the price level clearly reflects a fundamental change in the nature of the monetary regime – from a widespread popular demand for a metallic standard as the essence of sound money, to general acceptance of *permanent* monetary standards based on (inconvertible) paper monies. The world has indeed seen the triumph of monetary systems based on paper credit.[9]

In addition to the long-term upward trend in the price level visible in Figure 8.1, the new monetary standards have made another important difference for price level behaviour that is more easily seen in Figure 8.2.

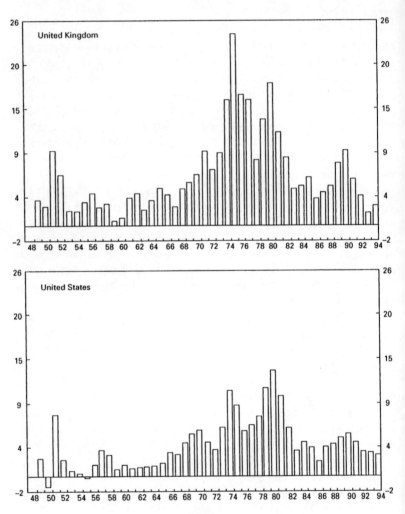

Figure 8.2   Annual Inflation: United Kingdom and United States
(in per cent)

This chart shows the annual inflation rate, based on the consumer price index, for the United Kingdom and the United States for each year since the late 1940s. Of course, with the upward trend in the price level exhibited in Figure 8.1, it is not surprising that the inflation rates exhibited in Figure 8.2 are generally positive. Beyond this, however, there is a key phenomenon to which I want to draw attention – with the passing of metallic monetary standards, we have seen the death of deflation.

The last time there was an annual drop in consumer prices in the United States was in 1954, with the end of the Korean War, a recession, and a substantial decline in world commodity prices. For the United Kingdom, there has been no year in the post-war period when consumer prices have recorded a measurable decline; you have to go back to the 1930s. For other industrial countries, the story is the same. Germany and Japan saw small declines in consumer prices in 1986, when their general inflation rates were quite low and there was a large drop in world oil prices. Broadening the sample to the G-7 industrial countries, we find no further instances of an annual decline in consumer prices in the post-war era. Indeed, for all of the industrial countries in the post-war era, we can probably count on the fingers of one hand the number of years in which any country has recorded a measured decline in consumer prices. And, to the extent that we have seen any deflation, it has been very small and very brief. The last time that we saw a substantial and persistent decline in the general price level was in the early 1930s during the great depression.[10]

Given the evidence, I think that we have to conclude that deflation, like Rasputin, is indeed dead. Why? And, what should we make of it?

Why? I believe that the answer is clear – at least for deflation, if not for Rasputin. Under a metallic monetary standard, deflation had a broadly accepted and easily understood goal – to maintain, or in the most important cases, to restore the metallic value of the currency. Under a permanent paper currency standard, there is no comparable goal to attract the popular mind. Who now argues that the economy should be put through the intense pain of deflation in order to restore some measure of the general price index back to some arbitrarily prescribed level? What index? What level? It just doesn't have the popular appeal of restoring the pound or the dollar to its gold parity. And the mystique of the gold standard is now gone and cannot be resurrected. There is no popular demand to restore the 'barbarous relic' to the High Altar of the Temple of Mammon.

So what? Should we be sad about the death of deflation? He was an irksome companion; and there is really no persuasive evidence that his economic influence was positive, in comparison with a monetary regime that sustains a positive but very low long-run inflation rate. Nevertheless, we should recognize that with no practical means to generate much popular support to impose deflation on the economy, the long-term trend of the general price level will surely be upward.

On this issue, I part company from some of my academic and other colleagues who analyse optimal rates of deflation or consider various schemes to assure long-run price stability. Even in the countries with the strongest records for maintaining *low inflation*, there is no evident desire to push back past increases in the price level, as would be necessary to achieve long-run price stability. Without the popular support for deflation deriving from widespread acceptance of the mystique of metallic money, there is no practical means for achieving long-run price stability. Rather, with the triumph of paper credit, the practical task is to find a nominal anchor for monetary policy that will provide reasonable assurance of a very low, but probably still positive, long-run inflation rate.[11] I turn to that issue now.

THE SEARCH FOR A NEW 'MONETARY STANDARD'

The end of long-term price level stability with the popular abandonment of metallic monetary standards, and the death of deflation during the modern monetary era, have necessitated the search for new monetary standards. There is a large and growing analytical literature on this subject and on related issues such as the institutional virtues of 'independent' central banks in assuring low inflation. In practice, however, I believe that the search for new monetary standards is better understood as an historical than as an analytical process. Specifically, to understand where we are now in that process, and where we are likely to go, it is useful to review briefly the key monetary developments of the post-war era.

During the first half of this era, the effective monetary standard in most areas of the world was determined primarily by two key elements: by the monetary policy of the United States, and by the Bretton Woods system of pegged but adjustable exchange rates through which most countries effectively linked their monetary policies to that of the United States. In effect, for most other countries, pegging the value of domestic paper money to the US dollar became the substitute for the old metallic standard.

In a limited way the central currency of the Bretton Woods system, the US dollar, remained formally linked to gold; the United States adopted the commitment to convert official holdings of dollars into gold at the fixed price of $35 per ounce. This limited official link of the dollar to gold undoubtedly added to the political acceptability of an international monetary system based *de facto* on a dominant national currency. In many important respects, however, this substitute metallic standard was only a pale reflection of the original. No country retained gold coins or gold-backed notes as a significant part of the circulating medium of exchange. In the United States, the only country whose national currency was formally linked to gold for official international transactions, domestic holdings of gold for monetary purposes and the denomination of transactions or contracts in terms of gold were legally prohibited. In the aftermath of World War II, most other countries devalued their national currencies against the US dollar and hence against gold. Unlike the situations after previous major wars, there was no great push to restore the old gold parities or even to introduce new parities for a renewed metallic standard. The psychological importance of the metallic standard to the popular mind as the essential foundation of 'sound money' was seriously eroded.

Moreover, the monetary policy of the world's key central bank, the US Federal Reserve, was primarily determined by domestic objectives, rather than by adherence to the principles of the gold standard. In general, from the end of the war through the 1950s and 1960s, the Federal Reserve allowed the US money supply to expand to meet the demands of a growing economy; and it persisted in this general policy despite a cumulatively substantial decline in the US gold reserve. Thus, the effective monetary standard in the United States was really a *discretionary paper standard*. The effective monetary standard was determined by the sequence of decisions by the Federal Reserve about how to conduct monetary policy in the light of a variety of primarily domestic economic objectives. Occasionally, the commitment to the metallic parity of the dollar may have been something of a constraining influence on US monetary policy, but that influence was rarely decisive.

Through the mid-1960s, the Federal Reserve's monetary policy delivered a consistently positive but generally quite low inflation rate in the United States. Other countries that pegged their currencies rigidly to the US dollar generally experienced similarly positive but low inflation rates, with some rapidly growing countries (most notably Japan) generally seeing modestly higher inflation despite the maintenance of a fixed exchange-rate parity. Countries whose national monetary policies accommodated moderately higher inflation than was consistent with the maintenance of a fixed parity against the US dollar needed to make occasional downward adjustment in the parities of their currencies against the dollar. By recent standards, however, these adjustments were not particularly large or frequent. Only one major country, Germany, pursued a national monetary policy that necessitated upward adjustments in the value of its currency against the US dollar, once in 1962 and again in 1969. Thus, until the late 1960s, there was no general clamour against the monetary policy regime managed by the Federal Reserve, either at home or abroad. There was no popular demand to impose deflation on the US economy and on the world economy. There was no general call for a return to the rigours of a real gold standard. During the 1950s and 1960s, the dollar reigned supreme. The metallic monarchs no longer held sovereign sway over the effective monetary standard, even if many of their relics happened to be buried at Fort Knox or in the basement of the New York Federal Reserve.

When the Federal Reserve did tighten US monetary policy, its purpose was usually to resist the rise of inflation, not to induce actual deflation or to defend the gold parity of the dollar. For example, when the Federal Reserve tightened US monetary policy in 1957, it was because of concern about an inflation rate that had risen to the then-uncomfortable level of 3 per cent. When the US economy fell into a deep recession in 1958, the Federal Reserve eased monetary policy. Concern about the loss of gold may have been one factor that contributed to the Federal Reserve's tightening of monetary policy again in 1960, but a more important concern was the perception that the recovery was proceeding at a sufficiently rapid pace that inflationary pressures might re-emerge.

The first four years of the long US expansion that began in May 1961 proceeded at a vigorous pace and with low inflation. The Federal Reserve maintained monetary policy in a quite accommodative stance. The decline in US gold reserves was viewed as a problem – to be addressed by other measures. Only when inflationary pressures began to pick up visibly did the Federal Reserve turn to a tightening of monetary policy in the 'credit crunch' of 1966 which temporarily slowed the pace of expansion. The substantial and persistent tightening of monetary policy that the Federal Reserve undertook in 1969, which precipitated the end of the expansion, was motivated by concern with an unacceptable rise in the rate of inflation to over 6 per cent. The recession of 1970–1 led to a significant easing of US monetary conditions, and this stance of monetary policy was maintained despite increasing evidence of deteriorating conditions for the US dollar in the foreign exchange market. Indeed, at the time, people spoke of a policy of 'benign neglect' toward the dollar on the part of the US authorities. It is clear that domestic concerns – about growth and inflation – dominated the conduct of US monetary policy.

Meanwhile, as the US inflation rate accelerated in the late 1960s, other countries became less satisfied with a monetary standard dominated by the policies of the US Federal Reserve. Dissatisfaction grew during 1970–1 as

US monetary policy remained directed toward domestic economic objectives and paid little regard to the rapid worldwide expansion of dollar-dominated liquidity. Recycling of dollar liquidity through the Eurodollar market helped magnify this problem. The crisis came during the summer of 1971 when, during a six-week period, the deterioration of US reserves on an official settlement basis amounted to more than the total reserves held by any other central bank in any previous year. On August 15, President Richard Nixon announced the imposition of domestic wage and price controls, introduced an across-the-board import surcharge, formally closed the gold window, and *de facto* floated the exchange rate of the dollar. The Bretton Woods system, and more generally the monetary standard based on broad international acceptance of the discretionary policies of the US Federal Reserve, had been dealt a mortal blow.

There was a brief effort to resurrect that system, formalized in the Smithsonian – an event which Richard Nixon described as 'the greatest monetary agreement in the history of the world'. It survived barely more than one year. With a continued rapid expansion of dollar-denominated liquidity, and with the boom in economic activity ongoing in all of the industrial countries, global inflationary pressures began to mount. Other countries, most importantly Germany, became fed up with the rise of domestic inflationary pressures that could not be contained so long as their currencies remained pegged to the US dollar and so long as the US Federal Reserve continued to pursue an expansionary monetary policy. In March 1973 the Bretton Woods system and the dollar-denominated world monetary standard gasped its final breath.

It is noteworthy that when the dollar-based world monetary system finally broke down in the early 1970s, there was no attempt to move back to national monetary systems or an international monetary system based on metallic standards. Indeed, by common consent, gold was formally written out of the international monetary system in the Second Amendment of the IMF's Articles of Agreement. The essential requirement for a metallic monetary standard – the popular demand for its institution and maintenance – had disappeared.

Even in retrospect, it is difficult to say how much of an effect in restraining inflation should be attributed to the limited role played by gold under the Bretton Woods system. Arguably, the commitment to maintain the gold parity of the dollar was a restraining influence on US monetary expansion before the early 1970s. Also, the role of gold contributed to the international acceptability of a dollar standard, with the understanding that US monetary policy was subject to some external discipline. And the dollar-based system of pegged exchange rates (together with a low-inflation policy of the Federal Reserve) arguably imposed a useful discipline against inflation in many countries. Certainly, average inflation rates in all countries moved up significantly in the 1970s; and in most countries inflation has only recently, or not yet, been reduced to the generally low levels that prevailed during the 1950s and 1960s.

However, during the period of the Bretton Woods system, there was no general desire, in the United States or elsewhere, for the Federal Reserve to run a generally deflationary monetary policy, as probably would have been required to sustain the official gold price in the face of rapidly expanding volumes of world output and trade. In the United States, people seemed quite happy with a low but still positive inflation rate. Most other countries either maintained rigid pegs of their currencies to the US dollar or occasionally had to depreciate. Worries about the long-run sustainability of the official gold price (the Triffin problem) were met with proposals to expand the effective gold base of the international monetary system by creating 'paper gold' in the form of Special Drawing Rights (SDRs) at the International Monetary Fund. The remedy of changing the official gold price (as permitted under the IMF's Articles of Agreement) was employed only as the system was collapsing in 1972. There was no stomach to employ the classic mechanism for sustaining a metallic standard – general and significant price deflation. In this critical respect, the old gold standard was already dead.

THE EMERGING MONETARY STANDARD

Since 1973, the functioning monetary standard in the world economy has continued to be a *discretionary paper standard*, but it has not been a single world standard dominated by one prominent national currency. Rather, under the regime of floating exchange rates that replaced the Bretton Woods system, many countries have chosen to operate their own discretionary paper standards in pursuit of their own, primarily domestic, economic objectives. Some countries, of course, have chosen to peg the exchange rates of their national currencies to those of partner countries and have accordingly discretionary monetary standards that are dominated by that commitment. Leaving aside this complexity and focusing on the major countries that maintain separate national monetary standards, it is fair to say that the effective monetary standard has been determined by the sequence of choices about how to conduct monetary policy directed at a variety of economic objectives.

Two main objectives appear to affect monetary policies in large countries in the modern era of discretionary paper standards: monetary policies generally seek to keep the general rate of price inflation under reasonable control; and, subject to this constraint, monetary policies seek to support sustainable real growth in the economy. Figures 8.3 through 6 provide some relevant information on this score for Germany, Japan, the United Kingdom, and the United States.

Although it may be a little difficult to see, there is a general pattern of monetary policy behaviour that is common to all of these figures. When the inflation rate begins to accelerate significantly, monetary policy is tightened, as reflected in a significant increase in short-term interest rates. Subsequently, economic activity begins to decline under the impact of tighter monetary policy. Somewhat later, when the monetary tightening appears to be achieving its intended goal, the inflation rate also declines and generally keeps falling for a while as the economy begins to recover. Monetary policy, as indicated by short-term interest rates, generally begins to ease when the economy falls into recession; this sometimes happens before the cyclical peak in the measured inflation rate (but when there is reason to believe that inflation is on a downward track). Monetary policy generally retains a relatively easy stance through the initial stages of recovery. Then the cycle repeats as inflationary pressures begin to rise in the later stages of the expansion.

There are, of course, important differences in this general pattern across countries and over time. In both of the upsurges of inflation in 1973–6 and again in 1978–81, the Bundesbank acted early and aggressively to tighten monetary conditions. In both episodes, the rise of inflation in Germany was significantly better contained than in the other three countries. In the first episode, the monetary policy response to the rise of inflation was relatively lax in both Japan and the United Kingdom; and this was reflected in the substantial rise of inflation to annualized rates of over 20 per cent in both countries. During the second episode, monetary policy reacted more forcefully to contain the rise of inflation in both Japan and the United Kingdom. In contrast, in the United States, monetary policy did better in containing the rise of inflation during the first episode, although not as well as in Germany; but, in the second episode, US monetary policy did worse. The US economy and much of the world economy paid a significant price for correcting this mistake in the severe tightening of US monetary policy that was necessary in the early 1980s to restore the Federal Reserve's credibility.

Learning the lesson from this bitter experience, during the long expansion that began in late 1982, the Federal Reserve acted to contain any early

162

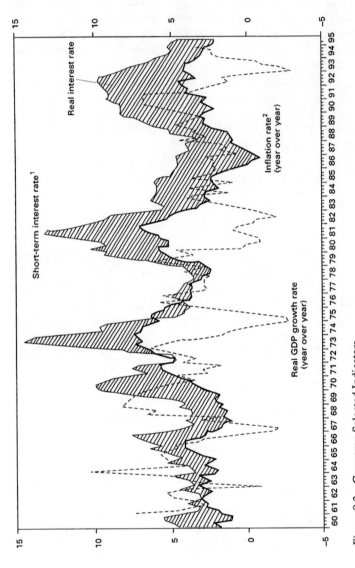

Figure 8.3   Germany: Selected Indicators
(in per cent)

[1] 3-month interbank deposit rate; quarterly average.
[2] CPI; quarterly average.

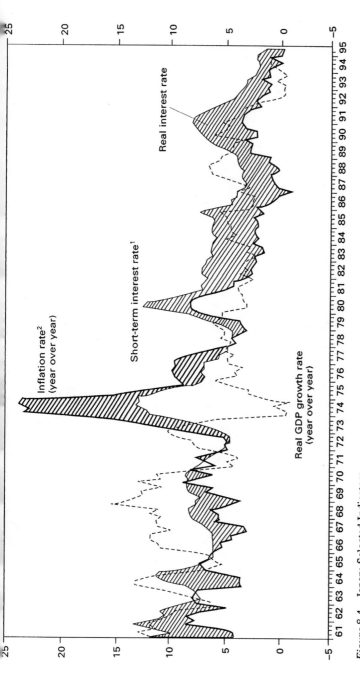

Figure 8.4 Japan: Selected Indicators
(in per cent)

[1] Money market rate; quarterly average.
[2] CPI; quarterly average.

164

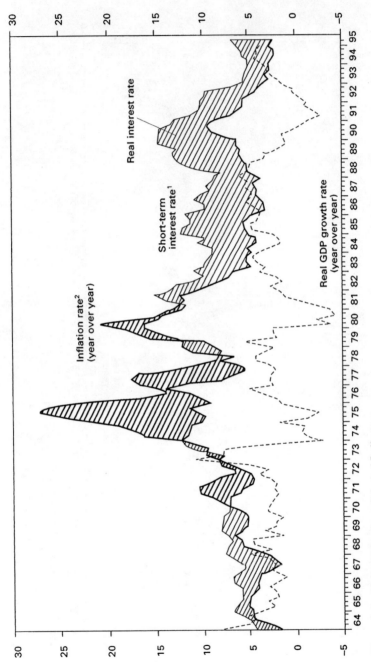

Figure 8.5 United Kingdom: Selected Indicators
(in per cent)

[1] 3-month Treasury bill rate; quarterly average.
[2] CPI; quarterly average.

165

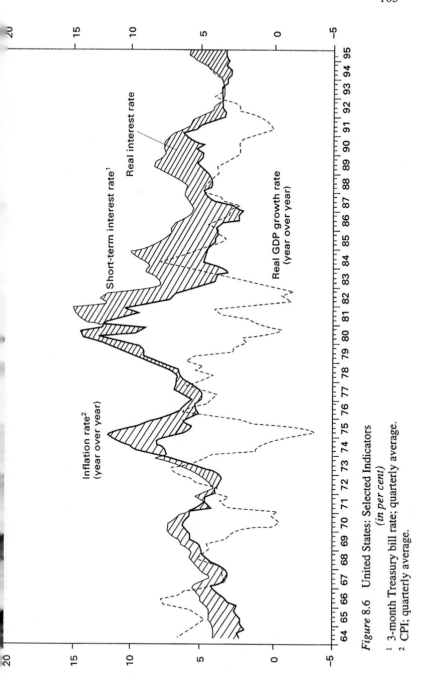

Figure 8.6   United States: Selected Indicators
(in per cent)

[1] 3-month Treasury bill rate; quarterly average.
[2] CPI; quarterly average.

resurgence of inflation and, in the late 1980s, acted relatively early to tighten monetary conditions as inflationary pressures began to rise. The peak of US inflation in 1990 was less than half of the peaks in 1974 and 1980, and the recession of 1990–1 was comparatively mild. Unfortunately, many other industrial countries did not do so well in containing the inflationary overheating of their economies in the late 1980s; and, in the necessary corrections brought on by monetary tightening, they suffered relatively severe recessions. In part, however, this may have been attributable to the fact that inflationary pressures in the late 1980s showed up more in asset prices than in goods prices or wages.[12] This novelty made the problem more difficult to diagnose, delayed the necessary cure, and worsened the unavoidable side effects.

From the diversity of experience with discretionary paper standards adopted by various national monetary authorities during the past two decades, I believe that we may draw four important lessons.

First, policy makers and the general public have learned that there is no long-run trade-off between tolerating higher rates of inflation and achieving higher levels of economic activity or more rapid rates of economic growth. Earlier, based on evidence from long periods of overall price level stability, it had been believed that there might be such a trade-off, as exemplified by the statistical relationship in the well-known Phillip's curve. By the early 1970s, the influential work of Friedman and Phelps helped to persuade many economists there was no such long-run trade-off. People might be temporarily surprised by an increase in nominal demand and respond with increases in output as well as in prices. But, once expectations of inflation had been adjusted to a rise of actual inflation, there would be no long-run gain in output or employment.

In practice, I do not believe that it was primarily the theoretical analysis of Friedman and Phelps that changed minds on the idea of the long-run trade-off. Rather, it was the actual experience with higher rates of inflation in the industrial countries during the 1970s and early 1980s that persuaded the general public, and hence policymakers, that higher rates of inflation did not necessarily mean better economic times. Indeed, in some respects, the experience of the 1970s may even have given inflation an unduly bad reputation because adverse supply shocks contributed to the negative economic consequences associated with higher inflation. In any event, as a result of the experience of the 1970s, inflation lost its deceptive allure as a possible path to greater economic prosperity.

Second, it is also clear from the experience of the past two decades that disinflation, like the deflation of earlier times, typically has painful short-term costs for the economy. Among the industrial countries, experience consistently shows that significant reductions in the rate of inflation tend to be associated with relatively deep recessions.[13] Conversely, experience in many countries shows when the *level* of economic activity is abnormally high, prices (including asset prices) tend to rise relatively rapidly. Macroeconomists summarize these phenomena in the idea that there is a short-run trade off between economic activity and inflation.

However, I reject the notion – developed in many theoretical models – that we have generally positive inflation (in the leading industrial countries) because of a 'dynamic inconsistency problem'; that is, because policy makers cannot credibly commit themselves to avoid exploiting this short-run trade-off and, therefore, society is condemned to a sub-optimal equilibrium with unduly high inflation.[14] Rather, I prefer the explanation that without the psychological imperative of a metallic monetary standard, there is no effective way to generate popular support for *deflation* of the price level; and, accordingly, the long-run average inflation rate is necessarily positive. During an expansion, there is a natural tendency for inflationary pressures to rise as the economy gathers strength. Sensible monetary policy may contain the rise of inflation for some time and gain thereby the benefits of a more durable expansion. Eventually, however, a mistake is made, and inflation gathers momentum. Then, the necessary monetary cure brings on at least a significant slowdown in economic growth and often a recession. In this process, there is a statistical association between higher levels of activity and higher rates of inflation; but there is not necessarily any effort of monetary policy to exploit the 'trade-off' that appears to be suggested by this statistical association.

Third, experience indicates that national policy authorities and the general public are willing to accept the short-term economic costs of disinflation in order to reduce inflation to low positive rates. Of course, most policy makers may not want to admit this too explicitly; but the facts clearly show that tightening monetary policy to dis-inflate the economy has significant short-term costs for activity and employment. Nevertheless, the experience of the past two decades clearly demonstrates that the policy authorities in most countries are prepared to pay the price when it is necessary in order to reduce the inflation rate to politically acceptable levels.

Indeed, inflation rates in the industrial countries generally peaked in the 1970s or early 1980s and have recently been distinctly lower than they were a decade or so ago. This is not an accident. It is a consequence of choices that have been made about the conduct of national monetary policy under the prevailing discretionary paper standards. These choices generally have enjoyed popular support. Governments that have successfully brought down inflation (or supported their monetary authorities in such efforts) have not generally been ejected from office; governments that have presided over significant increases in inflation have often not fared so well.

Thus, broadly speaking, the public no longer accepts deflation, but neither does it tolerate ever-accelerating inflation. When the rate of inflation rises above some generally acceptable level, the public expects that effective action will be taken to reduce the inflation rate, even at the expense of some negative impact to the shorter-term level of economic activity. The practical implication is that while a return to long-run price level stability may not be feasible because of a general lack of political support and tolerance for price deflation, discretionary paper monetary standards may well be consistent with low positive inflation rates over the longer term.

To use an analogy, the old-time monetary regimes based on metallic standards and with occasional sharp price deflation were like old-fashioned dentistry – dentistry without painkillers. That is no longer acceptable. The more modern practice, which involves occasional disinflation, is dentistry with painkillers. It is not necessarily pleasant, but it is accepted as necessary.

Fourth, recent experience suggests that there is growing understanding of the desirability of monetary policies that guard against a significant upsurge of inflationary pressures as the best way to avoid both the costs of inflation and the pain of dis-inflation. To run such a policy, the monetary authority must be appropriately forward looking. Because of the lags in the effects of monetary policy, monetary conditions must be tightened as the economy approaches the level of activity at which inflationary pressures are likely to emerge; but the tightening should not be so much and so soon that the expansion is killed-off prematurely. The prudent tightening of monetary conditions undertaken in 1994 in the United States, the United Kingdom, and Australia – in advance of any increase in measured price inflation – is evidence that this important lesson is being learned.

It is also relevant that an increasing number of countries, including the United Kingdom, are adopting explicit objectives for monetary policy stated in terms of low long-term inflation rates. The adoption of such inflation targets, of course, is not a substitute for pursuit of the policies that will deliver low inflation; and the adoption of such targets is not logically necessary to establish or maintain a low-inflation monetary standard. Nevertheless, the adoption and acceptance of such targets, together with the implementation of an appropriately forward-looking monetary policy, can be an important signal that a low-inflation monetary regime is in operation.

In summary, the recent trend of monetary developments in the industrial countries is a relatively hopeful one. Undoubtedly, we have seen the triumph of paper credit. All of our experience under discretionary paper money standards for the past fifty years suggests that we will probably have to live in the longer run with a positive trend in the general level of prices. However, experience does not indicate that the trend for the inflation *rate* is forever upward under such monetary standards. Rather, in accord with popular demand, national monetary regimes seem to be moving toward the delivery of relatively low long-term inflation rates.

IMPLICATIONS FOR THE INTERNATIONAL MONETARY SYSTEM

So far I have dwelt on the implications of the triumph of paper credit for the nature of national monetary systems and the behaviour of national price levels. To conclude I would like to turn to the implications of the widespread adoption of discretionary paper standards at the national level for the nature and operation of the international monetary system. Again, it is useful to take an historical approach.

In this, the fiftieth anniversary year of the Bretton Woods conference that established the International Monetary Fund and the World Bank, one often hears the complaint that since the collapse of the par value system in the early 1970s, there really has been no international monetary system. It should be recognized, however, that under the metallic monetary standards that prevailed prior to Bretton Woods, there also was nothing that could really be described as an international monetary system. There was, of course, some communication and cooperation among key central banks and important private banks on a variety of international financial issues. Sometimes, cooperation was quite extensive, most notably in the efforts after World War I to reconstruct national monetary systems and financial institutions in a number of European countries. But there were no formally agreed international rules of the game for the world monetary system, and there was no institution to supervise the operation of these rules. Nevertheless, under the old metallic standards, in contrast to what we have seen recently, exchange rates among major currencies generally remained highly stable over long periods of time, for example, the exchange rate between the sterling and the US dollar. How was this possible for much of the period before Bretton Woods, without formal rules of the international monetary system and without an effective mechanism to enforce these rules? Why is the same seemingly not possible today? What, if anything, could be done to change this situation, if such change were desirable?

In considering these questions, I believe that it is essential to recognize that under the old metallic standards, the fundamental character of the international monetary system was the by-product of the national monetary standard adopted by various countries. If two countries adopted the same metallic standard for their national currencies, then the international exchange rate between their currencies was automatically fixed (within the cost margins for transporting metallic bullion) by the relative amount of that metal in each country's national currency unit. For example, when the United States and the United Kingdom were both on the gold standard between 1879 and 1914, the exchange rate was effectively fixed within a narrow range around $4.86 to the pound. Foreign exchange market transactions were, of course, dominated by exchanges of dollars for pounds and not by shipments of gold. But, in terms of the basic conception of the system, people did not think of the international exchange value of the dollar as being determined by pegging the exchange rate of the dollar against the pound sterling. Rather, because the dollar was fixed in terms of gold and because sterling was fixed in terms of gold, by convenient accident the exchange rate between the dollar and sterling was also fixed.

Under metallic monetary standards, when different countries were on two different metallic standards, gold and silver, the exchange rate among their currencies was not automatically fixed. Rather, it fluctuated along with the world relative price of these two metals. In fact, however, for several centuries until late in the last century, the world relative price of gold and silver moved within a fairly narrow range, almost always lying between 15 to 1 and 16 to 1. This is a much smaller range of fluctuation than is now typically observed for nominal or real exchange rates among major national currencies. Why was the range of fluctuation in the relative price of gold and silver before 1870 so narrow, and why should not the same situation prevail for exchange rates among national currencies under modern paper standards?

Part of the answer is that when both metals were being widely used as monetary standards, stocks of these metals held for monetary use were very large relative to annual production. Demands to hold stocks of money also tended to be quite stable in an era of generally stable prices. This imparted considerable stability to the relative price of gold and silver.

Even more important was the maintenance of bi-metallic monetary regimes prior to 1870 by several important countries. The monetary exchange ratios in these bi-metallic regimes were generally set between 15 to 1 and 16 to 1. For a country running a bi-metallic system, a small shift in the world price of gold and silver, above or below the ratio set in the monetary standard, would induce, via Gresham's Law, the country to shift its *de facto* monetary standard either entirely into gold or entirely into silver. This happened when the United States raised the monetary ratio of silver to gold from 15:1 to 16:1 in the 1830s. Analytically, the effect was to introduce long horizontal sections to the schedule which plots the world demand for the stock of gold relative to the stock of silver (on the horizontal axis) against the world relative price of gold and silver (on the vertical axis), corresponding to the monetary ratios of different countries maintaining bi-metallic standards. With many countries maintaining bi-metallic standards with ratios in the range between 15:1 and 16:1, the result was to stabilize the world relative price of gold and silver within this range for several centuries. When bi-metallism was generally abandoned in favour of the gold standard in the early 1870s, stocks of silver previously held for monetary use flooded on to the world market, and silver lost half of its value against gold within 25 years.

In the modern era of paper currency standards, it remains true that the national monetary standard must perform in a manner that is broadly acceptable to the general public. But does such 'broadly acceptable performance' imply a significant popular demand that the national monetary standard should deliver stability of the exchange rate of a country's national money against the national monies of other countries?

In a number of European countries, especially on the continent, there is strong sympathy for a system of pegged exchange rates, at least among European currencies. Since the collapse of the Bretton Woods system at the world level, there have been several European efforts to construct a zone of exchange rate stability. Since 1979 these efforts have been formalized in the Exchange Rate Mechanism (ERM) of the European Monetary System (EMS). Despite the formal widening of the bands for exchange rate fluctuation in the summer of 1993, most of the remaining participants in the ERM continue to place considerable emphasis on limiting exchange rate fluctuations. Moreover, for the future of the European Union, the Maastricht Treaty provides for the construction of a European Monetary Union (EMU) with the ultimate goal of a common currency and with a European Central Bank (ECB) to manage monetary policy for this common currency.

However, the effort to create a European Monetary Union should not be thought of as an isolated attempt to provide an enhanced mechanism for fixing exchange rates among European currencies. EMU is clearly part of a much broader effort to create a more united Europe – economically, socially, and politically.[15] Those who favour a closely united Europe also generally favour EMU, both for what they expect to be its likely substantive contribution to stronger economic integration and as a key symbol of a deeper union in other important dimensions. Those who are sceptical about a tight, multi-dimensional European union also tend to be sceptical about EMU, for both substantive and symbolic reasons.

What type of monetary standard is a European Central Bank likely to establish when, and if, it comes into being? It will not attempt to reinstate a metallic monetary standard. Rather, as provided in the Maastricht Treaty, the ECB will operate a discretionary paper standard. By law, the objective of price stability will have priority. In effect, the intention is to create a central bank that will pursue, at the European level, the same monetary policy objectives that the Bundesbank has pursued in Germany. Any tendency for inflation to rise above a very low rate will be resisted aggressively, but inflation will probably not be zero; and, subject to the condition that inflation is acceptably low, monetary policy will not be indifferent to economic activity. As with Bundesbank policy at present, pursuit of primarily domestic objectives for European monetary policy implies that the ECB will give relatively little weight to stabilizing exchange rates *vis-à-vis* key non-European currencies.

Turning from the situation within Europe to the international monetary system, there appears to be little prospect of moving back toward a more 'rules-based' system that would deliver substantially greater fixity of exchange rates among the currencies of the three largest countries. As previously discussed, when the popular will demanded metallic standards at the national level, stability of exchange rates among national currencies came along as a by-product. However, with the widespread acceptance of discretionary paper standards at the national level, pegging of exchange rates among national currencies can only come as a consequence of deliberate decisions to adjust national monetary policies to the needs of maintaining exchange rate pegs and, correspondingly, to divert national monetary policies from other objectives.

Under the Bretton Woods system, most nations did pursue national monetary policies consistent with the pegging of exchange rates to the US dollar. But that was when the US economy held a preponderant position in the world economy, when the US dollar retained a formal link to gold, when there was widespread confidence that US monetary policy would maintain a consistently low inflation rate, and when the heritage of thinking from long experience with metallic monetary standards had accustomed the popular mind to the idea that fixed exchange rates among national currencies were an integral element of the natural order of international monetary affairs.

Now, after more than two decades of floating exchange rates among the world's major currencies, the basis for the establishment and maintenance of an international system of pegged exchange rates has been seriously and irrevocably eroded. The US economy remains the world's largest, but its position is no longer so commanding that pegging to the US dollar appears to be a natural choice for other important industrial countries. With the official banishment of gold from world monetary affairs, there is no neutral asset with a long history of monetary stability that provides the political and psychological basis for an international system of pegged exchange rates. After a general upsurge in the 1970s, inflation rates in the industrial countries have generally been reduced to levels close to those prevailing in the 1950s and 1960s.

For several important countries, it also is not perceived that the monetary policy implied by pegging the exchange rate to the US dollar would deliver satisfactory performance in terms of key domestic objectives, in comparison with what would be, and has been, achieved by an independent national monetary policy. In particular, after the general upsurge of inflation during the 1970s, inflation rates in most industrial countries have been substantially reduced and, during the 1990s, are running close to the levels prevailing in the 1950s and 1960s. Successful efforts to reduce national inflation rates, however, are rightly seen as accomplishments of national monetary policies and not as the by-product of the disinflation that has also been achieved in the United States. Thus, with the ascendancy of independent discretionary paper standards, the old mechanisms that formerly translated popularly accepted national monetary standards into an international system of fixed exchange rates have ceased to operate; and, with the gearing of national monetary policies to key domestic objectives, the international monetary system has necessarily shifted to a regime of floating exchange rates among major national currencies.

Indeed, following this line of argument, it is questionable whether the *international* gold standard system could have been sustained politically in earlier times if that system had been understood primarily as a mechanism for fixing exchange rates among national monies. Consider the situation in the United States during the deflation of the mid-1890s. In the summer of 1896 in a massive circus tent at 63rd Street and Cottage Grove Avenue, about half a mile from my office at the University of Chicago, William Jennings Bryan railed against the injustices of the gold standard and called for the free coinage of silver: 'Thou shall not crucify mankind upon this cross of gold'. With the effects of deflation crushing particularly hard on the rural areas of the country, Bryan carried every state south of the

Mason–Dixon line and west of the Mississippi and almost won the presidential election.

For Bryan and his supporters, the monetary demon was gold and the eastern banks and financiers who supported the gold standard.[16] For those on the other side, however, the gold standard was the pre-eminent guarantee of 'sound money' and Bryan and his proposal for the free coinage of silver were the inflationist threat. In the event, the majority of electoral votes lay in those states that felt less intensely the pain of deflation and that worried more about the inflationary effects of a return to silver. Imagine, however, what the political situation would have been without gold, but with a pegged exchange rate of the US dollar to sterling. In that case, the demon exerting severe deflationary pressure on important sectors of the US economy would not have been the need to maintain the gold standard as the essence of 'sound money'. Rather, the deflationary effort would have been needed to sustain the exchange rate of the dollar against the paper currency of 'perfidious Albion'. With the campaign issue phrased in these terms, Bryan might well have won the election.[17]

Attempting to draw such conclusions for the mid-1890s, of course, is highly speculative. In contrast, for the mid-1990s similar conclusions may be reached at extremely high levels of confidence. In the largest industrial countries, there is obviously no widespread popular demand to adjust monetary policy to the needs of fixed exchange rates with other major currencies, at the expense of the broadly accepted domestic goals for monetary policy. National monetary authorities probably have some limited latitude in this area, as the linkage of monetary policy to key domestic objectives is not very precise; but public opinion in the largest countries is not prepared to accept painful decisions about national monetary policy that have unpalatable consequences for economic growth or domestic inflation on the grounds that they are needed to stabilize exchange rates.[18]

For example, at the time of this lecture (October 1994), the US dollar has recently been weakening against both the deutsche mark and the Japanese yen and, on a real effective basis, is near to the lower end of its trading range of the past six years. In the present situation, the American public probably does not favour an excessively weak dollar, even if it might benefit US exporters. The US Congress and the general public seem to accept the recent actions of the Federal Reserve to tighten US monetary conditions, on the grounds that such tightening is needed to forestall an overheating of the economy and a future rise in inflation. The financial sector has generally applauded these moves. However, it is highly doubtful that the general public, the Congress, or even the US financial sector would applaud a sharp tightening of US monetary policy for the exclusive purpose of strengthening the dollar in the absence of any plausible threat of an increase of inflation.

Conversely, in Germany, the public has generally approved of the reduction in short-term interest rates that the Bundesbank has engineered since the summer of 1992. These monetary policy adjustments have been consistent with evidence that inflationary pressures are receding and have also contributed to prospects for recovery in the German economy following the recession that began in late 1992. One of the ancillary effects of this easing of German monetary policy has probably been to reduce upward pressures on the deutsche mark against the US dollar. If inflation continues to decline in Germany, and German money-supply growth slows somewhat further, additional easing of short-term German interest rates might be undertaken and would probably meet with approval in German public opinion. However, the Bundesbank would not pursue, and German public opinion would not approve, further short-term interest rate reductions undertaken for the purpose of easing exchange market pressures on the US dollar if such easing appeared to conflict with the key domestic objectives of German monetary policy.

This basic point applies far more generally to other countries with floating exchange rates and to other situations. The main focus of popular concern with national monetary policy in the largest industrial countries is on the domestic objectives of growth and low inflation; and stabilizing exchange rates is, at most, a secondary concern of national monetary policy. This is not a choice that has arbitrarily been made by the national monetary authorities or that these authorities are free to alter on their own initiative. Rather, national monetary policies must be conducted in a manner that is generally consistent with objectives that the general public is prepared to accept. For the largest industrial countries, these broadly acceptable objectives do not place much weight on stabilizing exchange rates, especially when this requires sacrifices in terms of key domestic goals of monetary policy. Thus, in my view, the international monetary system is likely to continue to be dominated by a regime of floating exchange rates among the major currencies during the modern era of the triumph of paper credit.

Notes

1. For many countries, maintenance of a pegged exchange rate provides the effective monetary standard. However, countries with such standards peg the exchange values of their currencies to the currencies of other countries which run 'discretionary paper standards'; and countries that maintain exchange rate pegs occasionally change these pegs or even shift to their own

     independently managed discretionary standards. Accordingly, the monetary standard for the world economy is now effectively a 'discretionary paper standard'.

2.   Gresham's Law says that 'the cheap money drives out the dear'. The increase in the relative monetary value of gold to 16 to 1 in 1834 made gold 'cheap' and made silver 'dear' for monetary purposes in the United States, in comparison with relative values in the world bullion market. Accordingly, it became profitable to melt down silver coins (of full weight), trade silver bullion for gold bullion in the world market, and import gold for minting into coin in the United States.

3.   In the so-called 'crime of 1873', the US Congress eliminated the principle of the free coinage of silver (at a price equivalent to 16-to-1 with gold). Although this measure effectively ended the legal basis for bimetallism in the United States, it was not a controversial matter at the time. Later, however, when the world relative price of silver fell significantly below 16 to 1 *vis-à-vis* gold, the call for resumption of the free coinage of silver became the battle-cry of those who favour a more inflationist (or less deflationist) monetary standard. For an interesting discussion of these events, see Milton Friedman's *Monetary Mischief: Episodes in Monetary History* (New York: Harcourt Brace Janovich, 1992).

4.   The logarithmic scale employed in Figure 8.1 diminishes the apparent magnitude of some of these fluctuations, in the interests of showing later price level developments on the same Figure 8.1.

5.   In both the US and the UK, real economic growth was relatively strong (by past historical standards) during the hayday of the gold standard in the century preceding the First World War. Growth of real per capita income has been somewhat stronger in these two countries since the Second World War; and, across the broad range of industrial countries and many developing countries, real growth has been particularly robust during this latter period. However, as many important factors influence long-term real economic growth, it is analytically dangerous to attribute differences in long-term growth rates to differences in monetary standards.

6.   See De Long and Summers (1986) for a general analysis of changes in the cyclical behaviour of the US economy over time. Meltzer and Robinson (1986) in their specific analysis of the effects of the gold standard conclude that it was in general less satisfactory than modern monetary standards in delivering output and (shorter-term) price stability. They note, however, that their results need to be interpreted with a degree of caution.

7.   During the era of metallic monies, there were examples of paper currencies that did gain acceptability, for example, in some of the American colonies and in China. However the inflation that often accompanied the substitution of paper monies for metallic standards, such as the spectacular episode of the French asignats, contributed to a general distrust of non-metallic monies.

8.   Bordo and Kydland (1996) argue that the gold standard should be interpreted as a 'contingent' policy rule under which it was popularly understood that the standard would be maintained during normal times but might be departed from in emergencies such as major wars. When such departures occurred, it was understood that the standard would be resumed once the emergency had passed.

9. In the twelfth century, the pound sterling had a value equal to $11\frac{1}{2}$ troy ounces of pure silver, one-half ounce being taken as seigniorage. Several debasements of the English coinage occurred during the next 400 years, with the result that the silver value of sterling was reduced by slightly more than half by 1526. Hawtrey (1928) argues, however, that these debasements essentially offset the rise in the value of silver relative to wages. Debasements during the reigns of Henry VIII and his son, Edward VI, were truly inflationary, with the silver value of the monetary unit reduced by nearly two-thirds in about 25 years. This debasement was substantially but not entirely reversed under Queen Elizabeth I when the silver content of the pound sterling was restored to about 75 per cent of its value in 1526 or about one-third of its value in 1200; that is, the pound sterling was restored to a value of about 4 troy ounces of silver, and it retained more or less this value in terms of silver for the next three centuries. By the end of the gold standard era (in 1930), the pound sterling was actually worth more than 4 troy ounces of silver, as the price of silver had declined significantly in terms of gold. In 1994, however, the pound was worth barely 1/4 of an ounce of silver. Thus, measured in terms of silver, the sterling has lost 95 per cent of its value in the past 65 years, in comparison with a cumulative decline in value of about two-thirds during the preceding six centuries.

10. It is widely recognized that indices of consumer prices tend to give an upward bias to measures of inflation because they fail to account adequately for improvements in quality and for the introduction of newer and lower-priced varieties of many products. Correcting for this bias, there might be a few more years where consumer prices registered small declines in some countries during the past half-century. However, we have not seen periods of substantial and persistent declines in the general price level, as used to occur with some regularity in the century and one-half preceding World War II.

11. It is generally recognized that there is some upward bias to consumer price indices as measures of the 'true' inflation rate because of shifts of consumption toward goods with declining relative prices, because of difficulties of taking full account of improvements in quality of existing goods and services, and because of the introduction of new goods (whose prices often decline before they become represented in measured price indices). All told, these measurement problems might well mean that a 1 per cent annual rise in the official consumer price index actual means stability in the true measure of consumer prices. However, these measurement issues do not really strengthen the case for price stability as a realistic objective for monetary policy under modern discretionary paper standards. All industrial countries have seen substantial increases in the level of consumer prices during the past 50 years as a whole; and, with no more than the possibility of one or two exceptions, every industrial country has seen significant increases in the *true* level of consumer prices in each of the past five decades. Nowhere is there any indication of determined efforts to drive down the true level of consumer prices once it has risen. The essential element of long-run price stability – a mechanism to force a reversal of inflation once it has occurred – is wholly absent in the modern era.

12. For a discussion of this issue, see the International Monetary Fund's *World Economic Outlook* for October 1992 and for May 1993, and 'Asset Markets

in the 1980s: Causes and Consequences', by Garry J. Schinasi and Monica Hargraves, in *Staff Studies for the World Economic Outlook* (Washington, D.C.: International Monetary Fund) December 1990, pp. 1–27.

13.   Circumstances appear to be different in countries experiencing very rapid rates of inflation. Experience shows that the economic pain and dislocation associated with hyperinflation is usually very large. When effective measures are taken to end a hyperinflation, the short-term effect is often a rapid improvement in economic activity. See Vegh, Carlos (1992) 'Stopping High Inflation: An Analytical Overview', IMF *Staff Papers*, September pp. 626–95.

14.   Robert Barro and David Gordon (1983) provide the classic presentation of the 'dynamic consistency problem' as the reason for a positive inflation rate. This idea has generated a large subsequent literature, and undoubtedly it has made a fruitful contribution to monetary theory and to macroeconomic analysis.

15.   Charles Goodhart (1995) provides an illuminating and persuasive discussion of the importance of the political dimension in the movement to create the European Monetary Union.

16.   Since the market value of an ounce of gold was about 30 times that of an ounce of silver in the mid-1890s, 'free coinage of silver' at a monetary ratio of 16 to 1 would have implied significant inflation. Bryan and his supporters, however, did not see it exactly that way. They did not support a paper money standard, which everyone would have understood to be inflationary. Rather, they argued for a return to the bi-metallic standard that had legally prevailed until silver was de-monetized by 'the crime of 1873'. Thus, the psychological appeal of a metallic monetary standard was very strong even among those who favoured greater inflation (or less deflation).

17.   Symmetrically, when Britain decided to return to the gold standard after the First World War, the issue was explicitly stated in terms of a return to the pre-war parity for sterling against gold – not in terms of a return to the parity of sterling against the US dollar (which had remained fixed to gold throughout the war).

18.   For further discussion of the international monetary system and of the difficulties of moving back towards a 'rules-based' system with significant greater fixity of exchange rates among major national currencies, see Mussa, Michael, et al. (1994) 'Improving the International Monetary System: Constraints and Possibilities', IMF *Occasional Paper* No. 116 (Washington, D.C.: International Monetary Fund) December.

References

Barro, Robert J. and David B. Gordon (1983) 'Rules, Discretion and Reputation in a Model of Monetary Policy', *Journal of Monetary Economics*, Vol. 12, No. 1, July, pp. 101–21.

Bordo, Michael D. and Finn E. Kydland (1996) 'The Gold Standard as a Commitment Mechanism', in Tamim Bayoumi, Barry Eichengreen, and Mark Taylor (eds) *Modern Perspectives on the Gold Standard* (Cambridge: Cambridge University Press).

De Long, James B. and Lawrence H. Summers (1986) 'The Changing Cyclical Variability of Economic Activity in the United States', in Robert J. Gordon (ed.) *The American Business Cycle: Continuity and Change*. National Bureau of Economic Research, Studies in Business Cycle Research, Vol. 25 (Chicago: University of Chicago Press).

Friedman, Milton (1992) *Monetary Mischief: Episodes in Monetary History* (New York: Harcourt Brace Janovich).

Goodhart, Charles (1995) 'The Political Economy of Monetary Union', in Peter B. Kenen (ed.) *Understanding Interdependence: The Macroeconomics of the Open Economy* (Princeton, New Jersey: Princeton University Press) pp. 448–505.

Hawtrey, R.G. (1928) *Currency and Credit*, 3rd. ed. (New York: Longmans, Green).

Meltzer, Allan H. and Saranna Robinson (1989) 'Stability Under the Gold Standard in Practice', in Michael D. Bordo (ed.) *Money, History, and International Finance: Essays in Honor of Anna J. Schwartz*. National Bureau of Economic Research Conference Series (Chicago: University of Chicago Press) pp. 163–202.

Mussa, Michael et al. (1994) 'Improving the International Monetary System: Constraints and Possibilities', IMF *Occasional Paper*, No. 116 (Washington, D.C.: International Monetary Fund) June.

Schinasi, Gary and Monica Hargraves (1993) 'Asset Markets in the 1980s: Causes and Consequences', in *Staff Studies for the World Economic Outlook* (Washington, D.C.: International Monetary Fund) December.

Staff of the International Monetary Fund, *World Economic Outlook* (Washington, D.C.: International Monetary Fund) October 1992 and May 1993.

Thornton, Henry (1802) *An Enquiry into the Nature and Effects of the Paper Credit of Great Britain*.

Vegh, Carlos (1992) 'Stopping High Inflation: An Analytical Overview', *IMF Staff Papers*, September, pp. 626–95.

9 Ethics and Morals in Central Banking – Do They Exist, Do They Matter?*

Otmar Issing

HENRY THORNTON AND CENTRAL BANKING

Money and interest rates have always been discussed in an ethical and moral context. For a long time charging interest was considered disreputable, and at times liable to hard secular and ecclesiastical punishment. The second Lateran Council, for example, decided in 1139:

> Furthermore, we condemn that practice accounted despicable and blameworthy by divine and human laws, denounced by Scripture in the Old and New Testaments, namely, the ferocious greed of usurers; and we sever them from every comfort of the church, forbidding any archbishop or bishop, or an abbot of any order whatever or anyone in clerical orders, to dare to receive usurers, unless they do so with extreme caution; but let them be held infamous throughout their whole lives and, unless they repent, be deprived of a Christian burial.[1]

Even if those times are past, it remains questionable whether – to quote the well-known Austrian capital theorist Eugen von Böhm-Bawerk – charging interest has ever lost its 'moral stigma' completely. A central banker should therefore think three times before he talks about questions of ethics and morals, as he represents an institution which not only lends money against interest but also compels its customers to hold interest-free deposits – at least where (non-interest-bearing) minimum reserves exist.

---

* My first approach to this topic is *Ethik der Notenbankpolitik – Moral der Notenbanker* ('Ethics of central bank policy, morals of central bankers') in H. Hesse and O. Issing (eds) (1994) *Geld und Moral* (Money and Morals) Munich: Verlag Vahler: I would like to thank Geoffrey E. Wood for valuable suggestions. This lecture was delivered at City University, London on 23 November 1995.

Or is it thought to be less reprehensible if it is banks which are charged interest?

The authority of Henry Thornton shows a way out of this dilemma, as it was he who introduced interest rates into the theory of the monetary process and who cast into a scientific mould the relations between money, prices and interest that are intuitively familiar to every banker (Schumpeter, 1954, p. 707).

Henry Thornton personifies several elements which are of great significance for central bank policy. By his famous work *An Enquiry into the Nature and Effects of the Paper Credit of Great Britain* he ushered in a new era in the development of monetary theory (Hayek, 1962, p. 36). As a successful banker – one of his brothers was, incidentally, a director of the Bank of England and from 1799 to 1801 its governor – he knew the practical sides of the money business, and as a Member of Parliament for 33 years he took great interest in the problems of monetary policy, particularly in connection with the financial crises caused by the war with France. His ideas challenge the monetary policy maker to this day (Hetzel, 1987, p. 15). Finally, Thornton was also a man who at times devoted six-sevenths of his considerable income to charitable purposes and who spent much time writing religious pamphlets – his 'Family Prayers', which appeared posthumously, were a sort of 'Victorian bestseller' (Laidler, 1987). An obituary characterised him as follows: 'A more upright, independent, and truly virtuous man has never adorned the Senate' (Hayek 1962, p. 33).

Can there be a better platform for discussing issues of ethics and morals in connection with central bank policy than a lecture dedicated to his name? The following passage from his *Paper Credit* (p. 259) could be displayed in any central bank as a code for a policy of sound money even today:

To limit the total amount of paper issued, and to resort for this purpose, whenever the temptation to borrow is strong, to some effectual principle of restriction; in no case, however, materially to diminish the sum in circulation, but to let it vibrate only within certain limits; to afford a slow and cautious extension of it, as the general trade of the kingdom enlarges itself; to allow of some special, though temporary, increase in the event of any extraordinary alarm or difficulty, as the best means of preventing a great demand at home for guineas; and to lean to the side of diminution, in the case of gold going abroad, and of the general exchanges continuing long unfavourable; this seems to be the true policy of the directors of an institution circumstanced like that of the

Bank of England. To suffer either the solicitations of merchants, or the wishes of government, to determine the measure of the bank issues, is unquestionably to adopt a very false principle of conduct.

ETHICS, ECONOMIC ETHICS, MONETARY ETHICS?

For years interest in 'ethics and morals' has been booming. Following a spate of conferences and publications, the subject matter is becoming increasingly complex, and in the process a multiplicity of ethical subdivisions is replacing general economic ethics in the area of research concerning ethics and economics. These subdivisions reflect both increasing specialization and the opening up of new areas of academic pursuit. (Schmitz 1988, p. 374, differentiates, for example, currency ethics from monetary ethics and financial ethics.) The findings of general economic ethics or its various specialized forms are linked with a whole series of moral codes of behaviour; corporate ethics, for example, has given rise to published statements in which moral codes of conduct are formulated as a guide for management.

After all these efforts, is there really now a need for monetary ethics, and a moral dimension to central bank policy based on them? The answer seems somewhat banal: the consequences of decisions on currency issues and monetary policy are far-reaching, and are generally measured in more than just purely economic terms. No modern school of ethics can ignore the consequences of actions; the responsibility of central bankers therefore ends up in the inter-dependent web of technical regularities and explicit or implicit evaluations. Conversely, it is inevitable that this gives rise to an ethical dimension to central bank policy and to moral criteria governing the actions of monetary policy makers.

This paper is not an attempt to establish and categorise a form of ethics for central bank policy and a moral code for central bankers (for a general overview see Hesse *et al.*, 1988, pp. 13 ff.). Instead, it addresses the much-less-ambitious question of how far and in what way ethical and moral aspects could, or perhaps even should, play a role in central bank policy.

COMPETENCE VERSUS MORALITY?

The categories of ethical reflection and a moral way of thinking are associated exclusively with human nature. In his 'Nicomachean

Ethics' (Book II, 1103b) Aristotle sets out the essential principles of ethics:

> Since, then, the present inquiry does not aim at theoretical knowledge, like the others (for we are inquiring not in order to know what virtue is, but in order to become good, since otherwise our inquiry would have been of no use), we must examine the nature of actions, namely how we ought to do them; for these determine also the nature of the states of character that are produced, as we have said.
>
> *(The Works of Aristotle, Vol. II, p. 349)*

The morally worthy man stands over and above the competent man. Thus:

> the case of the arts and that of the virtues are not similar; for the products of the arts have their goodness in themselves, so that it is enough that they should have a certain character, but if the acts that are in accordance with the virtues have themselves a certain character it does not follow that they are done justly or temperately. The agent also must be in a certain condition when he does them ... These are not reckoned in as conditions of the possession of the arts, except the bare knowledge; but as a condition of the possession of the virtues knowledge has little or no weight ... Actions, then, are called just and temperate when they are such as the just or temperate man would do; but it is not the man who does these that is just and temperate, but the man who also does them as just and temperate men do them.
>
> (Book II, 1105a ff. *The Works of Aristotle*, Vol. II, pp. 350 ff.)

That was how Aristotle treated the relationship between technical knowledge and moral attitudes and clearly conceded priority to morals. If I may be allowed to skip over 2000 years of philosophizing and venture to address the direct 'application' of this theory, I would like to ask the following two questions: is placing morality before ability justified in central bank policy, and is it right to choose the morally virtuous man before the technically qualified man or even instead of him? Are professional competence and moral integrity in fact mutually exclusive? Does Aristotle's maxim, rather, not tend to be based on a construed, an artificial conflict?

The general assumption sometimes made by advocates of public choice – that a form of 'marginal morality' prevails on the way up the ladder to success, with the result that the degree of morality in the upper hierarchical levels is on average relatively low (Tullock 1965, p. 22) – remains unaffected by this. According to this theory, Aristotle's postulate – which

further develops the demand of his mentor Plato and which calls for the
realisation of the ideal state by making philosophers king – could only be
achieved if the morally virtuous but technically inept were appointed to
managerial positions. Quite apart from the practical difficulty of finding
this person with a certain degree of reliability – and of regularly checking
to see whether or not his morality remains intact in this leading position –
this approach leads to an irreconcilable contradiction, since the highly
virtuous person chosen will be absolutely unable to reconcile his moral
principles with his responsibility for actions whose consequences he, as
someone unacquainted with the discipline concerned, can in no way
foresee.

To develop this idea just one stage further, this means to qualify a lack
of the relevant technical knowledge in a position of responsibility as
immoral. But it is not easy to define the technical competence necessary
for any given job in a complex world, as any one person never possesses
more than a certain share of the available knowledge. Consequently, the
highly qualified expert who trusts his own (limited) ability and knowledge
exclusively but has little respect for the opinion of others could actually
represent a particular danger where he can make or at least influence
decisions which are important for other people.

This is a serious objection in a world which is dominated by uncertainty, not only with respect to the correct analysis of a given situation,
but even more so with respect to assessing the future effects of monetary
policy measures. There has always been a broad spectrum of opinion in
academic circles, and making a compulsory selection based on absolute
and unquestionable superiority seems to be possible only for the person
who is immune to critical reflection. If, like F. Hahn, one believes that
monetary theory as a basis for a scientifically oriented central bank
policy is more of a framework than a completed building, it will be
difficult to avoid moral concepts when absolute, one-sided dogmatic
positions are to be assessed. On the other hand, the central-bank policy
maker cannot delay his decisions until academics have reliably solved all
the problems: decisions always have to be made in advance of a full
understanding of the real problems. Under moral aspects, such an
acknowledgement, of course, is no excuse for arbitrary deliberations and
decisions.

In a world of uncertain knowledge, technical demands and moral categories become fused in a mixture which is not easy to unscramble, if it can
be done at all. Standing Aristotle's sequence on its head makes the morals
of the expert an essential but subordinate condition relative to his technical
ability. However, is the moral attitude more than just an appendage, which

is to be welcomed in individual cases, but which, in the end, is unnecessary – and under certain conditions actually detrimental – to the satisfactory functioning of society?[2]

From the point of view of utilitarianism – in the sense of teleological ethics or so-called consequentialism – this conflict disappears, for it judges actions by their consequences, and not by their motives or intrinsic qualities (Brittan, 1983, p. 334). In the specific case of central bank policy the question is: must – or at least should – policy makers possess moral qualities in addition to their technical knowledge? If they must or should, how are these qualities to be defined? Is a moral attitude, as such, actually essential?

PERSONS OR RULES?

In the numerous well-known works on the history of individual central banks, persons often stand in the foreground. For example, large sections of David Marsh's book on the Deutsche Bundesbank and its predecessors constitute a series of biographical impressions prefaced, for good reasons, by a list of the 'dramatis personae' (Marsh, 1993, p. 7). In his official history of the Bank of England John Fforde sees in its long history a reason for the significance of events which reflect the influence of persons. 'For reasons lying deep in British habits of self-satisfaction, these circumstances of prolonged birth were widely presumed to endow the result with a special virtue, enhanced with a flavour of prestige, power, expertise and mystery' (Fforde, 1992, p. 4). This may be illustrated by a rather curious incident: in his negotiations with the government Montagu Norman, a dominant twentieth century central banker, was anything but overscrupulous in his methods; this man, who was 'ever the master of ambiguity' once sank unconscious into the arms of the Chancellor of the Exchequer, 'thus literally disarming the opposition' (King, 1993, p. 8).

A certain bias towards the personality story is no doubt to be expected from the journalist. Nevertheless, the theory of the striking significance of individual persons cannot simply be dismissed. For example, the policy of the Reichsbank under Hjalmar Schacht serves time and again as proof of the personality theory (Müller, 1973). And in a study of monetary policy in the United States Sherman Maisel (1973, p. 107) comes to the conclusion: 'Monetary policy does not merely reflect monetary doctrine; it is strongly influenced by the personalities in the Federal Reserve System and by their interaction, as well as by their responses to external suggestion and pressures'.

This list could probably be extended almost indefinitely – in time and place. If, however, individual people with their individual opinions are actually to the fore in monetary policy, is it not the inner attitude, the morals of central bankers, which is essential? If this is true, what is this moral attitude, and what provides it with monetary policy relevance? Considerations of this nature result, on the one hand, in a quest for the motives of the people concerned; and on the other hand, they give rise to the query as to whether the personal attitude is of any relevance to the outcome of policies. For example, Milton Friedman emphasizes in his commentary on the attitude of Schacht and Norman, to which he adds Benjamin Strong of the Federal Reserve and Governor Moreau of the Banque de France (to whose memoirs he refers), that they were convinced that they were acting in everyone's interest and were capable of working together to solve the underlying economic problems of the western world. In discussing this point of view, Friedman wrote: 'Though of course stated in obviously benevolent terms of doing the 'right thing' and avoiding distrust and uncertainty, the implicit doctrine is clearly dictatorial and totalitarian' (Friedman, 1962, p. 229).

Irrespective of whether Friedman was actually right or wrong in his assessment of the moral aspect, the question concerning the actual monetary policy results in an institutional arrangement in which individual persons and, more to the point, 'such' persons who possess powers of this kind would on no account be definitively answered by this. Incidentally, although an individual is sufficiently branded by the adjectives mentioned, his 'moral position' is still in no way fully characterized.

However, this may be enough of this – at best anecdotal – approach. There is little to be gained from a closer look at the relevant individual cases and from the ensuing problem of generalisation, principally because the various individuals concerned have acted under quite different conditions, or to be more precise, under very different constraints.

If more is involved than the degree of fame of persons with whom institutions are often identified in public, and if the question arises as to the content of monetary policy, the individuals initially take a back seat in the analysis, and the monetary policy regime concerned and its institutional determinants move into the foreground.

As in other cases, however, positive statements and normative demands often overlap here, too. Thus, many constraints on central bankers' individual room for manœuvre are conceivable – in the extreme case of which, monetary policy decisions are strictly linked to objective factors. The classical gold standard can be taken as the most important example of an institutional arrangement in which the course of monetary policy was essentially set by the obligation to exchange currency for gold, despite all the flexibility which individual authors had been at pains to devise (see, for example, Bloomfield, 1959).

However, normative points of view come to the forefront in the case advocated by the Chicago School. In his work 'Rules versus Authorities in Monetary Policy', Simons (1948) deals with a whole programme, namely the call for the replacement of dangers to the liberal order in general and to the monetary system in particular, caused by individuals and their preferences by proposing that policy be guided by clear and binding rules. Milton Friedman takes up this idea in his 'Program for monetary stability' and establishes his k-per cent rule, which in its demand for as steady a monetary growth as possible, even over very short periods, is designed to prevent any discretionary room for action whatsoever.

Persons and their attitudes have no place in this system. According to the advocates of strict rules, it would also be much too risky if a society had to rely on the knowledge and morals of central bankers and grant them appropriate discretionary room for action. Karl Brunner's vision of central bank policy makers (1981, pp. 18 ff.) is of people who have always been surrounded by a peculiar and protective political mysticism, which in turn is expressed in an essentially 'metaphysical approach' to monetary policy. Central bank policy is presented as an esoteric art in which only the initiated can participate. Such an attitude, he argues, is, firstly, dangerous because it exposes monetary policy to almost limitless exploitation for political purposes; and, secondly, this arrangement is all the more questionable as the choice of incumbents is (in his judgement) at best arbitrary, and the filling of executive posts with competent people is the exception rather than the rule.

These criticisms have been supplemented by the contribution of public choice, according to which it should be assumed that self-interest has precedence in the case of central bank executives, too. The result is that, where a choice has to be made, personal gain, such as increased prestige, will come before public welfare (Acheson and Chant, 1973). This line of investigation therefore provides a further argument for the view that, wherever possible, such an important task as monetary policy should not be entrusted to the discretion of 'personalities'.

Rules which are binding are therefore the better alternative – particularly according to the findings of the public choice theory – as they replace the 'rule by men' (Friedman, 1962, p. 235) with the 'rule by law' (Hayek, 1971, pp. 185 ff.) in an important policy area. Simons (1948, p. 169) elevates established rules somewhat excessively when he actually endows them with 'moral qualities':

In a free-enterprise system we obviously need highly definite and stable rules of the game, especially as to money. The monetary rules must be compatible with the reasonably smooth working of the system. Once established, however, they should work mechanically, with the chips falling where they may. To put our present problem as a paradox – we need to design and establish with the greatest intelligence a monetary system good enough so that, hereafter, we may hold to it unrationally – on faith – as a religion, if you please.

Accordingly, in the extreme, monetary policy is to be entrusted to a fully anonymous mechanism; while in a somewhat less rigorous form it requires the expert, or technocrat in the positive sense of the term, to operate the 'apparatus' in line with clear instructions. The internal acceptance by the expert of the standards prescribed from outside still does not establish any moral quality (Kliemt, 1985, pp. 240 ff.). Nevertheless, one will not be able to deny the 'operator', who is comparable with the pilot of an aircraft, personal characteristics and therefore possibly a professional ethos beyond his professional qualities. The significance of those, however, in the case of monetary policy remains a moot point.

The reason for establishing monetary policy rules is to achieve the actual objectives of monetary policy by first limiting or, indeed, eliminating room for the discretionary action of individuals. From that point of view any rule is all the more attractive, the more it increases the probability that major goals will actually be realised. The extent of the demands made by Simons (1948, pp. 181 ff.) on such a set of rules may again be seen in the following quotation:

> To assure adequate moral pressure of public opinion against legislative (and administrative) tinkering, the monetary rules must be definite, simple (at least in principle), and expressive of strong, abiding, pervasive, and reasonably popular sentiments. They should be designed to permit the fullest and most stable employment, to facilitate adjustment to such basic changes (especially in technology) as are likely to occur, and, secondarily, to minimize inequities between debtors and creditors.

If any monetary policy rule could actually meet such demanding criteria, it would be quite irresponsible not to put this proposal into practice. It is particularly the advocates of public choice who expect such irresponsible opposition from central bankers, because the establishment of strict rules would rob the latter of any aura of technical experts and reduce them to the status of semi-automatons. If, when the *status quo* of room for discretionary action was being subsequently defended even under such conditions, individual interests were seen to be given priority over those of the public at large, such an attitude must immediately be described as 'immoral'.

By analogy, this reproach would have to be levelled at the advocate of the unconditional application of rules if the implementation of his suggestion is not only unable to deliver the forecast results and, consequently, the more or less 'promised' improvement, but possibly raises the risk of instability. At any rate, hardly anyone would identify himself today with the claim made by Simons.

Friedman's demand for a rule which would legally commit the central bank to increasing the money stock annually by a constant percentage and, what is more, at as steady a rate from month to month as possible essentially promises – much more modestly – protection from major monetary disturbances and a marked reduction in short-term monetary uncertainty and instability (Friedman, 1960, p. 99). If, for the moment, one disregards the institutional prerequisite which Friedman considers essential for the absolute control of the money stock, not the least of these preconditions being the complete restructuring of the entire banking system, there is sufficient evidence today to show why the money stock rule could not produce the results claimed. This objection is justified, firstly, by the heated debate over the 'right' definition of the money stock which has prevailed among monetarists since then and, secondly, by the fact that unforeseeable financial innovations can decisively change the economic content of a statutorily fixed growth rate for a money stock aggregate laid down a very long time in advance.

It is not surprising that, under these circumstances, scholars have progressively turned their backs on the idea of simple rules. At first, relatively makeshift safety valves in the form of proviso clauses were used, which in the case of serious deviations – for example, exceeding particular unemployment rates – are to permit or even demand a departure from the prescribed path.

Later, interest was increasingly focused on so-called feedback rules, whose fundamental idea is that the appropriate form of action dictated to the central bank in the sense of an endogenous flexibility be amended by a number of automatic feedbacks, thus continuing to deny central bank management its discretionary scope. Approaches of this kind hardly go beyond the level of academic seminars and therefore form a basis on which the implementation of statutory regulations could not conceivably be substantiated.

TIME INCONSISTENCY AND CONSERVATIVE CENTRAL BANKERS

Friedman, to mention just the best known monetarist, identified a major problem but was unable to offer a satisfactory solution. There can hardly be anyone left who doubts that the ideal rule has still not been found (see also Loef, 1993, pp. 153 ff.).

Is, then, our only hope with the paper standard that a responsible central banker will make the right decisions in the interest of the common welfare? There are hardly any convincing reasons for relying on this mixture of resignation in the search for the effective institutional arrangement and of confidence in the selection of the right people. Firstly, monetary policy makers who have been granted full powers of discretion are not in a position appropriately to evaluate the flood of frequently contradictory information and accurately to assess the time-lags before the measures taken begin to work. Secondly, monetary stability in a monetary policy regime of this kind will fail if only because in the long run the central bank will hardly be able to resist the pressure from political groups who seek 'generous' monetary expansion to accommodate their own inflationary behaviour.

Finally, monetary policy makers who fully reserve decisions over future action to their own discretion fall into the trap of time inconsistency. Under these conditions economic agents will expect that a central bank will for example later compromise pay agreements which were agreed on the basis of expected price stability, so as to exploit the potential gains in employment realisable by monetary-policy expansion. In this scenario, which is interesting under aspects of game theory, inflation will be higher than it would be in the case of a strict, though unavailable, rule without there being any improvements in output and employment because the economic agents have anticipated corresponding action on the part of the central bank.

Some authors have thought to overcome this dilemma by appointing 'conservative central bankers' (Rogoff, 1985). Such a person attaches more importance to monetary stability than does society as a whole. This approach fits into the principal-agent model in which society (the principal) transfers the fulfilment of a task to be performed in its interests to persons (agents) chosen for the purpose (Fratianni, von Hagen, Waller, 1993).

The model of the 'conservative central banker' must, however, be seen as an almost futile attempt to revive the 'personality theory'. The solution even to the question of how one is reliably to find the person with the desired qualities must remain just as unsatisfactory as any supposed guarantee of protection against the *ex post* opportunism of a person once he has been selected. This is especially the case if a long term of office and protection against dismissal are among the basic institutional preconditions of a regime in which one expects central bank management to defend the value of money in situations of real or imaginary conflict between price stability and other economic policy objectives.

Incidentally, with the figure of the conservative central banker, a quality of person is meant whose relationship with moral categories is not to be overlooked. If, in a process which is difficult to operationalise effectively, society somehow chose the person with the right convictions, it would be morally essential that subsequent actions fulfilled this expectation. However, whether this expectation is justified, as least *ex ante*, would probably not, or at least not only, be based on the great preference for monetary stability which the person concerned had previously announced in one way or another. Instead, it would have to be concluded from his entire personality structure. Should and could one place the fate of a country's monetary policy on this supposition alone?

However, the model of the conservative central banker which has emerged in textbooks can, on closer analysis, be even less easily dismissed as no more than theoretical conjecturing than it was at first sight; time and again demands are openly voiced in political circles for this or that opinion to be given greater emphasis in monetary policy. However, the objections already mentioned apply to every attempt to make the real or, more likely, alleged preferences of the persons involved the basis of monetary policy decisions.

If moral issues in the widest sense were made the criteria of selection, monetary policy decisions would inevitably also be morally evaluated. One can easily imagine how, for example, in times of recession or of a trade-off – albeit only a short-term one – between inflation and unemployment, central bank policy would inevitably be drawn into the political struggle with ideological dimensions: does the 'social conscience' announced in an expansionary policy or the determination to preserve monetary stability earn a higher moral rating? Is there, shall we say, also a 'moral' trade-off between these two types of behaviour?

IMPOSED GOAL AND INDEPENDENCE

Monetary stability as a public good has no advocate in the everyday pursuit of politics and differing interests. The idea of entrusting the

fulfilment of this task to the selection of the right persons alone is un-
convincing for the reasons already mentioned, especially as the question
arises as to why the political authorities, which for opportunist reasons are
not themselves in a position to defend monetary stability, should transfer
the important instrument of their monetary policy to persons whose decisions could result in conflicts with their own objectives and, in extreme
cases, the loss of their own (government's) powers.

Evidently a more stable institutional arrangement is required, one which
can also function with the 'wrong' people in emergencies. If a society
thinks the objective of monetary stability is important, although always
under threat in the political process, the only solution is to be found in an
arrangement which takes the monetary system out of the political sphere
as far as possible. If the fixed link of the creation of central bank money to
a naturally scarce asset, as under the gold standard, is ruled out because of
the known disadvantages and if a strict monetary rule cannot produce the
desired stability either, there is only one way left. That is to transfer
responsibility for monetary policy to an independent central bank and at
the same time to commit the latter to the clear objective of maintaining
monetary stability (Issing, 1993).

Advocates of public choice, and all those economists who, following
the enlightenment of Scottish origin, support the programme of 'econ-
omising on virtue', declare they are dissatisfied with this system. They
believe that the independence of the central bank is reconcilable with the
condition of democratic control only if there are sanctions for central
bankers who do not pursue the objectives they were appointed to observe
(Vaubel, 1990, p. 945). This approach endeavours to link the pursuit of a
public mandate with that of the individual's interests; that is, it establishes
the appropriate incentives (Neumann, 1992). Conceivable here would be,
for example, a mixture of a threat of punishment up to and including dismissal for failure, on the one hand, and bonuses for achievement of the
objective of price stability, on the other.

This model was implemented in New Zealand in 1990 (see Issing, 1993,
pp. 26 ff.). The central bank was committed to the goal of price stability;
in an agreement between the finance minister and the central bank governor, the exact modalities are laid down before the governor is appointed. If
the governor does not fulfil the stipulated mandate, he can be prematurely
dismissed at the request of the minister.

The appeal of this regulation is obvious, not least because there is no need
to waste time thinking about the moral conduct of the person concerned:
under such a regime one can expect that anyone, regardless of his individual
qualities, will try to achieve the prescribed macroeconomic objective.

Unfortunately, an arrangement of clear objectives, independence in implementing policy, and the threat of sanctions in the case of failure, which is so attractive at first sight, loses a great deal of its simplicity and therefore persuasiveness on closer analysis. It is reasonable to say that punishments only make sense if the person concerned can actually be shown to be responsible for undesirable developments. From the central bank's point of view, however, major influences on the price level – such as increased indirect taxes, deteriorations in the terms of trade or inflationary wage agreements – represent exogenous factors. Only in a world of completely flexible prices could one expect monetary policy to compensate immediately for such effects through restrictive pressures. In the real world such an undertaking would not only be futile, that is the rise in the price level could in no way be prevented by monetary policy, but the overall economic costs would also be unbearably high. With the inclusion of proviso clauses for exogenous factors – which, incidentally, has also been done in the case of New Zealand – the arrangement loses its intended unambiguous character. The failure to meet the target becomes subject to interpretation and is therefore hardly 'litigable'. This is all the more true as the allocation of responsibility for monetary policy decisions has to take account of the sometimes considerable time-lags before measures take effect.

As with the strict monetary rule, it is the intention of the public choice approach to establish the right incentives to eliminate all risks to an objective in the public interest which can arise from personal preferences. However justified one may think the approach in principle, one can have little hope of finding an arrangement which is absolutely 'crisis-proof'. As in all institutions, persons are likely to play a role in central banks, too; their attitude, or their 'morals', if you like, will always influence the measures taken and, consequently, the outcome of monetary policy (see also Hausmann and McPherson, 1993, pp. 672 ff.).

This attitude or morals can, admittedly, also change under the influence of the institution. In connection with the model of the conservative central banker, the danger of moral hazard was described above, that is a person prior to his appointment to the central bank board could pretend to be more stability-minded than is consistent with his actual inclinations and his subsequent conduct in practice. The converse is, of course, also conceivable. Under the influence of the institution and its past, his personal preferences may change in favour of a greater priority for monetary stability. What personal predisposition is required before a 'Becket effect' of this kind actually materialises is a moot point, as is the question of how resistance to the influence of the institution and its functions is to be morally defined.

CENTRAL BANK CONSTITUTION AND CENTRAL BANK POLICY

Ethical categories and moral aspects are expressed, firstly, at the level of
the central bank constitution and, secondly, at that of the individual and
collective behaviour within the prescribed institutional framework.

In looking for the best possible institutional arrangement it is 'the ethics
of forming an appropriate opinion in matters of constitutional political
economics' that is involved, and 'not ethical questions concerning the
content' (according to a commentary by H. Kliemt). The competent
authority in this sphere is not the central bankers themselves but the legisla-
tor and, initially, politicians. One cannot deny that there is an ethical-moral
dimension to considering the intention of reserving recourse to the banknote
printing presses, and the transfer of monetary policy responsibility to an
independent central bank. This certainly does not only apply whenever
one – like A. Glucksmann (1993) – elevates, say, the preference of the
Germans for a stable currency to the rank of a 'currency religion'.

If the ideal of a perfect regulatory system, which precludes any discretionary latitude and leads in a more or less automatic process to the
desired results, remains barred, success will always depend on the persons
responsible. It would then be naive and, in view of the possible consequences, too risky simply to count on the central bankers' 'morals'. On the
other hand, scepticism that – through appropriate incentives – the known
defects of adhering to rules could be successfully overcome, more or less
through the backdoor, by 'subduing selfish interests' will probably be
difficult to avoid. However, the public choice approach probably falls
short in any case by assuming an all-too-simple motivation structure, and
in underestimating the influence of the institution (see also Simon, 1993).
In a concluding résumé of his deliberations North (1991, p. 140) says that
the public choice approach cannot be the complete answer as informal
restrictions inevitably also play a role. Our knowledge of the interaction
between culturally based standards of behaviour and formal rules may still
be rather limited. This probably also applies to the sphere of central bank
policy.

Notes

1. Tanner N.P., S.J. (ed.) (1990) *Decrees of the Ecumenical Councils, Vol. 1,
   Nicaea I to Lateran V* (London) p. 200.
2. Sen (1987, pp. 2 ff.) refers to the two different substantiations of economics.
   The one approach deals with matters of ethics, the other (engineering) with
   the functioning of the economy. Developments in modern theory have
   largely driven the ethical approach into the background, to the detriment of

economics and ethics. Bringing the two closer together again promises substantial 'rewards' (Sen, 1987, pp. 88 ff.).

References

Acheson, K. and J.F. Chant (1973) 'Mythology and Central Banking', *Kyklos*.
Aristotle (1952) *Nicomachean Ethics, The Works of Aristotle*, Vol. II (Encyclopædia Britannica).
Bloomfield, A.J. (1959) *Monetary Policy under the International Gold Standard: 1880–1914* (New York).
Brittan, S. (1983) 'Two Cheers for Utilitarianism', *Oxford Economic Papers*, No. 35.
Brunner, K. (1981) 'The Art of Central Banking', in H. Göppl and R. Henn (eds) *Geld, Banken und Versicherungen* (Money, banks and insurance enterprises) (Königstein).
Fforde, J. (1992) *The Bank of England and Public Policy 1941–1958* (Cambridge).
Fratianni, M., J. v. Hagen and C. Waller (1993) 'Central Banking as a Political Principal-Agent Problem', Centre for Economic Policy Research, Discussion Paper Series No. 752.
Friedman, M. (1960) *A Program for Monetary Stability* (New York).
Friedman, M. (1962) 'Should there be an Independent Monetary Authority?' in L.B. Yeager (ed.) *In Search of a Monetary Constitution* (Cambridge, Mass.).
Glucksmann, A. (1993) *Lieber die Mark als noch einmal Hitler* (Better the Mark than another Hitler), Rheinischer Merkur of September 3.
Hausmann, D.M. and M.S. McPherson (1993) 'Taking Ethics Seriously: Economics and Contemporary Moral Philosophy', *Journal of Economic Literature*.
v. Hayek, F.A. (1962) Introduction in H. Thornton, *An Inquiry into the Nature and Effects of the Paper Credit of Great Britain*, ed. F.A. v. Hayek (London).
v. Hayek, F.A. (1971) *Die Verfassung der Freiheit* (The constitution of freedom) (Tübingen).
Hesse, H. et al. (1988) *Wirtschaftswissenschaft und Ethik* (Economics and ethics), in *Wirtschaftswissenschaft und Ethik* (Economic and ethics), ed. H. Hesse, Schriften des Vereins für Socialpolitik, new series, Vol. 171 (Berlin).
Hetzel, R.L. (1987) 'Henry Thornton: Seminal Monetary Theorist and Father of the Modern Central Bank', Federal Reserve Bank of Richmond, *Economic Review*, July/August.
Issing, O. (1993) 'Central Bank Independence and Monetary Stability', Institute of Economic Affairs, Occasional Paper 89 (London).
King, M. (1993) 'The Bundesbank: A view from the Bank of England', in Deutsche Bundesbank, *Auszüge aus Presseartikeln* (press excerpts) No. 25 of April 2.
Kliemt, H. (1985) *Moralische Institutionen* (Moral institutions), (Munich).
Laidler, D. (1987) 'Thornton, H.' in *The New Palgrave, A Dictionary of Economics*, edited by J. Eatwell, M. Milgate, P. Newman (London).
Loef, H.-E. (1993) *Zwei Geldbasisregeln im Vergleich – Möglich-keiten für eine regelgebundene Geldpolitik in Europa?* (Comparison of two rules for a monetary base – opportunities for a rule-based monetary policy in Europe?), in D. Duwendag and J. Siebke (eds), *Europa vor dem Eintritt in die Wirtschafts-*

und Währungsunion (Europe prior to entry into economic and monetary union), Schriften des Vereins für Socialpolitik, new series, Vol. 220 (Berlin).

Maisel, S.J. (1973) *Managing the Dollar* (New York).

Marsh, D. (1993) *The Bundesbank* (London).

Müller, H. (1973) *Die Zentralbank – Eine Nebenregierung* (The central bank – a subsidiary government) (Opladen).

Neumann, M.J.M. (1992): *Bindung durch Zentralbankunab- hängigkeit* (Linkage through central bank independence), in H. Albeck (ed.) *Wirtschaftsordnung und Geldverfassung* (Economic order and monetary constitution) (Göttingen).

North, D.C. (1991) *Institutions, Institutional Change and Economic Performance* (New York).

Rawls, J. (1971) *A Theory of Justice* (Cambridge, Mass.).

Rogoff, K. (1985) 'The Optimal Degree of Commitment to an Intermediate Monetary Target', *The Quarterly Journal of Economics*.

Schmitz, W. (1988) *Währungsethik – eine tragende Säule der Wirtschaftsethik* (Monetary ethics – a mainstay of economic ethics), in H. Hesse (ed.) *Wirtschaftswissenschaft und Ethik* (Economics and ethics), Schriften des Vereins für Socialpolitik, new series, Vol. 171, (Berlin).

Schumpeter, J.A. (1954) *History of Economic Analysis* (New York).

Sen, A. (1988) *On Ethics and Economics* (Oxford).

Simon, H.A. (1993) 'Altruism and Economics', *The American Economic Review*, Papers and Proceedings.

Simons, H.C. (1948) 'Rules versus Authorities in Monetary Policy', Reprint in: ibid, *Economic Policy for a Free Society* (Chicago).

Thornton, H. (1802) *An Enquiry into the Nature and Effects of the Paper Credit of Great Britain*, ed. F.A. v. Hayek (London) (1962).

Tullock, G. (1965) *The Politics of Bureaucracy* (Washington).

Vaubel, R. (1990) 'Currency Competition and European Monetary Integration', *Economic Journal*.

Index